MYTHOLOGY FOR TEENS

MYTHOLOGY
FOR TEENS

CLASSIC MYTHS IN TODAY'S WORLD

WRITTEN AND ILLUSTRATED BY ZACHARY HAMBY

Prufrock Press Inc. • Waco, Texas

Library of Congress Cataloging-in-Publication Data

Hamby, Zachary, 1982-
 Mythology for teens : classic myths in today's world / Zachary Hamby.
  p. cm.
 Includes bibliographical references and index.
 ISBN-13: 978-1-59363-363-9 (pbk.)
 ISBN-10: 1-59363-363-7 (pbk.)
 1. Mythology, Classical. I. Title.
 BL725.H24 2009
 292.1'3--dc22

                    2008049537

Cover Image: ART156889
Verdier, Francois (1652-1730)
Jupiter Orders Mercury to Release Io. Oil on canvas. 135.5 x 189 cm. MV 7121.
Chateaux de Versailles et de Trianon, Versailles, France
Requested resolution : 2000 X 2000 pixels
© Reunion des Musees Nationaux / Art Resource, NY

Copyright ©2009, Prufrock Press Inc.

Edited by Lacy Compton

Cover and layout design by Marjorie Parker

ISBN-13: 978-1-59363-363-9

Printed in the United States of America.

At the time of this book's publication, all facts and figures cited are the most current available. All telephone numbers, addresses, and website URLs are accurate and active. All publications, organizations, websites, and other resources exist as described in the book, and all have been verified. The author and Prufrock Press Inc. make no warranty or guarantee concerning the information and materials given out by organizations or content found at websites, and we are not responsible for any changes that occur after this book's publication. If you find an error, please contact Prufrock Press Inc.

Prufrock Press Inc.
P.O. Box 8813
Waco, TX 76714-8813
Phone: (800) 998-2208
Fax: (800) 240-0333
http://www.prufrock.com

Dedication

To Homer, Ovid, Virgil, and Zorn

"Give me the voice

to tell the shifting story of the world

from its beginning to the present hour."

Ovid, *Metamorphoses*

TABLE OF CONTENTS

PREFACE

Welcome to *Mythology for Teens*, a textbook that presents ancient myths in the form of reader's theater plays. Additional materials explain the myths' relevance to teenagers (and others) who live in our modern world. The focus of this book is Greek and Roman mythology. Unfortunately, not every Greek and Roman myth can be explored. This isn't (and doesn't claim to be) a complete collection of myth. It's a sampling—a sampling that hopefully will leave the reader hungry for more. I hope you enjoy reading, learning, and acting from this book. I have designed it for education, as well as entertainment. Please feel free to contact me with comments and suggestions.

—Zachary Hamby (mr.mythology@gmail.com)

ACKNOWLEDGMENTS

This project began out of desperation—a desperate mythology teacher struggling with a difficult curriculum. The problem was one of interest: How do you capture the interest of teenage learners day after day? The plays collected into this book are my answer to that question. It has been a successful answer, one that turned a class once dreaded into one I love to teach.

Now these plays are presented to you for use in your own classroom. If your students are anything like mine, you will see the same results. I would like to thank all of the people who have been instrumental to this book's creation.

I give special thanks to: Edith Hamilton, without whose dry prose I would have never been inspired; a former teacher named Zorn, who gave me an outlet; Keri Franklin and Carolyn Hembree, who encouraged me to pursue publication; the Ozarks Writing Project; Don and Carolyn Hamby, my father and mother, for their encouragement; Rachel Hamby, my wife, for her patience, support, and quote-checking skills; and the many, many students who have come through my door.

TEACHER'S GUIDE

This book presents myth in ancient and modern contexts. As I mentioned before, it is not intended to be a comprehensive textbook of mythology. Out of many Greco-Roman myths, only six are present. I selected these six for their ancient importance (why they were important to the Greeks and Romans) and their modern applicability (why they should matter now). After being exposed to these selections, students should leave the book with a healthy understanding of Greco-Roman myth.

Each chapter is geared toward a theme or issue that will be its focus. The reader's theater play makes up the main part of each chapter. When read aloud, these plays run between 25–40 minutes. Some of the myths are so long that here they are broken up into two plays to accommodate their length. In addition, there are several other follow-up sections that add to the reader's sphere of reference. Most sections include discussion questions, asking the students to analyze what they have read. Every chapter includes additional activities, some of which ask the students to draw, research, write, act, present, read, or watch outside material. These activities, designed with the intent of stimulating creativity, help to further the students' understanding and enjoyment of the myth. My goal has been to breathe life into the old bones of myth through interactive learning.

Even though they can be read and enjoyed individually, the reader's theater plays should be read with a group or "full cast" to utilize their maximum potential. The variety of voice and interpretation adds a whole new dimension to the written word and links the learners together in a common experience. During this process, students become active participants as they are asked to interpret the text before them. Linguistic processing and audio processing combine, resulting in maximum comprehension. The group-learning atmosphere also makes the reading more enjoyable.

Let me stress that these plays can *never* replace the original works. As hard as I try to maintain the themes and tone of the poets, I will never be as good at telling Homer's story as Homer. If your students enjoy the version read here, please encourage them to seek out the original source.

That being said, these plays are as faithful as they can be. As you might imagine, fitting a complex story into a 30-minute play is a challenging task. Needless to say, a few of the stories' peripheral details have been lost, but the core is intact. At times I have condensed events; at others I have combined or eliminated characters. For that I personally apologize to all of the dead poets who brought us these stories. If you truly wish to have the full flavor of the original, read the original. If you wish to have the condensed, but not-skimping-on-the-feel-and-emotion-of-the-story version, you can't beat these plays.

Writing these plays has been a process of translation, and during this process, I'm sure a little bit of my own voice has snuck in. I've tried to make the plays' dialogue as engaging as possible for modern teenage audiences, while leaving it archaic enough to still be challenging. I've avoided phrases such as "S'up, fool!" (I *know* that would register with teenagers), but also shied away from lofty language that would trip up the tongue, such as "Begone, thou ill-tempered harlot!" It's a balancing act to challenge the student's intellect without insulting it.

As for the actual reading of the play, you, the teacher, should act as the casting director. You know which student will fit best with each part. I strongly encourage *you* to participate in the play as well. This is helpful in breaking down a learning barrier. Instead of leaving students to learn on their own, you are becoming a participant and experiencing with them. In my own classroom, I commonly choose to be the narrator.

Emotion cues in parentheses such as (*frightened*) or (*angrily*) come at the beginning of important lines. Even those students who are not strong readers can still participate (and should be encouraged to do so). Sound effects are indicated (*booming thunder*) in the script and can be performed by the whole class.

Reader's theater has experienced plenty of success in lower grades, but its usefulness in middle or high school is relatively unexplored. A common rationale is this: Older students will not like activities geared toward younger students. I am here to tell you that this is not the case. Teenagers enjoy acting, playing, and creating just as much as elementary students.

Even though they would hate to admit it, they're still kids inside. One draw to reader's theater for teens is that it *appears* easy. Reading aloud seems like an "easy assignment." But, when students are handed parts in a play, they are presented with a complex task: They must take the written word, interpret it, and present it for others to hear—all in a matter of seconds. This process looks less like an "easy assignment" and more like active learning.

Reader's theater is not the only way to experience literature, but it is a great way to create a classroom learning experience where everyone laughs and learns together. As you implement this book into your own classroom, please keep these things in mind. Students will value knowledge when you make it applicable to *them.* I haven't yet encountered a class that didn't enjoy participating, experiencing, and learning from these stories as they are presented here.

Note on Supplemental Materials

For the films recommended to accompany certain sections, I've tried to steer clear of R-rated material (*Troy* and *JAWS* being the exceptions). The majority of the recommended films are either rated PG or PG-13. Please preview each film to determine if its contents are appropriate for *your* classroom. You also may want to consider showing just sections of these films applicable to the discussions. In many cases, the films are long and student interest may be lost if they are shown in their entireties.

INTRODUCTION
Why Study Mythology?

Myths are ancient stories that have been handed down from generation to generation in a particular culture. The suffix -ology means "the study of"; therefore, mythology is the study of myth. By studying the myths of a culture, a person can learn how people in that culture thought, lived, and expressed themselves.

Myths began as religious stories—stories that explained why the universe worked the way it does. Most people today use the word myth to indicate a story that is false. Ancient people took their myths as truth. It's just that for many cultures the religious beliefs associated with the myths have fallen away. A myth stripped of its credibility is still not a lie. It becomes a story, and in many cases, a good story. Today when we read the myths of the ancient Greeks and Romans, we do not do so for any religious significance. The religion is gone, but the story remains.

It's also important to understand how mythology works. Only through reading and studying myths can you understand the process. How is a myth made? How do myths shape a people? What messages do myths send to future generations? When you understand this process, you can look at your own culture and ask, "What will our message be? What mark will we leave on an ever-changing world?"

History is deeds. Myth is words.

What are our words for the future?

DISCUSS

- Think about television. If a teenager in the year 3001 discovered a week's worth of modern-day television programming, what would he or she think of our culture?
- Is our entertainment industry (film and television) a clear reflection of us as a people?

WRITE

Write a dialogue in which two or more futuristic commentators try to determine what life was like in our day and time. The only tool they have for determining this is a week's worth of modern television programming.

From Greek to Me

Who were the Greeks? On the surface it seems like an easy question. The ancient Greeks were the people who inhabited ancient Greece. That's one answer. But, what were they like, and, more importantly, why should we care? To answer the second question, let's list some things that got their start in ancient Greece: science—the Greeks were the first scientists; philosophy—the Greeks were the first philosophers; democracy—ancient Athens provided the first working model of a democracy; drama—the Greeks were the first real playwrights and actors; and history—the Greeks were the first historians. And, these are only the things they started. We failed to mention the items that the Greeks didn't necessarily start but nearly perfected: poetry, architecture, politics, mathematics, sculpture, and war. Is there anything this people didn't do? There are a few things—but they covered most of the important points. What about all of those civilizations that came after the Greeks? What about the Roman Empire, the British Empire, the United States of America? Didn't they accomplish something as well? Certainly. But, that *something* is firmly planted on Greek bedrock.

Textbooks talk about the melting pot of America, or how a multitude of cultures have come together and blended into the American people. That's true. Your ancestors could have come from any possible point on the globe, but when they became an American, they claimed Greek descent.

More than 2,500 years ago the ancient Greeks set forth all of the ideals we hold so dearly: freedom of thought, freedom of speech, and freedom of expression. To the ancient world, nothing was a more shocking thought than freedom. Just a little more than 200 years ago when the American colonies decided it was freedom they wanted above all else, it was *still* a shocking idea. If it weren't for the Greeks, would there have been a United States of America? Maybe not.

Because the ancient Greeks were successful in so many different areas, there must have been some key ingredient, some secret recipe for these astounding breakthroughs. Indeed there was, and it was relatively simple: *The Greeks questioned everything.* Without questioning there is no learning, no progress. The Greeks were the first to grasp this concept.

It's beyond our modern mindset to understand how ancient man was wired: He was designed to *not* question. Kings didn't want their subjects questioning their right to rule. Slave owners didn't want their slaves questioning what life would be like without slavery. Questioning was dangerous business. Even in Greece, the birthplace of constant questioning, too much questioning could get you into trouble. Socrates, the philosopher most famous for his questioning, was condemned to die. The charge? Corrupting the youth of Athens with the questioning plague.

Yet, they couldn't help themselves, those Greeks; they had to understand it all—life, war, politics, art, architecture, even the universe. Once they questioned the old ways, they thought of new ways. History is made when things change, and things changed in ancient Greece. The rest of us have been merely riding on their coattails ever since.

This period we were just discussing is known as Classical Greece, the time when all of the movers and shakers in Greece got to moving and shaking. It all happened about 500 years before Christ. But, all of this sounds more like *history* when the subject of this book is supposed to be *mythology*.

Hopefully, you're impressed by how intelligent, modern, and classy the Classical Greeks were. (I mean, anything with the word *classical* in it has to be highbrow, right?) But, the thought-provoking, chin-stroking, universe-questioning Greeks of Classical Greece didn't write the myths we associate with Greek mythology. They came from an older time, a time in Greece that embarrassed most classy Greeks—a time when men weren't philosophers or scientists. Strong kings ruled the lands, not the people. Debates were settled by chariot and spear instead of rhetoric. Warriors, not thinking men, were the toast of Greece. Bards wandered the countryside, singing of mighty battles. These previous Greeks weren't as smart or sophisticated as the Classical Greeks, but they could tell a good story. Some call their time the "Dark Age" of Greece—not a flattering name. The Classical Greeks will be remembered for their knowledge and the Dark Age Greeks will be remembered for their sheer imagination. Their keeps have crumbled. Their armies lie as bones in barrows. Their stories are all that is left of them. Words have endured—words that come out of the past like voices from a cave.

Greek myths, as in most cultures, originated orally—told or sung for the pleasure of the listener. In this form they managed to stay alive, passed from parent to child as the only heirloom of the previous generation. When the miracle of the written word arrived, the old oral tales were still there, fully developed, begging to be written down. Through the preserving power of writing, we still have them today.

Although many things developed in Greece, one institution that failed was organized religion. The Greeks certainly had plenty of stories about gods; they even prayed to these gods. They had temples and oracles and offered sacrifices. What they lacked was a strict religious code. They had no Ten Commandments, no set of scriptures, no dogma attached to their gods. There was nothing to tell them what to do, when to do it, or why they should do it. Because this code never developed, the Greeks weren't a terribly religious people. The fault for this might lie within the nature of the Greek gods themselves. The gods frequently became angry—shaking, flooding, and striking the Earth with fire. They acted on whims. The gods could love you one day and hate you the next. They also became jealous of humans—jealous of their beauty, their talent, and their wives. Such amoral gods failed to produce a moral code.

If the gods did have one thing going for them, it was their physical perfection. They were imagined as human in appearance—perfectly formed humans. When you look at Greece's neighboring cultures, you start to see what a unique idea these humanized gods were. In Egypt, the gods were towering animal-headed creatures—phantoms you might see in a nightmare. In India, the gods had the same anamorphic make-up—maybe an elephant head or six-slithering arms. Definitely *not* human. Unfortunately, being beautiful on the inside was not the Greek gods' specialty. They suffered from "human" weaknesses—greed, rage, lust, and jealousy.

Some researchers have posed a theory. Maybe the reason the Greek gods are so human in action and appearance is simply that the Greeks couldn't imagine anything higher or more worthy of worship than themselves. Maybe the Greeks were saying that gods aren't the measure of all things. Humans are. Edith Hamilton (1942) puts it like this: "The Greeks made their gods in their own image" (p. 8).

This would have been blasphemy anywhere else, but not in Greece.

By the time the Classical Greeks came on the scene, their ancient religion had been reduced to rituals—going through the motions. People were seriously starting to doubt the gods. Flat-out rejecting the old myths, the intellectual set started exploring new ways to get in touch with the universe. Their own people demoted the Greek myths from fact to fiction. But, this didn't hurt their popularity any. In fact, it helped it in a way.

Socrates and his student Plato, although they couldn't endorse the myths as true, developed a new use for them. In their eyes, the myths were still meaningful if people looked at them as metaphors. They were the science of the previous generation. Playwrights in Athens knew their usefulness as well. They used retellings of myth as their way of examining human nature. Even though myth was losing its credibility, Homer, the Dark Age chronicler of the Trojan War, was still revered as Greece's greatest poet. In fact, the *Iliad*, Homer's mythical account of the war at Troy, was the closest thing to a Bible the Greeks had. Political and philosophical arguments could be settled by a quote from its passages. Achilles, Agamemnon, and Hector were *the* examples of manly excellence. In a story filled with gods and goddesses, the Greeks saw the human factor as the truly important one.

The way the Classical Greeks viewed their myths is not far off from how we will view them. We're not looking for gods; we're looking for men and metaphors. We're not looking to understand the heavens. It would be enough to just understand ourselves.

An Accurate Picture of Ancient Greece

This book will use the term *Greece* to indicate the many city-states that once inhabited the region called Greece today. The sad truth is that from its earliest times until long after its Classical period, a unified concept of Greece did not exist. Instead it was every city-state for itself.

As for city-states, the name almost says it all. They were cities, but also held the power of states. The leader or leaders of a city also ruled the regions outside that city's walls. During the Greek Dark Age, kings and queens governed these areas. Later when the idea of democracy prevailed, a council of elected elders ruled in some cities. In times of war, the countryside peasants would retreat behind the walls of the city for protection.

The geographical layout of Greece, multiple mountain ranges surrounding plains, kept the city-states from easily interacting with one another. A city-state's culture often developed in different ways than its neighbor's culture, leading to mutual distrust and alienation. City-states spent most of their time warring with one another over land or other trivial matters. The thought of a unified country ever coming out of these squabbling states seemed impossible.

Most of what we know about the ancient Greek city-state comes from Classical Athens. When some people say *Classical Greece,* they basically mean *Classical Athens.* Athens set the cultural trend for the rest of the city-states, who simply adopted Athenian ideas and entertainments. The agora, a central marketplace where farmers and merchants sold their wares, was the lifeblood of the Greek city. Most cities would have a citadel or keep reserved for their ruler at the height of the city. In Classical Greece, most cities also had a gymnasium (a sports complex/spa/park combination) where male citizens could stay fit in case of war. Exercise and competition were done in the nude, so no women were allowed to participate. Wealthy boys were expected to be educated in all of the latest learning. If they were especially privileged, they might become a student of a philosopher like Socrates or Plato. They were expected to be cultured young men—their days filled with studying Homer and composing their own poetry. Mastering the lyre, a small harp, also was a requirement of the Athenian gentleman. In Athens, keeping up on the latest political and philosophical ideas was a common pursuit and almost a full-time job. During the festival of Dionysus, citizens would crowd to the city theatre, where they would catch an all-day marathon of the latest dramas by Sophocles or Euripides. In spite of this intellectual atmosphere, women and slaves still held almost no rights.

In the Dark Age of Greece (the setting for all of our myths), the same Greek city-states existed but were not nearly as cultured. The only information about this time comes from the myths themselves. City-states were ruled by powerful kings, who were at times barbaric and ruthless. Under their rule, not even males had any inherent rights. Bandits and beasts roamed the roads, and travel was dangerous. Although women enjoyed more freedom than they would in classical times, they were open to more risks as well. Rape was common. Men, women, and children could easily be kidnapped and sold into slavery.

It was a hard life—for almost everyone. In a way, the myths that emerged from this time were the Greeks' method of dealing with the untamed world around them.

CHAPTER 1
The Hero

THE TALE OF PERSEUS

Cast

Perseus *(Young hero from Argos)*

Acrisius *(Elderly king of Argos, Perseus' grandfather)*

Danaë *(Perseus' young mother, Daughter of Acrisius)*

Dictys *(Kindly fisherman)*

Wife *(Wife of Dictys)*

Zeus *(Ruler of the gods)*

Athena *(Goddess of wisdom and battle)*

Hermes *(Messenger god)*

Medusa *(Evil creature who lives at the edge of the world)*

Gorgon *(One of Medusa's foul sisters)*

Sister One *(One of the gray sisters)*

Sister Two *(One of the gray sisters)*

Sister Three *(One of the gray sisters)*

Atlas *(Titan that holds up the sky)*

Polydectes *(Evil king of a faraway realm)*

Andromeda *(Beautiful princess)*

Oracle of Apollo *(Prophetess of Delphi)*

Man *(Man in the crowd)*

NARRATOR: Acrisius, King of Argos, traveled afar to the Oracle of Delphi seeking knowledge of the future. He had a beautiful daughter, Danaë, but, as all kings do, he desired a son. Because he was heavy with age and had no wife, he traveled to the oracle to ask it how he might procure a great heir to his throne.

ORACLE: *(distantly)* Enter . . .

ACRISIUS: Oracle of Apollo, it is said that you speak the word of the God of Truth. I have come begging a question of you. Please hear me, and answer me my riddle.

ORACLE: You may speak, Old Man. But, you may not find happiness in the answer.

ACRISIUS: *(pausing)* I have no son to receive my throne. If I do not produce a successor, my kingdom will fall into ruin. My wife has died many years before now. Tell me, Oracle, what must I do?

NARRATOR: At this, the oracle's eyes grew white, and her voice became low, yet filled with the power of the gods.

ORACLE: *(deeply)* Your daughter shall have a son. He will be a great man, known by all of Greece.

ACRISIUS: *(relieved)* Thank you, oh, thank you. That is excellent news.

ORACLE: Halt! That is not all. This son of your daughter comes at a price. It will be at his hands that you will die.

ACRISIUS: *(shocked)* That cannot be.

ORACLE: I have spoken.

NARRATOR: King Acrisius returned to Argos in a stupor. What could he do? He desperately needed an heir, but in his heart he feared death more than anything. He therefore resolved to make sure his daughter would have no son.

DANAË: *(surprised)* Father? You've returned so soon?

ACRISIUS: *(coldly)* Danaë, come with me.

DANAË: Where are we going? What's going on?

ACRISIUS: Guards, lock her below.

DANAË: Father! *(weeping)* What have I done to deserve this?

ACRISIUS: *(to himself)* I will put her where no man can touch her.

NARRATOR: So, the cowardly Acrisius had a house built for his royal daughter—a house that the light of the sun would never touch—hidden underground. And, there she dwelt, weeping day after day in her subterranean prison. It was there that Zeus, looking down from Olympus, saw her.

ZEUS: *(amorously)* What a beautiful maiden! Why does she weep? I must comfort her.

NARRATOR: Under the Earth, Danaë looked up and saw sparkling pieces of gold falling into her prison from nothingness. It was the form of Zeus.

DANAË: A shower of gold!

NARRATOR: She ran forward and let the gold fall upon her—touch her—caress her.

ZEUS: I am in the gold, Danaë. It is I, Zeus, Lord of the Sky.

DANAË: I don't understand.

ZEUS: Do not be sad. You will bear a great son from me—a son who will set you free.

NARRATOR: At this, Danaë grew silent, and the gold continued to fall. Many months later, she found herself with child. She did not tell the guards who brought her food. She kept it hidden. And, when the day came to give birth, she did so as quietly as possible—for she feared her father's wrath. And, so was Perseus born.

DANAË: I will name you Perseus. Zeus is your father, little one. You shall do great things in this world.

NARRATOR: Danaë kept the baby a secret longer than any would imagine. He grew into a golden-haired toddler in the confines of the underground room. He learned to play quietly and to hide when the guards came with food. Danaë took little for herself, instead giving Perseus most of the food. But, it could not stay a secret forever. The guards heard laughing one day and reported it immediately to the king. Acrisius' worst fears had come true. The son of prophecy had been born—right below his very nose.

ACRISIUS: *(madly)* Fool girl! Is this the respect I receive? Raising you from a babe? I should stick you with my own sword!

DANAË: Father! No! *(weeping)*

ACRISIUS: Harlot! Who is the father? Who could have reached you? I was so careful! I sealed you in! No one could have reached you.

DANAË: Zeus reached me, Father.

ACRISIUS: *(quietly)* Zeus . . .

NARRATOR: Acrisius could no longer put the boy to death as he had planned. This child was a son of Zeus. The king knew he would be struck down before he removed his sword from the scabbard. But, if the boy were to meet with an untimely accident, no one would be the wiser. Accidents happen after all—even to princes. And so, Acrisius made a great wooden trunk and placed Danaë and the boy inside.

ACRISIUS: Go to a watery grave! I curse you!

NARRATOR: He set the chest out to sea, sure that Poseidon, Lord of the Depths, would claim his human sacrifice. But, Poseidon was no fool and knew his Olympian brother's wishes, so he guided the wooden trunk safely through the turbulent waters—to a faraway shore where he knew it would be found by the kind fisher folk that lived there.

DICTYS: Look! There in the surf!

WIFE: A bit of driftwood perhaps?

DICTYS: I will bring it in with the net. *(scuffling sound, sound of door opening)* Ahhh!

DANAË: Ahhh!

WIFE: A woman?

DICTYS: And her child!

NARRATOR: Danaë and Perseus were found by the kind fisherman Dictys and his wife. Having no children of their own, the poor pair took them in as their daughter and grandson. It was a happy time for mother and son—when they were able to forget the past. Over the years Perseus grew to be a handsome young man with the glory of his immortal father shining in his eyes. Danaë, free of her prison, had become more beautiful than ever, and word of her famed looks spread throughout the land. News of it even reached the ear of Dictys' brother, Polydectes. Now, Polydectes had much more ambition than his kind-hearted brother and through cunning and force had become ruler of the tiny island kingdom. He was ruthless, and his greed knew no bounds. Upon hearing of Danaë, he came to claim this beauty for himself.

POLYDECTES: (imperiously) Hello, brother. How goes it down here in the filth?

DICTYS: (angrily) What do you want? Have you come to gloat?

POLYDECTES: You have been keeping secrets from me, Dictys. I hear you have a certain . . . treasure that you have hidden from my sight.

DICTYS: I assume you speak of our daughter.

POLYDECTES: You have no daughter, fool. Who is this woman you keep? I must see her for myself.

(sounds of footsteps; we hear Perseus laughing)

NARRATOR: As the two brothers spoke, the young mother and son ran into view up the narrow beach.

DANAË: (huffing/puffing) Perseus, you always beat me. What a fast son I have!

PERSEUS: Oh, mother, I was even lagging behind. I didn't want to beat you too badly.

DICTYS: Danaë! Perseus!

DANAË: Oh, I am sorry. I didn't know we had a visitor. Hello, sir, I am Danaë.

POLYDECTES: Beautiful—I am Polydectes, ruler of this realm.

DANAË: Your majesty, this is my son—

POLYDECTES: (interrupting) I have never before seen a woman as dazzling as you.

PERSEUS: (forcefully) And I am Perseus.

POLYDECTES: Surely, my sweet, you will come to my palace with me and be my wife.

DICTYS: (angrily) Polydectes!

DANAË: My lord, I have no need for a husband. My boy is my only love.

POLYDECTES: (pause) I see. (under his breath) An obstacle that can be easily removed.

NARRATOR: His advances thwarted, Polydectes left in a huff. After he was gone, Dictys and his wife stared at Danaë in shock.

DICTYS: You should not have refused him, Danaë.

WIFE: He is an evil man. He will try to harm you and Perseus.

DANAË: Why should he want to do that?

DICTYS: He wishes to have you as a trophy, and you have rejected him. His anger is legendary. He has sent many men to their deaths for his vanity.

PERSEUS: I'm not afraid of him.

WIFE: But, you should be. His greatest desire has been to have the head of the monster, Medusa.

DANAË: (in shock) But, she cannot be killed! Her gaze turns men to stone!

DICTYS: Exactly. Think what a madman like Polydectes would do with a weapon like that!

PERSEUS: She couldn't be as bad as all that.

WIFE: She is, boy, she is. For hair she has writhing snakes. She does not live alone either. She also has two Gorgon sisters, and they cannot be killed!

DICTYS: He has sent man after man to retrieve the head of Medusa. All because of his lust for power. Now, you, Danaë, seem to be the desire of his black heart. He will kill many men to get to you as well.

NARRATOR: Danaë pondered these things in her heart. She loved nothing more than Perseus. She would do anything to ensure his safety. What was marriage to a man she did not love? Little when compared to the life of her son. In the dark of night, Danaë made her way to Polydectes' palace and pledged herself to him. The next day, it was declared that a royal wedding was to occur immediately. The entire kingdom was in attendance. Perseus could not bring himself to go inside and brooded outside the great hall.

DANAË: Perseus, what are you doing out here?

PERSEUS: Why, Mother? How can you marry that man?

DANAË: It must be done. We must give him what he wants.

PERSEUS: I refuse.

DANAË: It is not your choice to make. I have made mine.

POLYDECTES: *(walking up)* Ah, my queen-to-be, what are you doing out here with the riffraff? You no longer have to associate with such people. You are a queen.

PERSEUS: *(Seething)* And what am I?

POLYDECTES: Ah, *Persiun*, I'm glad you could make it. You were extended a special invitation after all—from the high to the lowly. It was such a select guest list—not even my poor brother was able to make it. Nothing puts me off my lunch like the smell of fish.

PERSEUS: *(angrier still)* He's too good for you.

POLYDECTES: *(laugh)* Certainly. Now, tell me, what have you brought as a present? Surely, you did not bring shame upon your mother by offering her nothing on her wedding day?

PERSEUS: I—I—

POLYDECTES: Some fish heads perhaps—a gown made from a bit of old net. Poor, poor Persiun, you look as if you could cry.

PERSEUS: *(determined)* I will bring a present, you snake, one that you have always desired . . . the head of the Gorgon!

DANAË: Perseus! No!

POLYDECTES: *(laughing)* Medusa? How will you catch her, boy? With one of your nets?

PERSEUS: I will bring it back, and you shall look into her eyes and see your own demise.

POLYDECTES: *(not laughing anymore)* A strong promise, boy. I will be sure to inform all present. That way when you return empty-handed, I will declare myself shamed and have you put to death.

DANAË: No! Perseus, take it back!

PERSEUS: Goodbye, mother. I will return—I will come back for you.

POLYDECTES: *(laughing)* Fly, fool. Hurry home. I await you with open arms.

NARRATOR: Perseus fled the palace, his mother in tears. He had no idea how he was going to accomplish such a task. In despair, he sat on the beach and wept. The sound of soft footsteps raised his eyes from the sands. A tall, powerful woman—one he had never seen before—was standing in front of him.

ATHENA: Do not despair, Perseus. I heard your promise back there.

PERSEUS: Why shouldn't I?

ATHENA: Because you are a child of Zeus, just like me.

NARRATOR: Then he met her gaze and saw beyond her human disguise. It was Athena, goddess of war—his sister.

ATHENA: I have come to tell you to take heart. Your quest is not as impossible as you may feel it to be.

PERSEUS: How can I? You're a goddess. I'm just a boy—it doesn't matter who my father is.

ATHENA: It was I who turned Medusa into the creature she is today. Do not doubt that I know how to defeat her. On top of hope, I also give you this.

NARRATOR: She pulled forth a shining shield. Perseus gaped at its beauty. In its golden form, he saw himself reflected back.

ATHENA: You will use this to kill Medusa. No man may look on her face and live, but her reflection causes no pain.

PERSEUS: Thank you, but I have no way to kill a Gorgon.

NARRATOR: At that moment, there was a slight crackling sound in the air, and a young man stood beside Athena. On his cap and on his sandals fluttered four tiny wings. In his hand, he carried a golden staff.

HERMES: *(cough)* Sorry I'm late—trouble in the Underworld.

ATHENA: *(sighing)* This is Hermes. He has come to lead you to the Gorgon's lair. And, unless I am mistaken, he also has some gifts to bestow upon you.

HERMES: *(pause)* Of course, of course . . .

NARRATOR: The god rummaged in a sack slung at his side. The first thing he pulled forth was a mighty sword.

HERMES: *(proudly)* This is from me—a sword powerful enough to pierce the hide of the Gorgon.

PERSEUS: *(mesmerized)* Thank you.

ATHENA: And?

HERMES: And, what? *(pause)* Oh, yes, gifts from the Hyperboreans, the happiest people on Earth, that is.

ATHENA: They have heard of your quest and wish to help.

PERSEUS: How did—?

HERMES: Here we go—a magical cap to make you invisible—you'll need that—and some winged sandals—just like mine—and this wonderful magical wallet—no matter how much you put into it, there's always more room.

NARRATOR: Perseus stood speechless.

HERMES: It's mainly for when you cut her head off. Y'know, you can put the head in there. It's a mess otherwise.

PERSEUS: All I can say is, thank you.

ATHENA: No, thank you. Medusa has been at large for many years. She has become more evil than I ever imag-

ined. If it were my place, I would have taken care of her myself—but it is *your* destiny. Now, put on your sandals and your cap, take your shield and your satchel, and Hermes will guide you where you need to go. Hermes . . .

HERMES: Yes?

ATHENA: Guide him.

HERMES: Who?

ATHENA: *(annoyed)* Perseus!

HERMES: Where is he?

ATHENA: *(through her teeth)* He—put—the—cap—on—

HERMES: Oh, right. *(cheerily)* Come along, Perseus.

(sounds of beating wings)

ATHENA: Farewell, Perseus. You shall succeed—have faith.

NARRATOR: With his new sandals, Perseus flew beside the golden god, Hermes. The world spread out below them. They flew over great fields, churning seas, and high mountains, but no sign came from the messenger god as to where they were. Finally, Perseus gathered the courage to ask . . .

PERSEUS: *(shouting over the wind)* Are we there yet?

HERMES: Ah—forgot you were there for a second.

PERSEUS: Over here.

HERMES: Yes, right. *(cough)* Well, I don't know exactly where we're going.

PERSEUS: What do you mean?

HERMES: Well, what I mean is—we have to stop and ask for directions.

PERSEUS: To find Medusa?

HERMES: *(slowly)* No, actually to find the people who know where Medusa is. It's complicated.

NARRATOR: Perseus grew a little worried. Sure, Hermes was a god, but did he know what he was doing? Below, the Earth was growing flat and barren. Soon, Perseus feared it would end completely, falling off into the black nothingness of night.

HERMES: There he is!

PERSEUS: Who?

HERMES: Atlas, of course.

NARRATOR: And there he was, the titan who holds up the skies, groaning forever under the great weight. Perseus and Hermes flew close, and Perseus balked at Atlas' size—as big as a mountain.

ATLAS: (groaning) What now, Hermes? Another curse from Zeus?

HERMES: Just some directions. This is Perseus.

ATLAS: (grunts) Where to?

HERMES: We seek the Gray Women. They alone know where the Gorgons live.

ATLAS: You seek the Gorgon's head, eh? Good luck to you. (grunts) I will tell you where to find the Gray Women, but you must make me one promise.

HERMES: (to Perseus) Are you getting this?

ATLAS: When you pass back this way, let me look on the face of the cursed one. I have borne this burden for an eternity, and I desire rest—even if it means my own destruction.

PERSEUS: I promise.

ATLAS: (relieved) Thank you. You can't believe how much this thing weighs.

NARRATOR: Atlas told them how to find the Gray Women, three old sisters who all shared one eye. They lived at the edge of dreams, on a dark, desolate plain. And, they did not give information lightly. Because they lacked sight themselves, they loved to take it from trespassers. As Hermes and Perseus saw the first signs of that dark land, they felt fear rising up in their hearts.

HERMES: Here's the trick. All three sisters share an eye. They take turns sticking it into their empty sockets. They fight over it quite a bit. They are all three jealous of each other, and their greed will be their undoing.

PERSEUS: What must I do?

HERMES: You have on a cap of invisibility. Sneak into their midst and steal the eye. Once you have it, they will tell you whatever you wish to know.

PERSEUS: What if I fail?

HERMES: Well, let's not think about that. Just make sure you don't.

NARRATOR: Before long, they saw the black plain where the three sisters lived. They sat in a circle around a bubbling cauldron. Perseus saw one remove the eye and hand it to her sister. He shuddered.

HERMES: (whispering) Go on. I'll stay here. Don't mess up.

NARRATOR: Perseus nodded and walked forward into the midst of the three Gray Sisters.

SISTER ONE: (cackling) Tell me, sister. What became of that delicious young man who came to our realm yesterday?

SISTER TWO: (witchily) Ah, yes, I remember him well.

SISTER THREE: We made a stew of him, did we not?

SISTER ONE: Yes, yes, I remember now—a fine stew. (pause) Give me the eye, love, I wish to see what creature I feel walking our way.

SISTER TWO: Certainly, sister, I will give you the eye when it is your time. I have just received it. I see no creature.

SISTER ONE: I feel it. A large creature. Give me the eye, so that I might spring upon it.

SISTER TWO: (growling) No, it is mine.

SISTER THREE: Sisters, give me the eye. I will see for us all.

SISTER ONE: (shrieking) No, give it to me, to me!

(sounds of old women squabbling)

SISTER TWO: Where is it? You took it! I have it no longer!

SISTER ONE: You lie! I did not take it! I will cut out your tongue!

SISTER THREE: You both lie, and you keep it from ME!

PERSEUS: (loudly) I have it.

SISTERS ONE–THREE: (gasps) Who are you?

PERSEUS: My name does not matter. Just know that if you do not tell me what I wish, I will crush this eye in my hand.

SISTER ONE: The eye! No!

SISTER TWO: Tell it what it wants to know!

SISTER THREE: We must!

PERSEUS: I wish to know where to find Medusa, the Gorgon.

SISTER ONE: To the east, the east.

SISTER TWO: Past the Mountains of Fire.

SISTER THREE: Yes, yes, that is where you will find her. Now, give us the eye.

PERSEUS: Here! I throw it upon the ground. You can fight for it among yourselves!

SISTER ONE: It's mine!

SISTER TWO: I saw it first!

SISTER THREE: Miiiiiiiine!

(sounds of old women squabbling)

HERMES: Nicely done.

PERSEUS: Thank you.

HERMES: I guess you won't need my help any longer. Follow the directions they gave you. You will be able to tell by the stench when you are near.

PERSEUS: But . . .

HERMES: Remember, Medusa is not the only Gorgon. Her "sisters" have suffered the same fate as her. Do not attempt to kill them. They are immortal, yet they do not possess her power. Remember your shield, and you can't go wrong.

PERSEUS: I'm glad you have faith in me.

HERMES: Ah, you're a resourceful lad. You'll make it. Well, I have to be off. I've loved adventuring with you, but the dead have been piling up. Farewell!

NARRATOR: And, with his golden staff spinning in his hand, Hermes disappeared. Perseus followed the directions that the three sisters had given him. Soon he smelled the stench of decaying bodies, and a black mountain rose up before his view. There on the peak, he saw the three Gorgons sleeping. They were all fearsome creatures, but Medusa stood out above the others. He was careful to only look at the reflection in his shield. Snakes writhed where hair should be. The terrifying scales of her skin rose and fell with her shallow breathing. She was a monster.

PERSEUS: I have to get in close.

NARRATOR: Perseus flew in, landed, and quietly crept toward the sleeping sisters. Before he had taken three steps, he saw the reflection of Medusa rise.

MEDUSA: *(hissing)* Foolish creature! You have disturbed my rest! Now, I will send you to Hades.

NARRATOR: He was shaking. In his shield, he saw her charge. He felt the sword heavy and still in his hand. He waited. With all his might, he swung his weapon.

(snicker-snack of the blade)

MEDUSA: Ahhhhhhhhhh . . .

NARRATOR: He felt its sharpness pierce her neck, and he realized that he had succeeded. But Medusa's dying cry had awoken her two immortal sisters. They rose up on their haunches and hissed.

GORGON: *(beastlike)* Murderer!

NARRATOR: Quickly, Perseus gripped the severed head of Medusa. The snakes still writhed and bit his hand, but his grip did not falter. Careful not to meet its gaze, he slipped it into his satchel, and, just as Hermes said it would, it engulfed the head and then shrank back to its original size.

GORGON: *(roars like a lion)*

NARRATOR: He took to the air as the Gorgons ran to their dead sister's body. He heard them wailing behind him as he flew away. He had done it!

PERSEUS: I have to thank Atlas for his help.

NARRATOR: As he passed the great titan, Perseus hailed him.

PERSEUS: Atlas!

ATLAS: *(grumbling)* Who is it?

PERSEUS: It is I, Perseus. I have returned with the head of the Gorgon like I promised.

ATLAS: *(excitedly)* Have you, boy? The weight of the skies has grown so heavy. I can stand it no longer. Please, show it to me.

NARRATOR: Perseus brought Medusa's head forth from his satchel. Atlas met its gaze. He turned to stone with these final words on his lips:

ATLAS: *(fading away)* Thank you.

PERSEUS: I've got to get back to Mother.

NARRATOR: And, back he flew—as fast as the winged sandals could carry him—back over the barren fields, the high mountains, and the roaring seas. But, as he crossed the sea, he heard a cry.

ANDROMEDA: *(screaming)* Heeeeelp! Help me!

NARRATOR: A beautiful young woman was alone on an island, tied to a stake in the ground. Perseus landed and ran to her.

PERSEUS: What's the matter?

ANDROMEDA: *(crazily)* A serpent, a serpent is coming for me! Quickly!

NARRATOR: Her name was Andromeda. A terrible sea serpent had been terrorizing the people of her country. An oracle had told them in order to stop the beast they must sacrifice Princess Andromeda. But, Perseus knew none of this yet. He only saw a beautiful woman in need of his help.

PERSEUS: There. You're free.

ANDROMEDA: Too late. *(frightened)* Here it comes!

NARRATOR: Perseus turned to face the giant snake. He was no longer the Perseus of before, self-doubting and weak. He was the slayer of Medusa, the son of Zeus. The great beast of Poseidon rose from the brine—red eyes, scales dripping saltwater, and a pink mouth, yawning wide, full of tiny teeth. Once again, he felt the blade swing from his side. It tore through flesh. Through half-closed eyes, he saw the limp body fall back into the water.

ANDROMEDA: *(stunned)* I can't believe it! Who are you?

PERSEUS: Perseus—but we must go—quickly! Let me take you back to your family.

ANDROMEDA: My family? No. They were the ones who put me out here to die. Take me with you.

NARRATOR: With this, Perseus smiled. He took the princess into his arms and flew back to the kingdom of Polydectes as quickly as his winged feet would take him. He and Andromeda found Dictys' hut abandoned. Neighbors told Perseus that after he had left, his mother had fled the palace, rejecting the king's proposal. The king in a fury had sent his guards after her. Dictys had helped hide Danaë, and they had fled to a faraway temple where they were allowed sanctuary. Polydectes had been furious. Perseus knew what he now must do. He left Andromeda at the hut, kissing her before he left. He had a meeting with the king.

POLYDECTES: Men, I have called you here today for a great purpose. My pride has been scorned. A woman has made a mockery of me. I have spent these last weeks preparing an army to march on the land that hides her from me. You are here for that purpose. *(sound of door opening)*

POLYDECTES: *(in shock)* Perseus? It can't be!

PERSEUS: I have come back, and I have brought what I promised.

POLYDECTES: No, I won't let this happen.

PERSEUS: You can do nothing to stop it. Die now.

POLYDECTES: Seize—

NARRATOR: Polydectes froze in mid-speech, his arm thrown forward in anger—so had the rest of the men in the hall stopped—forever turned to stone. At the door, Perseus stood, averting his gaze, holding the writhing head of Medusa aloft one final time. He had fulfilled his promise.

News spread quickly that the King had died. Danaë, Dictys, and his wife were sent for. They rejoiced when they saw the noble Perseus again and showered him with kisses and handshakes.

Athena was there as well, visible only to Perseus, and she took the head of Medusa from him. Zeus placed it on a shield, which he gave to Athena. To this day, it still stares forth from her mighty armor. Dictys, once a poor fisherman, was made king of Polydectes' realm. Perseus and Andromeda were married on the very shore where he and his mother once washed up. After the ceremony, Danaë stood apart from the rest, crying to herself.

PERSEUS: Mother, this is a happy occasion! What's the matter?

DANAË: Oh, Perseus. I miss my home. Argos is where I belong.

PERSEUS: Well, we have righted things here. Why shouldn't we return there?

DANAË: *(crying)* Perseus, you are the best boy a mother could ask for.

NARRATOR: Danaë, Perseus, and his new bride returned to Argos and sought out Acrisius, the king. There was a great celebration going on—a great bout of games. They stopped and asked the people if they knew of Acrisius.

MAN: He is the king no longer. He was driven mad and fled the palace. No one knows where he is.

DANAË: Perhaps it is better this way.

NARRATOR: So, they resolved to make their home in Argos. As they walked through the festival, Danaë felt her spirits rising. She was home. Perseus and Andromeda were deliriously happy. They had found each other. Feeling like a young boy again, Perseus entered the discus contest. Andromeda laughed at his antics as he joked inside the ring. *(laughing)* With his swift arm, the same arm that had slain the Gorgon and the great sea serpent, he let the discus sail. *(whistling sound)* There was a commotion among the crowd. The discus had gone awry, into the bystanders and had killed a man. It was the mad King Acrisius—killed by Perseus' discus. Oracles never lie.

DISCUSS

- What qualifies Perseus as a hero?
- The fisherman Dictys' wife is never actually named in the story. What does this tell you about women in ancient Greece?
- The tale begins with a prophecy and ends with its fulfillment. What does this ending add to the story?

DRAW

Draw a map of Perseus' journey, making sure to highlight all major points of interest.

WATCH

Watch *Clash of the Titans* (1981) directed by Desmond Davis. The film is loosely based on the Perseus myth. What changes have the filmmakers made?

The Hero

Two heroes enter the stage. The hero on the right is wearing a red cape. He has a chiseled chin and bulging muscles. You know, if prompted to, he could stop a speeding bullet or leap a tall building in a single bound. The hero on the left is wearing a simple dress and a cloth wound tightly around her head. Her face and hands are wrinkled from the years she has spent laboring in the ditches of Calcutta, caring for the sick and dying. She has touched the lives of millions worldwide, but her footing is so weak she can barely stand.

Who is the *real* hero?

Obviously, there are many different definitions of the word *hero.* For some, it might mean a political or religious figure. For others, a beloved relative or friend. It might even mean comic books and spandex to a few. But, some heroes don't have supernatural powers, some heroes haven't changed the world, and some heroes aren't even famous.

What are the tried-and-true qualifications of a hero?

At some point a hero has impacted another person's life. Heroes are personal. Affecting the lives of thousands is great, but one is enough. Heroes are trailblazers. Heroes overcome great challenges. Heroes have all of the weaknesses the rest of us have—greed, fear, hate—but they have mastered and defeated them. Heroes make their heroic deeds look easy, even though they're not.

Zeus (Roman Names: Jupiter, Jove)

Lord of the Sky, Rain-Bringer, Cloud-Gatherer

After leading his brother and sister gods in a revolt against their forefathers, the Titans, Zeus became the unquestioned ruler of the heavens. His feared weapon is the thunderbolt, and his palace on Mt. Olympus is a place of peace, where all gods are welcome. Zeus is the husband of the goddess Hera, but it's not in his nature to be faithful. Time and time again, he enters into disastrous affairs with other goddesses, nymphs, and mortal women. Zeus is the all-father. Almost all of the second generation of gods claim Zeus as their father. Many of the mortal heroes are children of the god as well. Zeus' bird is the eagle.

Many people have asked, "Are heroes born or made?" Does everyone have the hero capability lying dormant inside him or her? Or, are heroes only a certain type of people, the ones destined to do great things? Don't ordinary people do heroic deeds all of the time? They stop a child from drowning. Their kind words keep a woman from committing suicide. They save a man from going hungry. Until they were placed into these situations, they might not have known if they were heroic or not.

Our culture talks about heroes so much, it's almost cliché. When you're asked to write about heroes for the 500th time, you might roll your eyes. But actually, this topic is one that *should* be run into the ground. We should never forget the sacrifices made in the past and in the present to preserve our safety, freedom, and happiness. If writing "My Hero Is . . ." essays until your hand falls off is the way to remember that, so be it.

Heroes inspire more heroes. It's a side effect of their actions. Seeing them do their best inspires us to do our best. The heroic spirit is kept alive and reborn for a new generation.

All of these points are important to consider. Someday you might want to be a hero yourself. You'll need to know how this whole hero thing works. Along the way, you also might discover that heroes aren't confined to the lofty heights of Mt. Olympus or even the Batcave. They might be everyday people right here on Earth—a lot closer than you thought.

Maybe your definition of a hero doesn't match this one. Maybe you want more qualifications. For you, heroes may only be linked to sports or music or politics. Because heroes are personal, it's up to you to determine your personal definition. That way it will be easier to spot them when they come along.

What does it take to be a hero for you?

DISCUSS

A new museum is being opened. It is solely dedicated to five heroes who have shaped your country. You and your classmates have been selected to decide which five figures will be inducted to *The Hall of Heroes.* Each person should nominate one person. Discuss your choice with your classmates. Then vote on the five inductees. If there is a discrepancy, continue to vote until you reach a consensus. Then, answer the following questions:

- What were some of the different qualifications used to justify your nominees?
- Who are the heroes of your society? Explain.
- Are heroes born or made? Defend your answer.

Spider Sense Tingling!

To the Greeks, heroes were mortals who showcased superhuman capabilities. Although it was only for a brief time, Heracles (Hercules) held up the enormous weight of the sky by himself, Atalanta could beat any other mortal in a foot race, and Perseus could fly—with a little help from his winged sandals. Gods could have done all of these things as well, of course, but heroes were human, and this made all the difference.

The concept of the hero has taken a more down-to-earth route over time. Mother Theresa, Martin Luther King, Jr., and Mahatma Gandhi are three excellent examples of the modern hero. But, what would the ancient Greeks think about this? Gandhi didn't slay a hydra, Martin Luther King,

Jr. was not present at the Trojan War, and Mother Theresa couldn't even chuck a spear. Therefore, the Greeks would conclude, these are not heroes at all.

What happened? Our definition is basically the same: Mortals doing amazing things, things that no other human thought possible. The modern concept of these "amazing things" must have changed. Now we're more interested in heroes who can reform society than those who can wrestle lions. But, didn't we have the Greek concept at one point? Where has it gone? Where have all the boulder-tossing, monster-fighting, maiden-saving, sky-flying heroes gone?

Read a comic book lately?

Superheroes are an invention of the 20th century—handsome men and beautiful women, possessing extraordinary capabilities, who vow to fight for truth, justice, and the American way. Multicolored spandex, capes, weird gadgets, masks, and secret lairs—it's all very exciting, but where did it come from? Just like the superheroes they feature, comic books have a secret identity, a hidden origin that they may not want revealed. But now, their secret is out. Superheroes aren't a new idea. They're a very ancient one—with a makeover.

Athena (Roman Names: Minerva, Pallas Athena)

Goddess of Wisdom and Battle

According to one tale, Athena was not actually born, but sprang fully grown from Zeus' head. This is symbolic of her distinction as Goddess of Wisdom. Athena's animal is the wisest of birds, the owl. As the leader of the Virgin Goddesses, those who will never marry, Athena refuses to let any man to be her master. When a new city-state was founded, there was a contest between Athena and her uncle Poseidon over who should be its patron god. The competition was fierce. To win the people over to his side, Poseidon formed the first horse from the crest of a wave. In order to one-up his gift, Athena created the bridle, a tool man could use to subdue Poseidon's creation. Because her gift was the wiser, the city chose Athena as their patron goddess. From this point on the city-state was called Athens.

Instead of monsters and armies, superheroes battle mutants and mad scientists. Instead of rescuing beautiful princesses, superheroes rescue school children from wrecked buses and mothers from burning buildings. Instead of being the children of gods, superheroes are the product of strange circumstances—radioactive chemicals, alien parentage, magical amulets, or simple mutation. However they came to be super, they are called upon to do good with their abilities, to protect the weak and downtrodden, and to defeat those who threaten peace.

Heroes haven't changed much on the inside—just on the outside.

The best way to weaken superheroes is through their alter egos, their secret identities. The bad guys may not stand a chance against Batman, but if they find out he is really Bruce Wayne, they have an advantage. The Greek heroes were human underneath it all as well. More often than not they fall victim to the same shortcomings the rest of humanity does—greed, lust, and pride.

Like the ancient Greeks, we need to feel that somewhere there exists a larger-than-life person who embodies a timeless ideal. Superheroes are a holdover of that need. When all other hope has vanished, who will save the day?

The Hero's Journey

Joseph Campbell (1970), an American psychologist and mythological researcher, wrote a famous book entitled *The Hero With a Thousand Faces.* In his lifelong research, Campbell discovered many common patterns running through hero myths and stories from around the world. Years of research lead Campbell to discover several basic stages that almost every hero-quest goes through (no matter what culture of which the myth is a part). He called this common structure the *monomyth.* Campbell identified many stages in his monomyth. For our purposes, we will only focus on a basic few.

The Call to Adventure

For heroes to begin their journeys, they must be called away from the ordinary world. Fantastic quests don't happen in everyday life. Heroes must be removed from their typical environment. Most heroes show a reluctance to leave their home, their friends, and their life to journey on a quest. But, in the end they accept their destiny.

Usually there is a discovery, some event, or some danger that starts them on the heroic path. Heroes find a mystic object or discover their world is in danger. In some cases, heroes happen upon their quest by acci-

---

Hermes (Roman Name: Mercury)

Messenger of the Gods

Hermes, the most mischievous and clever of the gods, also serves as a psychopomp (a guide of dead souls to the Underworld). One of the youngest gods, Hermes showed his ability to cause both trouble and delight at an early age. On the day of his birth, Hermes snuck out from his cradle and whisked away the cattle of his elder brother Apollo. Hermes was quickly found out and forced to return the cattle. But, in reparation for his actions against Apollo, the newborn god created a lyre from the shell of a turtle. He presented the stringed instrument to his older brother. Apollo's anger melted away, and he gifted Hermes with a magical sleep-inducing staff called the caduceus. Once Zeus realized his young son would cause nothing but trouble if he weren't constantly occupied, Hermes was given the job of Olympian Messenger. A winged cap and sandals were presented to him to assist him in his duties. Due to the nature of his job, Hermes appears most often of all the gods.

---

dent. Campbell (1970) puts it like this, "A blunder—the merest chance—reveals an unsuspected world" (p. 51).

The new world the hero is forced into is much different than the old one. Campbell (1970) described this new world as a

> fateful region of both treasure and danger . . . a distant land, a forest, a kingdom underground, beneath the waves, or above the sky, a secret island, lofty mountaintop, or profound dream state . . . a place of strangely fluid and polymorphous beings, unimaginable torments, superhuman deeds, and impossible delight. (p. 58)

This description may seem pretty vague, but think of all the various fantasy realms characters have entered throughout the years: Middle-Earth, Oz, Narnia, and Wonderland. It could even be outer space, a haunted house, or the Matrix. Regardless of the details, the new world is sure to be filled with adventure.

Entering the Unknown

As they embark on their journey, the heroes enter a world they have never experienced before. Very often it is filled with supernatural creatures, breathtaking sights, and the constant threat of death. Unlike the heroes' home, this outside world has its own rules, and they quickly learn to respect these rules as their endurance, strength, and mettle are tested time and time again. After all, it is not the end of the journey that teaches, but the journey itself.

Supernatural Aid

Supernatural doesn't necessarily mean *magical.* There are plenty of hero stories that don't have wizards or witches. Supernatural simply means "above the laws of nature." Heroes almost always start their journey with the help of a character who has mastered the laws of the outside world and comes back to bestow this wisdom upon them. This supernatural character often gives them the means to complete the quest. Sometimes the gift is simply wisdom. At other times it is an object with magical powers. In every instance it is something the hero needs to succeed.

As Campbell (1970) said, "One has only to know and trust, and the ageless guardians will appear" (p. 72). There are countless examples of this. Where would Cinderella be without her fairy godmother? Where would Luke Skywalker be without Obi-Wan Kenobi? As with these examples, the job of the supernatural assistor is to give the heroes what they need to finish the quest—not finish it for them.

Helpers

Every hero needs a helper, much like every superhero needs a sidekick. Without the assistance of their companions and helpers along the way, most heroes would fail miserably. Helpers aren't supernatural. They're everyday folks, operating under (not above) the natural conditions of the new world. The assistance they offer is practical yet indispensable. For example, in the Greek hero story of Theseus, Minos' daughter Ariadne, after falling hopelessly in love, helps Theseus navigate the Labyrinth. She does this by holding one end of a golden thread while Theseus works his way inward to slay the Minotaur. Without her help, Theseus would never have fulfilled his quest or found his way out of the maze once he did so.

Tests and the Supreme Ordeal

The heroes progress through a series of tests, a set of obstacles that make them stronger, preparing them for their final showdown. At long last they reach the *supreme ordeal,* or the obstacle they have journeyed so far to overcome. For example, for Theseus, slaying the Minotaur was his supreme ordeal.

Atlas

Atlas belonged to a race of immortal beings called the Titans, who ruled the world before the gods came into existence. Cronus, the father of Zeus, was the leader of his Titan brothers and sisters. Cronus feared a child of his own would one day overthrow him, so to prevent this from happening, he ate his children one-by-one as they were born. His wife, Rhea, managed to save one and substituted a rock for his supper instead. Zeus, the saved son, grew up in exile and returned to face his father. Forcing Cronus to vomit up his eaten brother and sisters, Zeus freed the gods, and together they waged a war against the Titans. When the gods emerged victorious, the Titans were punished or chained in the Underworld. Atlas, for his part in the war, was forced to stand between heaven and Earth, where the weight of the sky eternally rests on his shoulders.

All of the heroes' training and toil comes into play now. The journey has hardened them, and it's time for them to show their prowess. Once this obstacle is overcome, the tension will be relieved. The worst is passed, and the quest, while not officially over, has succeeded.

Reward and the Journey Home

Typically, there is a reward given to heroes for passing the supreme ordeal. It could be a kingdom. It could be the hand of a beautiful princess. It could be the Holy Grail. Whatever it is, it is a reward for the heroes' endurance and strength.

After the heroes complete the supreme ordeal and have the reward firmly in hand, all that is left is for them to return home. Just because the majority of the adventure has passed doesn't mean that the return journey will be smooth sailing. There are still lesser homebound obstacles to overcome.

Restoring the World

Success on a quest can be life changing for heroes and often for many others. By achieving victory, heroes have changed or preserved their original world; thus, that world's grateful inhabitants recognize them as a hero.

Heroes who finish quests return home also having grown in spirit and strength. They have proved themselves worthy for marriage, kingship, or queenship. Their mastery of the outside world qualifies them to be giants in their own. But, sometimes this growth has made them too big to fit back into their original world. Their taste for adventure makes them unsatisfied with ordinary life. Usually this problem, this desire for more than the normal world offers, will lead them to yet another adventure.

Although Joseph Campbell's monomyth works best with the traditional form of the quest—folk and fairy tales, myths, legends, and other fantasies—it can be applied to many different genres or types of stories. A quest does not have to include swords and monsters. It can just as easily occur in the real world. Even though a quest for the perfect Christmas present is far less mystifying than a quest for a golden fleece, the same stages easily can apply. The monomyth exists anywhere and everywhere. It is ageless and universal.

DISCUSS
- Find each of Joseph Campbell's monomyth stages in the story of Perseus, and discuss their importance.
- Find each of Joseph Campbell's monomyth stages in another book or film, and discuss their importance.

CREATE
Create your own hero's journey for an original hero. This hero can be in the ancient or modern world. (Make sure that his or her journey contains all of the elements of this structure.) Use the written word, art, or a combination of the two to express your hero's journey.

She's a Monster!

Medusa is a nasty customer, but she is only one of many creatures the Greeks used to populate their world. The ancient wilderness presented man with his biggest fear—fear of the unknown. No one knew what existed beyond his or her own little sphere of life. The Greeks had plenty

Medusa

Snake-haired and steely-eyed, Medusa the Gorgon possessed the power to turn any living creature into stone with her supernatural gaze. Medusa was not always a hideous creature though. Once she was a beautiful mortal maiden, who dared to meet her lover in the temple of Athena. Athena, being a virgin goddess, was deeply offended by this blatant disrespect for her holy place. Appearing in a flash of flame, Athena struck down Medusa's lover, transformed the maiden into a monster, and banished her to the ends of the earth. Because she was an enchanted being, Medusa's blood contained magical properties. When Perseus ended her life, another magical being sprang from her spilled blood, Pegasus, the famous winged horse. The head of Medusa now stares out from the aegis, Zeus' shield, which he allows his favorite daughter Athena to bear for him.

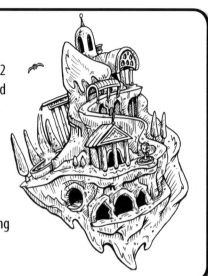

Mt. Olympus
The Heavenly Mountain of the Gods

The palace of Zeus on Mt. Olympus is the home of the 12 Olympian gods and goddesses. When the heavens and Earth were divided between his two brothers, Poseidon and Hades, Zeus declared that Mt. Olympus would be common to all. Here is where the gods have their great debates, sipping nectar and eating ambrosia. In the earliest myths, Mt. Olympus is still associated with the mountain in Greece that bears the same name. But, by later times, it was imagined to be a mystical place, floating high in the heavens.

of these wilderness monsters to chose from—harpies, sphinxes, Chimaeras, hydras, Cyclopes, and giant serpents. Ancient cultures all over the world, not only the Greeks, invented all kinds of razor-clawed, snaggle-toothed creatures, lurking just outside the known, waiting to gobble up unsuspecting adventurers. Perhaps these kinds of stories were designed to keep people close to home.

The unknown was and still is the playground of the imagination. Walking through a dark forest, walking through a dark alley, or even walking through a dark room is enough to start the imagination working. Living in a dark world, the Greek imagination started to work in the same manner. Without true knowledge of what actually lay just beyond the borders of life, their minds were given free reign.

Does the same thing still happen today? Are we still populating the unknown with fantastical creatures? At first you may think not. We're so much smarter, so much more advanced in our day and age. Monsters are entertaining for sure, but not a real threat. The *known* is getting pretty large, and the unknown is shrinking at a rapid rate. Soon there probably won't even be an unknown. Right?

Like I said, that may be what you *think*.

Think about the tabloids that feature those outlandish stories—headlines like *Batboy Found, Mother Gives Birth to 300 lb. Watermelon*, and *Devil's Face Appears in Man's Breakfast Cereal.*

A lot of people buy these magazines to laugh at them, but other people buy it out of curiosity. Could there really be a creature like a batboy? Exactly how would you give birth to a 300 lb. watermelon? And, why is the devil popping up in someone's Lucky Charms? It's proof that society still thinks there's an unknown. Some things are still unexplainable.

Plenty of completely sane people believe in Sasquatch or Bigfoot, a 10-foot-tall ape-man living undetected in the forests of North America. And, Bigfoot isn't the only unexplainable creature on record. His European counterpart, Nessie, the Loch Ness Monster, has a following as well. Could an immense dinosaur-like animal be living at the bottom of a Scottish lake? There's even a whole branch of science called *cryptozoology*, a combination of Greek root words that mean "the study of hidden animals," that researches mysterious or hidden creatures, as well as creatures that may have existed at some point but are extinct now (such as dragons).

Hades (Roman Names: Pluto, Dis)

Ruler of the Dead, Lord of the Underworld

Although he has been presented as one before, Hades is no villain. He is cold and calculating. He keeps to himself, only showing up in myth when he is sought out. Hades is more a recluse than anything else. He has little to do with mortal's lives. Their deaths are a different story. Hades is not Death himself; in other words he is not responsible for deciding when mortals die. A mortal's death is an assembly line: The Fates snip the threads of life, Thanatos (or death) causes the mortal to die, and Hermes leads the soul to the banks of the Styx. After the gods defeated their forbearers, the Titans, Hades was presented with a helmet of invisibility and given the Underworld to rule. Hades' Roman name, Pluto, came from the Greek word for wealth. The god was considered rich because of all of the precious metals that are found beneath the Earth.

If these "unsolved mysteries" aren't enough to convince you, let's look to the heavens. A certain group of people has been "watching the skies" for decades. You might ask, "Watching the skies for what?" Aliens, of course. Personal stories of abduction, blurry photographs of flying saucers, and mysterious patterns stamped into crops are enough to raise the question: Do extraterrestrials exist? Even scientists say there *could* very well be life on other planets. Have they been visiting us and trying to contact us these many years?

Whether you chose to believe in any of these creatures or not, you should still see that the possibility of their existence hinges on one thing—the unknown. Although no one has effectively proved that they *do* exist, no one can for sure say that they *don't*. Also think about where these

DISCUSS

- Is there a correlation between ancient Greek monsters and our own? Explain.
- What are some other examples of modern "unsolved mysteries"?

DRAW

Draw an ancient Greek tabloid cover (similar to the magazines mentioned earlier) complete with headlines from outrageous stories about outrageous creatures.

creatures live, on the edge of our comfort zone, places where our knowledge gets thin—deep woods, deep water, and deep space. Ours may look a little different than the Greeks', but we still have our own monsters of the unknown.

The Underworld

Often referred to as Hades (after its ruler), the Greek Underworld was an interesting concept. As its name implies, it existed below the Earth, and in several spots live mortals could actually enter the Underworld (if they dared). Hades was not Hell, or in other words, it was not only reserved for the evil of the world. All of the dead went to the Underworld, good and bad. There they would be judged according to their deeds in life. An eternal fate would be assigned to each soul. For those who committed heinous crimes, torture would be their destiny. Even for those souls who were not punished there, Hades was an unpleasant place. It was cold and lifeless, a dismal destination everyone would have to face someday. Perhaps this is why the Greeks were so focused on getting the most out of life.

CHAPTER 2

Battle of the Sexes: Women in Mythology

THE STORY OF ATALANTA

Cast

Atalanta (Hero of our story)

Meleager (Prince of Calydon)

King (Atalanta's father)

She-Bear (Wild mother bear)

Chief (Leader of a tribe of nomadic hunters)

Hunter (One of the Chief's tribesmen)

Centaur One (Brutish, half-horse, half-man creature)

Centaur Two (Another brutish, half-horse, half-man creature)

Uncle One (Meleager's uncle)

Uncle Two (Meleager's uncle)

Wild Boar (Supernatural beast sent by Artemis)

NARRATOR: There once was a king in Greece who wanted nothing more than a son. He was getting on in years, and at last his wife delivered him a child. But, his joy at this news was short-lived.

KING: (angrily) A daughter? I won't have a girl-child inheriting my kingdom! Take this child into the forests and leave it there! If I will have no son, I will have no heir!

NARRATOR: The servants rushed to carry out his orders, and the baby was left in the nearby woods. It was here that she was found by the most unlikely of nursemaids. A passing She-Bear, mourning the loss of her young cub, happened upon the infant girl.

SHE-BEAR: (surprised) A human child? Here in the forest? It will snow soon, and it shall surely die.

NARRATOR: The baby stirred something inside the beast, and she nuzzled the child with her warm snout and licked the dirt from its face.

SHE-BEAR: The humans have abandoned you. They are cruel and barbaric creatures, but I will take you for my own, young one, and I will raise you to have a nobler heart than those from which you came.

NARRATOR: The mother bear made good on her word and took the girl back to her den and raised the child as her own offspring. The She-Bear gave her a name in the language of the animals that meant "equal"—because the girl would be raised to be as much a bear as one had ever been. When the time came for the girl to walk, the She-Bear showed her how to run on all fours and how to stand up tall to intimidate an opponent. She showed her how to find grubs for sustenance. She showed her how to slap the silvery fish out of the swift-flowing stream. And so, the girl grew and grew.

ATALANTA: (young-sounding voice) Mother, why do I look nothing like you? Why do I not look like other bears?

SHE-BEAR: (laughs) Because you are not a bear. You are a human child.

NARRATOR: The girl's face wrinkled in disgust.

ATALANTA: Humans are cowards. They're the ones that come into the forests with their spears. What weaklings! They don't even have claws like you, mother.

SHE-BEAR: No, they do not, but neither will you.

ATALANTA: (disappointed) Awwwww. I was hoping they might grow in.

SHE-BEAR: No, you will be as unprotected as any other man. But, man's strength is not in his body—it's in his mind. He is tricky.

ATALANTA: I want to be strong!

SHE-BEAR: You will be, dear, you will be.

NARRATOR: One day, while mother and cub were drinking from a cool stream, the She-Bear froze.

SHE-BEAR: (whispering) Daughter, you must be still. There are men there on the other side of the stream. Can you smell them?

ATALANTA: (whispering) Yes.

SHE-BEAR: When I tell you, you must run.

ATALANTA: (frightened) No, mother!

NARRATOR: But, before either could move, a shrill cry came from the far bushes, and like a stinging fly, a spear shot forth and into the side of the She-Bear. She roared and fell upon the shivering girl.

SHE-BEAR: (badly hurt) Be still, be still.

ATALANTA: (crying) Mother, mother . . .

SHE-BEAR: (weakly) The men are coming, my dear. You must go with them.

ATALANTA: No, mother, I'm not one of them!

SHE-BEAR: Oh, you are, daughter. I was wrong to keep you from your kind. You must join them, but you must show them—you must be better. You must be kind and noble and fair . . .

ATALANTA: But, you—I won't ever leave you.

SHE-BEAR: (whispering) Good-bye.

NARRATOR: When the hunters rolled over the carcass of their latest kill, they were greeted by quite a shock. Curled into a weeping ball beneath it was a spindly little girl—naked, her hair a tattered mess.

HUNTER: (surprised) What's this?

NARRATOR: The little creature's eyes flicked open, and she lunged at them—sinking her teeth into the nearest man's leg.

HUNTER: (screaming) Ahhhhh! Get it off!

NARRATOR: It took two men to finally corral her. She kicked and scratched and cried like a wild thing. They finally pinned her to the ground, and her rasping breaths slowly started to subside.

HUNTER: (angrily) We should take no chances. Let us drown this evil thing at once!

CHIEF: (laughs) Evil thing? It is just a little girl.

HUNTER: Look what she did to my leg!

CHIEF: Is that why you are so quick to condemn her? She is alone out here—raised up by this bear. Now, we must raise her.

HUNTER: What? She will tear out our throats in the middle of the night!

CHIEF: Did you see her speed? Her agility? We will make her one of us.

NARRATOR: And so, the hunters took her back to their nomadic camp. She fought them the whole way—crying like the Furies—but they did not let go of her.

CHIEF: First thing she needs is a bath. Take her down to the river. Andreas, find her some clothes.

NARRATOR: For a time, the young girl resisted. She would be no human. She would not serve the men who killed her mother—but then the final words of the She-Bear came back to her little mind. She softened and allowed the hunters to adopt her into their tribe.

ATALANTA: I must live in their world, but I shall never be a part of it.

NARRATOR: The leader of the hunters saw this change in her. He noticed that she listened when he and the hunters spoke, and after time, he perceived that she understood their words. One day, he took her by surprise and spoke directly to her.

CHIEF: I am sorry that we killed the one that you love.

ATALANTA: (sadly) She was my mother.

CHIEF: What name did she give you?

ATALANTA: She called me "equal."

CHIEF: Then that is what we shall call you as well, little one. Atalanta is what you will be named for it means equal.

NARRATOR: And so, the wild girl grew up in the camp of the hunters. She learned to kill the animals with which she had once shared the forests—but did it with respect, never for sport. In time, her scrawniness dropped away, and she became tall and proud—the fastest, the smartest, and the fairest among the hunting tribes.

CHIEF: I believe our little Atalanta is growing up.

HUNTER: Why do you say that?

CHIEF: The men from the other tribes let their eyes linger upon her. They no longer think of her as our wild brat, but as a grown woman—one they desire.

HUNTER: I will kill them if they look at her in such a way!

CHIEF: (laughs) I remember how you wished her dead many years ago.

HUNTER: I was a fool. She is one of us now—our daughter and our sister.

CHIEF: True. She is even the best among us. She can throw farther and run quicker than any man here. Soon, she shall leave us, I fear.

NARRATOR: As the two spoke, the radiant form of Atalanta burst forth from the underbrush. Her hair had grown free and hung like a golden shower upon her shoulders. Her skin was tanned from the constant sight of the sun.

ATALANTA: Brothers! I have killed a boar!

CHIEF: Very good, Atalanta. Where did he fall?

ATALANTA: Not far. I will drag him here soon.

HUNTER: All by yourself?

ATALANTA: (defensively) I can do it.

CHIEF: You should never be ashamed to ask for help, Atalanta, or pride shall become a weakness.

NARRATOR: The girl snorted and disappeared back into the thicket.

CHIEF: She is independent to be sure.

NARRATOR: A faraway cry was sounded, and the two nomads' attention was turned. Three men on horseback came riding through the forest and into the village— two old men in traveling coats and a dark-haired young man.

UNCLE ONE: (shouting) Who is the leader here?

CHIEF: I am. What do you lords want with us? We are humble hunters.

UNCLE TWO: We come to offer you riches—in turn for your help.

CHIEF: We do not pledge our help to strangers. Tell us who asks.

MELEAGER: I do.

NARRATOR: The youth rode boldly forward.

MELEAGER: I come in the name of my father, King Oeneus. A savage beast has been ravaging our land—a giant boar—killing livestock, travelers, and any who try to hunt it.

CHIEF: Powerful beasts do not just appear without reason. Your father must have angered the gods.

MELEAGER: It is true. Artemis has cursed us. My father has forgotten her in his sacrifices.

CHIEF: We respect the will of Artemis, but I will admit we are poor and our people want for the things your riches could provide.

UNCLE ONE: Then you shall help us?

CHIEF: I will think on it. You may stay here tonight.

UNCLE TWO: (laughs) Stay here? No, thank you.

MELEAGER: Uncle, there is nothing wrong with staying here.

UNCLE ONE: Sire, you are a prince. You should not sleep with such dogs.

MELEAGER: I will stay, and you will not order me around. *You* may do what you will.

CHIEF: Come, young prince. We shall show you our simple ways.

NARRATOR: The young man dismounted. The chief shook his hand warmly and led him away. The two uncles stared sourly at one another. Through a faraway clearing, the huntress Atalanta was running—searching for her kill—and at that moment, it was eluding her.

ATALANTA: *(angrily)* It was there before! What has happened to it?

NARRATOR: At once, she stopped—and sniffed. Two creatures were in the thicket to the south; two loud, uncouth beings. Creeping on all fours, she inched toward them and peered out from a low-lying bush.

ATALANTA: *(whispering)* Centaurs.

NARRATOR: There were two great beasts in the thicket—9 feet tall, half-man, and half-horse. She had found her dead boar as well. They were making a quick meal of its red flesh. In one single movement, Atalanta sprang up, drew her bow, and notched an arrow into the string. The heads of the centaurs flicked up.

ATALANTA: *(gritted teeth)* Leave it alone or die!

CENTAUR ONE: *(beastlike)* What do we have here? A pretty little huntress!

CENTAUR TWO: *(beastlike)* Yes, it would seem so.

ATALANTA: I have given you your warning. You leave me no choice.

CENTAUR ONE: Perhaps we should teach her some manners.

CENTAUR TWO: She *is* a pretty thing.

NARRATOR: The centaurs raised their blood-wet lips into a howl and rearing their front legs started to charge. Two swift arrows split the air and found their marks in each of the beasts' necks.

CENTAUR ONE AND TWO: *(dying, coughing)*

NARRATOR: With a thump, the two huge bodies fell to the ground. Atalanta crept cautiously closer. She peered down at the decimated cadaver of her kill and wrinkled her nose.

ATALANTA: Beasts! *(spits)*

NARRATOR: Seeing that her prey had been ruined—she turned and ran quickly back through the wood. She smelled the strange horses in the village before she saw them. It was growing dark when she arrived. The hunters and some strange men were gathered around a campfire. They all stopped their talking when she walked up.

ATALANTA: Who are these strangers?

HUNTER: Ambassadors from Calydon. The chief is talking with their prince.

ATALANTA: *(spitefully)* What do such great ones want with us lowly hunters?

UNCLE ONE: Those are our sentiments exactly, but our impetuous nephew sees it otherwise. What are you? The village wife?

ATALANTA: *(hatefully)* I would watch my tongue if I were you, white-head. I will bear no man to be the master of me.

UNCLE TWO: *(laughs)* What man would want to? Where is your chief? What is taking so long?

NARRATOR: Atalanta gave the newcomers a vicious glance, but looked up to see the chief coming forth from his hut—his arm around a handsome young man.

CHIEF: Ah, Atalanta! You have returned!

NARRATOR: The prince stopped short, and he found a lump lodged in his throat. Before him was the most beautiful woman he had ever seen—the appearance of a goddess in earthly form—Artemis come to life.

ATALANTA: Why is he looking at me like that?

CHIEF: Ah, it seems that our young prince has noticed what you have failed to, Atalanta.

MELEAGER: No—I—just—*(cough)*

CHIEF: This is our sister-daughter Atalanta. We have raised her from a child.

MELEAGER: *(nervously)* It is a pleasure to meet you.

NARRATOR: The fumbling boy stuck out his hand, but the huntress only looked at it in anger.

ATALANTA: (angrily) Is this what I think it is? Have you decided to marry me off to this weakling? Look at him! He probably couldn't throw a spear 2 meters!

MELEAGER: (insulted) I don't think—

CHIEF: Atalanta! Be silent! We have not arranged a marriage. The prince has come to recruit hunters to take back with him to Calydon.

ATALANTA: Oh. I see. Well, then, boy, you have met the very best.

CHIEF: She is ever so humble, my lord. Tell me, Atalanta, where is the boar that you have killed?

MELEAGER: A wild boar? That is a mighty kill.

ATALANTA: That is nothing, princeling! I have just slain two centaurs as well.

CHIEF: My girl! That is most wonderful—and most dangerous! You could have easily been killed.

ATALANTA: No, I could not.

CHIEF: (chuckles) Very well. I know you are tired, but take the prince and show him some lodging.

ATALANTA: But—I—

CHIEF: Do as I say.

NARRATOR: Turning with a huff, Atalanta stalked away into the darkness.

CHIEF: There she goes, your highness. None of us may tame her. Perhaps you will have better luck.

NARRATOR: Meleager grinned and trotted off behind the girl. Like almost any man would, he was already falling quickly in love with the fiery young maiden.

MELEAGER: My name is Meleager.

ATALANTA: (angrily) I hope you don't think that I have to be nice to you. I have no intentions of doing so.

MELEAGER: Well, that's to be expected.

ATALANTA: I'm a fierce huntress—savage and brutal. You really should be afraid of me, you know.

MELEAGER: I am, I am—but you're not always savage and brutal, are you?

NARRATOR: The girl stopped and stared him down.

ATALANTA: Always.

NARRATOR: She took off again, and Meleager struggled to keep up.

MELEAGER: I think deep down you're probably kind and compassionate—

ATALANTA: I killed two centaurs today, boy. I am no princess. I was raised as a man.

MELEAGER: Yes, but you are a woman—perhaps you should start acting like it.

NARRATOR: Atalanta spun on her heel and grabbed the startled prince by the throat.

ATALANTA: Should I squeeze? I think so. Don't tell me what I should be.

MELEAGER: (hoarsely) All right! All right!

NARRATOR: The huntress released him and began walking again.

MELEAGER: They say that you were raised by bears.

ATALANTA: Not bears—a bear.

MELEAGER: I think that that's fascinating.

ATALANTA: Do you, princeling? Do you know what it's like to have your mother murdered before your very eyes? Do you know what it's like to be raised as the only woman in a group of men? Do you know what it's like to have people trying to tell you what to do and who to be?

MELEAGER: (softly) Yes. Actually, I do.

ATALANTA: Ha!

NARRATOR: They had reached a large hut. Atalanta angrily pulled open the flap and motioned to enter.

ATALANTA: Here you are, princeling—your palace.

MELEAGER: Thank you—and I understand.

NARRATOR: Meleager ducked into the hut, but Atalanta was soon behind.

ATALANTA: What do you mean you understand?

MELEAGER: What you've gone through.

ATALANTA: You cannot possibly understand—

MELEAGER: Will you let me speak? How will you ever know anything if you don't listen?

NARRATOR: Atalanta shut her mouth with a click and sank to the floor. The prince seated himself as well.

MELEAGER: You're angry at the world, because you were left alone. Well, I'm angry at the world for the same reason—only there are hundreds of people all around me.

ATALANTA: I don't understand.

MELEAGER: It's a long story—but I was cursed on the day I was born. The Three Fates came to my mother a week after my birth and prophesied my death. They told her that I would be dead when the log on the fire had been consumed.

ATALANTA: Obviously, they were wrong.

MELEAGER: Thanks to my mother. As soon as the vision of the Fates disappeared, she ran to the fireplace and put out the fire. Then she took the log—the one that symbolizes my life—and ever since has had it locked away.

ATALANTA: Congratulations. You can never die.

MELEAGER: I know that I *will* die someday—and so does my mother. And, it has driven her insane. She never leaves her room. She watches the chest with the log inside day and night. My father has considered her dead to him.

ATALANTA: Was she killed in front of your very eyes? I don't see how this is pertaining.

MELEAGER: Ever since I can remember, my mother has had a guard about me—someone to watch my every step. Over the years, this constant fear has destroyed her mind. Her love has turned to hate. She hates anything that could take me away from her. She has forbidden me to marry—threatening to destroy the log herself if I should do such a thing. And so, I am cursed to be alone the rest of my life.

ATALANTA: *(quietly)* I am sorry, but to me that would be a great thing—no one to ever tell you what to do.

MELEAGER: Have you never desired a companion? Someone to share your life with?

ATALANTA: No—never. I was raised wild, and I think I shall always be wild.

MELEAGER: I hope not. But, come, Atalanta. If nothing else, let us be friends.

NARRATOR: He held out his hand, and she glanced at it hesitantly, but then took it in her own.

ATALANTA: Agreed. Now, sleep, princeling. I have a feeling that you and I are going to be going on a long journey tomorrow.

NARRATOR: She was right. The next day, the chief pledged the help of the hunters to Prince Meleager of Calydon, and they made ready to depart.

MELEAGER: Atalanta, have you ever been out of Arcady?

ATALANTA: No, this has always been my home. What is Calydon like?

MELEAGER: A lot like this country—wild and free.

ATALANTA: Then I shall like it. How big is this boar, did you say?

MELEAGER: Men say that it is 10 to 12 feet tall.

ATALANTA: Men? Men always exaggerate.

NARRATOR: The two companions rode at the front of the procession—laughing and jibing. The chief rode with a satisfied look on his face.

CHIEF: Perhaps our little wild girl will find love after all.

NARRATOR: At the back of the procession, two old men rode with downcast looks upon their faces. They were the uncles of Meleager, the brothers of the queen.

UNCLE ONE: We do not need this rabble to kill the boar!

UNCLE TWO: Especially that female whelp. Look at her—flirting with the prince. Does she think that she will *ever* become a princess?

UNCLE ONE: Not if I have anything to say about it.

NARRATOR: They rode for many days until they finally came to the wilds of Calydon. They pitched their tents and made camp in the forest and prepared their weapons and their beasts for the hunt the following day.

ATALANTA: *(proudly)* I say that I shall be the first to slay the boar.

MELEAGER: Really? I think *I* shall get there first.

ATALANTA: *(playfully)* You? You are a woman! That beast is from Artemis. It will see your shaking hand and your pale face and know that it has nothing to fear.

NARRATOR: And so, the two stayed up late into the night of the eve of the great hunt. In spite of Atalanta's efforts, they had become fast friends. The morning broke light and crisp, and an early horn sounded that the hunt had begun. Meleager rode his magnificent steed into the forest, while Atalanta ran lightly at his side.

CHIEF: Hunters, stay close! Keep your spears before you! The boar will charge without warning.

NARRATOR: They went deeper and deeper into the wilderness. The prince's uncles and their men were obviously poorly trained for woodland travel and soon began to swear at the thick foliage.

ATALANTA: We have lost all element of surprise by your crashing through the underbrush! This is pointless!

MELEAGER: Quiet, uncles. We must not give our prey an advantage—

NARRATOR: His words were cut off by an otherworldly roar. The giant form of a hoary beast burst forth from the trees and tore through the men to the company's left. Bodies flew through the air, as the 12-foot-long tusks flung them like rag dolls.

ATALANTA: *(yelling)* Get away from him! He is mine!

MELEAGER: Atalanta, be careful!

NARRATOR: Atalanta and Meleager charged toward the boar, which was now trampling its victims into the ground. Its bloody snout lifted from the earth, and its red eyes stared at them menacingly.

BOAR: *(scary voice)* Do you know who sent me, mortals?

ATALANTA: She has sent you, and I will send you back to her, pig.

BOAR: I shall like to see you try.

MELEAGER: What are you saying to it?

NARRATOR: The roaring beast charged forward. Atalanta stood her ground. With it only paces from her, she leapt into the air and buried her spear into the back of its neck. It squealed a squeal of the souls tormented in Hades and stumbled to the ground. Meleager was there in a flash and drove his sword deep into its throat.

BOAR: *(rasping)* Artemis—will—be revenged . . .

NARRATOR: The red light of its eyes flickered and faded. Meleager and Atalanta smiled at each other in triumph. The rest of the party was quickly making its way over to the scene of the battle.

UNCLE ONE: Victory! The beast is dead, I see. To whom shall we give the body?

UNCLE TWO: He who dealt the killing stroke shall have it.

MELEAGER: It was Atalanta. She was the one who killed the boar.

ATALANTA: No, I must confess—I only injured it. It was the prince who killed it.

UNCLE TWO: As a prince should. How embarrassing it would be to have a ratty girl show him up.

MELEAGER: *(angrily)* Silence! I won't have you speak to her that way. *She* shall have the body. I could not have killed the boar without her.

UNCLE ONE: *(angrily)* Preposterous! Giving the body to a *girl*—a penniless urchin! Never!

MELEAGER: *(even more angry)* I have said my piece.

UNCLE TWO: *We* do not care about what you have to say. In fact, nephew, I believe it is time you ran home to your mother. We have business to settle here.

UNCLE ONE: Yes! Men, kill this scum! They have fulfilled their usefulness!

NARRATOR: The hunters stirred at once, but the Calydonian men moved in closely around them—weapons at the ready.

MELEAGER: *(shocked)* What are you doing?

UNCLE ONE: We can't have the kingdom knowing that we enlisted the help of *heathen hunters* to kill this beast. Surely you understand, nephew. Kill them at once! The girl as well!

MELEAGER: Noooo!

NARRATOR: Meleager drew his sword and jumped toward his grimacing uncles. Atalanta and the hunters, too, jerked into the fray. The battle went quickly. The trained Calydonian men were no match for the honed senses of the hunters. Their little band of troops began a retreat back to the city. Atalanta saw the bent form of Meleager and came to his side. He was kneeling by two covered bodies.

MELEAGER: *(quietly)* I killed them. They tried to kill you.

ATALANTA: They were evil men.

MELEAGER: They were my mother's brothers. Men run back now to tell my father the news. I have betrayed my family—for a woman.

ATALANTA: You have done the right thing! What is there to worry?

MELEAGER: I have killed the beloved ones of my mother. Her retribution shall be swift.

NARRATOR: He was right. The survivors from the skirmish soon reached the city walls wailing. When the queen heard the news, she tore her cloak—and furiously dug a hidden bundle from a dusty trunk. She raged as she threw it upon the roaring fire. Quickly the thin wrapping burned away, and a simple aged log was revealed beneath. She laughed the laugh of the mad.

Back in the clearing, Meleager fell to the ground.

ATALANTA: Meleager!

MELEAGER: *(weakly)* Artemis has had her revenge. The prophecy of the Fates has come true. I can feel it!

ATALANTA: *(frantically)* No! I can save you! I'm strong! I can save you!

NARRATOR: Atalanta cradled the body of her friend in her arms, and it began to glow. Meleager cried out in pain.

MELEAGER: *(weakly)* Atalanta—I love you—I always loved you . . .

ATALANTA: I know, my friend, I know.

NARRATOR: She held him tightly—as tight as she could—but her strength could not help her. She felt the weight of the prince disappear from her arms, and his body crumbled into ash.

Then—for the first time in her life, she wept. The legends of Atalanta did not end here. She went on to many mighty deeds. But, from this time on, she was a changed person. She did not swagger as she did before. She did not boast as loudly. She was never again afraid to take the help of a friend.

Women and History

If you want to start a heated debate among a group of men and women, just ask this question, "Who has it worse in the game of life, guys or girls?"

Then, step back.

History is made up of power struggles—rich against poor, country against country, country against self. But, what about men vs. women, guys vs. girls? Has there been a power struggle there?

At different points in history, women have received different degrees of freedom. Men *and* women in the past have placed restrictions on female clothing, female activities, and female etiquette. Fathers decided whom their daughters would marry. Husbands decided what wives could and couldn't do. Sons ran the homes in their father's absence.

Yet, even in the times of greatest restriction, powerful women still emerged from time to time. In the ancient world, Cleopatra was Queen of the Nile. In the Middle Ages, Joan of Arc, a simple peasant girl, led France to war. Queen Elizabeth I ruled in England during the time of Shakespeare, avoiding calls to get married so her husband could rule, and Queen Victoria ruled England for more than 50 years during the Victorian age. All of these women were years ahead of their time. The "fair sex" obviously has been struggling for equal treatment and rights for centuries. So, in America at least, have women finally gotten what they wanted and deserved?

DISCUSS

- How does Atalanta's story figure into the battle of the sexes?
- Atalanta's tale happens many centuries before the restrictions placed on women in Classical Greece. How do you think the Classical Greek women felt when they heard this story?
- How is Atalanta similar to the goddess Artemis? What is ironic about their relationship in this story?
- Did women destroy Meleager? Explain.

Artemis (Roman Name: Diana)

Virgin Goddess of the Hunt, Protector of Maidens and Wild Creatures

Artemis is often called upon by maidens who want nothing to do with men. Her silver arrows have slain many overzealous suitors. Artemis is also the twin sister of Apollo and revered as the Goddess of the Moon. At times her different duties contradict one other. Even though she is a hunter of animals herself, she often demands that mortals pay for killing defenseless beasts. In the most famous case, she demands that a Greek army offer her a human sacrifice in apology for trampling a family of rabbits. She asks for the life of the general's young daughter, a maiden. This is strange behavior for the protector of maidens.

DISCUSS
- Do you think men and women are finally equal? Why or why not?
- Why do you think feminism is such a hot topic between men and women?
- Sexism can also mean stereotyping the sexes. What are some male stereotypes? What are some female stereotypes?
- Who has the harder job in life: Guys or girls? Why? (Remember to step back.)

There are female construction workers, female doctors, and even professional female wrestlers. We have posters of Rosie the Riveter rolling up her coverall sleeve to show her bulging bicep. Her message: Women can do anything a man can. We have female judges, senators, and presidential hopefuls. It's strange to think that less than a hundred years ago women in America were still fighting for their right to *vote*. So, is the sexual revolution over? Some say yes. Some say no. Either way, the world has definitely changed.

Sexism refers to discrimination based on sex. It's a two-way street. An employer cannot refuse to hire applicants because of their sex. Over time the sexual stigmas surrounding certain jobs have faded away. Fifty years ago, there were "female" jobs like secretary, nurse, and stay-at-home mom. That's all changed. Men have entered female-dominated professions, and women have entered male-dominated ones. The lines of what a man and woman can't do have blurred.

Due to this shift, political correctness has forced us to neuter some of the words we use to describe these jobs. It can't be a mail*man* anymore; it's a mail*person*. There are no stewardesses; they're now flight attendants.

Some people think it's still not enough. Others think it's too much. The battle continues.

Women in Ancient Athens

Although Classical Greece was the fountainhead of democracy in the Western world, Greek women and slaves still held no rights. Only free males were considered citizens and given the right to vote in Athens. The sheltered life of Classical Greek women is hard to imagine for the liberated women of today. Women were kept confined to the house—only going out on special occasions such as the citywide festivals. When a woman was allowed outside, a male servant chaperoned her to protect her reputation. Greek women were encouraged to dress modestly with their robes fully covering their bodies. Most Greek men considered women to be mentally inferior. Education, they thought, would be wasted on the fragile female mind.

Girls were considered a burden rather than a blessing in most Greek houses. The poorer citizens who couldn't afford to feed a female child often abandoned the newborn outside the city. Fathers used their daughters to secure friendships, offering a dowry (money or goods) to prospective husbands. Girls were to be married off in their early teens to men most likely near 30. Unless she was extremely wealthy, a wife would be expected to spin wool for clothing, prepare meals for the household, and care for the children. A husband and wife usually occupied separate areas of their house, with the wife forbidden to enter the area where the husband entertained male guests.

Hestia (Roman Name: Vesta)

Goddess of the Hearth and the Home

Hestia never plays a part in any Greek myth. Even though she wasn't exciting enough to make it into their stories, the Greeks honored Hestia with their dinnertime prayers, asking her to bless their food and protect their homes. City-states had a central hearth dedicated to the goddess, where a holy fire forever burned. She is the third of the three virgin goddesses. In Rome she was the patron goddess of the Vestal Virgins, who kept the hearth fire of Rome forever burning.

Slaves were the second group who had no rights. The slaves of Greece were war prisoners captured from neighboring city-states. When one city-state defeated another, the able-bodied men would be killed and the women and children hauled away to a life of servitude. In some cases, poor families indentured themselves to a life of servitude to repay their enormous debts. Almost every Greek household had at least one slave. It was the job of the woman of the house to manage the slaves' duties.

Much like the early United States of America, Athens was committed to freedom yet turned a blind eye to the rights of women and slaves.

DISCUSS
- Men and women lived two separate lives in ancient Greece. Is there another period in time where this same division of the sexes occurred?
- How is this system of segregation unfair and unhealthy?

Atalanta's Race

Atalanta's story does not end with Meleager's death. Another of Atalanta's tales picks up where the first one left off. The following is the second part of her story.

After Atalanta's first adventure, news of the great boar hunt spread through Greece like wildfire. One day, a traveling bard sang her tale in the court of an old king. Singing of the ferocity of the killer beast and the huntress who slayed it, he recounted the early life of Atalanta. The old king looked up. He realized that this wild girl must be the daughter he abandoned in the woods long ago. He called for his messengers at once. "Bring my daughter back to me," he told them. "Maybe she can ease the burden of my old age."

When the messengers reached her, Atalanta received the news coolly, although inside she was shocked. She was a princess?

"Very well," she said. "Take me to this king."

Royal father and wild daughter were reunited. Through tears the king embraced Atalanta and begged her forgiveness. He expressed his joy at finding her again. But, his brow soon clouded. "I am growing old," he said, "and you are my only heir. You must claim your birthright and marry soon. Produce an heir for your kingdom."

Her heart sank. "Don't try to make me into someone I'm not, father. My heart is closed."

The king begged Atalanta to think of her people, instead of only herself.

"All right," she began slowly, "I agree to marry the man who can beat me in a foot race. Any who try and fail will pay with their lives."

Overjoyed, the king clapped his hands and sent the news out at once.

Word soon spread of the beautiful princess Atalanta and the kingdom that would be her dowry, and suitors flocked to the summons. Watching them flood into the city, Atalanta stared at their number in disbelief. "All of these men are willing to die for *me*?"

Man after man raced the royal huntress, but her swift feet never failed her. She left them far behind in the dust. Then, when their defeat was complete, they paid with their lives. Yet, more hopefuls continued to come. Atalanta began to fear she would spill the blood of all Greece's young men.

One day a suitor named Melanion appeared at court. Atalanta paid him little attention.

But, this suitor would prove to be different. Before journeying to Atalanta's kingdom, he had paid a visit to the temple of Aphrodite. Melanion had begged the goddess of love to help him win the fair maiden's hand. Aphrodite, annoyed by Atalanta's denial of love, presented the prince with three golden apples. "The allure of these apples cannot be resisted," she told him.

As the crowd gathered to watch the footrace between Atalanta and her newest suitor, Melanion slipped the three golden apples from his satchel. These would be the key to his success.

The princess and the Melanion lined up on their mark, and the signal came. Melanion ran for all he was worth, but Atalanta effortlessly pulled ahead. The prince launched the first apple, throwing it ahead and a little to the side. Surprising everyone (including herself), Atalanta darted off the path in pursuit of the shining apple. Melanion pulled ahead.

Apple in hand, the princess recovered her senses and retook the lead.

Melanion threw the second apple. Once again, she turned to the side to pick it up.

Now the finish line was in sight. There would be no other chances after this apple was thrown. The prince felt Atalanta on his heels. In a split second she would pass him.

He chose his spot carefully and lobbed the final apple far from the path.

Atalanta disappeared into the bushes to retrieve it.

As Melanion crossed the finish line triumphantly, he bent double to catch his breath and noticed the bare feet of Atalanta standing near him. Even with his trick, he still only beat her by a hair. He looked up. There she was, holding the three apples in her hands.

A sly smile spread across the princess' face. "Nice trick."

Melanion and Atalanta were happily married for a number of years, and before his death, the old king was able to see the grandson he had so desperately wanted. But, one day, roaming freely in the countryside, Melanion and Atalanta took shelter in the temple of Zeus and made love within it. As a punishment for their sacrilege, Zeus transformed the two lovers into lions. Atalanta was wild once again.

DISCUSS
- Do you think the second half of Atalanta's story complements or contradicts the first half of her story? Explain.
- Would you risk your life for a spouse and kingdom? Why or why not?
- What does the fact that Atalanta was "tricked" into marriage say about women?

Hebe
Goddess of Youth

Hebe is the most easily overlooked Greek goddess. Her only job on Olympus is to hold the holy cup from which the gods drink. Nectar, the magical liquid found within the cup, confers immortality on those mortals who drink it. Ambrosia, a food fine enough for divine lips, also is eaten on Olympus. Hebe is the daughter of Zeus and Hera. When Heracles (Hercules) completed his life of heroic deeds, he ascended to Olympus, where Zeus allowed him to drink from the holy cup. The hero then became a god, and Zeus presented him with a new wife, Hebe.

DISCUSS

• Apart from dolls, what other toys prepare children for life?

CREATE

Create a doll based on a mythological *female* you have read about using the handout on page 45. Use details about the mythological character to complete the Features and Accessories of your doll.

FEATURES

Features are actions that the doll can do. Perhaps your doll can speak a line, kick, jump, or bat its eyes. (Make sure these relate to the character you have chosen.)

ACCESSORIES

These are small, usually painted, plastic items that come with the doll. Create a vehicle for your doll. This can be a modern vehicle, but make it relevant to the character. Make reference to another toy that might go well with the one you have created. For example, Barbie has all kinds of extra accessories—beach houses, other doll friends, and pets.

DISCUSS

• If a child is happy living among animals, should he or she be removed from the "pack"?
• In Rudyard Kipling's *The Jungle Book*, Mowgli, a young boy, is raised by wolves. What other stories, new or old, contain instances of feral children?
• What are some common themes in these stories?

Mythological Barbie

There's a lot of thought put into toys. You may not notice it when you're growing up, but in some ways, toys are designed to prepare you for life. Many toys mimic adult behavior. Baby dolls, for example, are intended to teach girls about motherhood. Not every girl will end up being a mother, but the doll helps prepare her for that possibility.

Since she first rolled off the assembly line 50 years ago, Barbie, America's favorite doll, has given girls a concept of womanhood. Some have criticized Barbie for her plastically perfect body and impossible measurements, feeling that she gives girls unrealistic standards. Some have also criticized Barbie's flippant nature. After all, she *does* spend most of her time lounging in her Jacuzzi or going to the mall. To answer some of these criticisms, Barbie has recently gotten with the times. Instead of simply being a "trophy wife," Barbie has branched out into the workforce. Now Barbie can be a pilot, a brain surgeon, even a nuclear physicist.

If toys teach children about their roles in society, what would the dolls of other cultures be like?

Raised By a Bear

Girl, Raised By Bear, Returns to Family would make an interesting headline in the Sunday paper. Storybooks, instead of newspapers, are usually where you hear about this sort of thing. The fact of the matter is that *feral children* (that's the proper term) do exist. There have been rare cases where a child is discovered living with a group of animals as one of their own. The type of animal has varied to include dogs, wolves, monkeys, and, you guessed it, bears.

Zoologists admit that it is possible for a female animal to be so distraught over the loss of one of her young that she adopts a creature of a different species. If given the right conditions, an animal easily could adopt a human child. However, the odds of this happening are still far-fetched.

When the adopted children are discovered and forced to reenter the human world, the process is extremely difficult. The human child *thinks* he or she is an animal. He or she must be separated from the animal world and taught human ways. Success only comes when he or she can truly resist the call of the wild.

Mythological Barbie

Draw your Mythological Barbie's features and add accessories to the model on this page. List each choice that you've made. On a separate sheet of paper, draw the vehicle for your doll.

Features   *Accessories*

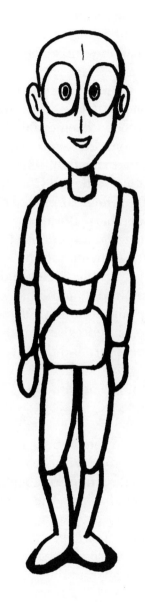

To Hunt a Boar

If you go to your local sporting goods store and look for a "Boar Hunting" section, you might be disappointed. What once was the most popular sport for gentleman now has all but died out—along with their quarry, the wild hog.

The hunting of all animals started out as a necessity. If you didn't hunt, you didn't have meat to eat. Over time, hunting became sport, an activity that is not necessary but still enjoyable. In the Dark Age of Greece, most people who hunted boar did so for adventure. It was a rite of passage for young men, a way of proving themselves capable for warfare. War against beasts wouldn't be much different from war against enemies. And, for the seasoned warrior, the wild boar proved a formidable opponent, one who could keep your skills sharp, during times of peace.

The boar hunting tradition carried all the way up into the Middle Ages of Europe. Men in medieval England were still hunting their game much in the same way as the Greeks did 2,000 years before. The hunter pursued the animal on foot, accompanied by his dogs, and overcame it by running, striking, and shooting. Of course, with the boar, whose tusks could easily rip open a hunter's stomach, it was best to hunt in a group, forming a ring of spears around the animal after it had been cornered by the hounds.

In his novel *The Sword in the Stone*, T. H. White (1938/1965) described a medieval boar hunt:

There was only one rule in boar-hunting. It was: Hold on. If the boar charged you, you had to drop on one knee and present your boar-spear in his direction. You held the butt of it with your right hand on the ground to take the shock, while you stretched your left arm to its fullest extent and held the spear tightly with it, as high up as possible. You kept the point toward the charging boar. The spear was as sharp as a razor, and it has a cross-piece about eighteen inches away from the point. This cross-piece or horizontal bar prevented the spear from going more than eighteen inches into his chest. Without this cross-piece, a charging boar would have been capable of rushing right up the spear, even if it did go through him, and getting at you like that . . . He weighed between ten and twenty score [110–120 lbs.], and his one object in life was to heave and weave and sidestep, until he could get at you and champ you into chops, while your one object was not to let go of the spear, clasped tight under your arm, until somebody had come to finish him off. If only you could keep hold of your end of the spear . . . you knew that there was at least a spear's length between you, however much he ran you around the forest. (p. 136)

DISCUSS

- How has the sport of hunting changed in the modern era?
- Do you believe in the principle of animal rights? Explain.

Greeks believed that a helmet or covering made from the boar's body contained the power of the beast. This went for any kill. Heracles, after defeating the Lion of Nemea, whose skin was impervious to weapons, took the beast's skin and wore it as a cloak, covering him with the same supernatural power.

The prestige of a hunt was enough to attract many noblemen, so it was no surprise that the Calydonian Boar, massive in size and strength, brought heroes running from all of Greece to compete for the honor of slaying it. Keeping this in mind, you might be able to imagine the shock of these noblemen when the prize of the kill goes to a penniless *girl*. But, her encounter with the boar was enough for Atalanta to prove that she was capable of any manly feat.

Boar hunting was not the only type of hunting enjoyed by ancient Greek men. The hunting of deer and rabbits also was popular. A pit or net trap would sometimes be prepared ahead of time. After the hounds had driven the animal into the trap, it was clubbed to death. Another tactic involved capturing a fawn and using it as a decoy for the mother deer. Once the doe was in the clearing, the hunter would release his hounds upon it. There is little pity to be found for animals in ancient Greece and Rome. Only the goddess Artemis stood up for the idea of animal rights.

The Fates

The Greek concept of life and death was embodied in the three eternal creatures they called the Fates. Often depicted as three old hags, these beings spin out the thread of life, measure out its length, and snip it loose when the appropriate time comes. The Greeks believed that the Fates held power even over the gods themselves. Not even Zeus can undo Fate.

Hogzilla?

Blood and fire shining from his eyes
and a neck stiff with bristles just like spear shafts . . .
In length his tusks were like an elephant's,
and bolts of lightning issued from his mouth,
and when he exhaled, trees turned black and died. (Ovid, 8/2004, p. 275)

Even though it sounds like Godzilla, this is Ovid's description of the wild Calydonian boar from his epic poem *Metamorphoses*. Because the people of Calydon ignored Artemis in their sacrifices, the goddess equips her beast with a deadly pestilence, the ability to wither vines and destroy whole fields of grain. He's a beast and a plague rolled into one—a very impressive combination. This is the beast that Atalanta is up against—not an everyday wild pig, but a destroyer of homes, crops, and lives. Luckily, Atalanta is up to the challenge.

Centaurs

Centaurs are half-man, half-horse creatures that are savage in nature. They are frequently the perpetrators of murder and rape and go absolutely wild when allowed to drink wine. Out of the many centaurs, only one learned to be good. His name was Chiron. The truth-loving god Apollo and his twin sister Artemis raised Chiron up from a colt and taught him all of their wisdom. When fully grown, Chiron became a trainer of heroes—coaching great names like Jason and Achilles. When Chiron attended a wedding feast with his centaur brethren, the hosts committed a terrible mistake and offered wine to the beasts. The centaurs became instantly uncontrollable and began to tear the host's palace apart. Heracles, another wedding guest, fought against the centaur horde, and in the process, wounded peaceful Chiron in the hoof. The centaur eventually died from this wound, yet in honor of his great accomplishments, Zeus placed him in the sky as the constellation we today call Sagittarius.

I mentioned Godzilla earlier for a reason. Atalanta's pig-on-steroids seems like he would be right at home in a Hollywood film. Such a film might have a plot like this: A group of unsuspecting teenagers plan a weekend camping trip. As they stop for gas, the weird locals try to warn them of a giant hog who roams the countryside. The teenagers shrug off this story as silly and continue their weekend. One by one they are picked off by "Hogzilla," the maniacal beast of which they were warned.

Movies about killer animals have enjoyed quite a bit of success, so much success that they're almost their own genre. It all started with *JAWS* (1975), when Steven Spielberg and his animatronic shark made beach-goers terrified to go into the water. Lots of imitations have followed. Spiders, anacondas, prehistoric crocodiles, lions, grizzlies, squids, birds, radioactive lizards, and even the family St. Bernard have all been the featured creature in this type of movie. It's easy to see that the human world is still a bit nervous about what's lurking out there in the wild. One of mankind's deepest, darkest fears is a fear of nature. But, haven't we conquered nature? Don't we have our warm homes and bolted doors? Sure, we do. But, put a human and a hungry mountain lion in the middle of a forest and see which one comes back alive.

Hollywood has played off this fear and made some big-time money in the process. Of course, the predators in films aren't your everyday, normal-sized variety. Directors decided a long time ago that bigger *is* better and also scarier. Godzilla is a *giant* lizard. King Kong is a *giant* ape. Jaws is a *giant* shark.

So, now we're back to Atalanta's Calydonian boar. Not only is it an animal to be feared, but it's a *giant* animal to be feared. Here is a beast with all of the primal instincts necessary to rip you limb from limb, amplified beyond imagination. For the Greeks this would be downright horrifying. They were forced to think: If placed in her shoes, would they be as brave as Atalanta? Would they stand firm as it charged toward them, lightning flying from its eyes and fire from its tusks? Or, would they turn tail and run away like a girl?

Or, should we say *unlike* a girl?

DISCUSS
- Name some of the horror movies centered on killer animals. What elements do they have in common?
- Think of a book or film that centers on a character vs. nature conflict. Why is this conflict necessary to the point?

DRAW
Draw a movie poster for a movie featuring a larger-than-life animal. Title your movie, and depict a dramatic scene in your drawing.

WATCH
Watch *JAWS* (1975) directed by Steven Spielberg, and analyze the ways in which the director enhances suspense. What other movies have been influenced by this approach?

CHAPTER 3

A Twist of Fate

OEDIPUS REX

Cast

Oedipus *(Young prince)*

Jocasta *(Queen of Thebes)*

Tiresias *(Blind prophet of Thebes)*

Laius/Old Man *(King of Thebes)*

Polybus *(King of Corinth)*

Servant *(Servant to Polybus)*

Shepherd *(Servant to Laius)*

Sphinx *(Supernatural creature)*

Guard   *(Watchman of Thebes)*

Creon   *(Brother of Jocasta)*

Maidservant *(Servant of Jocasta)*

Oracle   *(Oracle of Delphi)*

NARRATOR: In the midst of a howling storm, Jocasta, the queen of Thebes, gave birth on the darkest night of the year. Grouped about her in a sweaty bundle, her maidservants attended her, dabbing her fiery face, and ushered her wailing son into the world. Shaking hands finally held him aloft for the bleary-eyed mother to see.

MAIDSERVANT: *(frightened)* She is weak—she may not even live to see the dawn. This child is cursed to be born on such a night.

JOCASTA: *(weakly)* The king—tell the king—his son is born . . .

NARRATOR: The maidservant jerked her head toward the door, and a young midwife left to carry out the queen's orders. She gazed sadly at her mistress. Jocasta was nearly a child herself, barely 16—the king a man of 30. It would be a pity if a royal mother died at such a young age. Flashes of lightning ticked off the seconds until Laius, the king, came bursting into the stifling room. He had been eagerly awaiting the birth of his heir. The maidservant displayed his child to him, and he took it into his arms.

LAIUS: *(anxiously)* A boy?

MAIDSERVANT: Yes, your majesty.

LAIUS: *(overjoyed)* Praises to Zeus! Oh, my young pretty, you have done your husband well.

NARRATOR: He put a hand to her streaked face.

JOCASTA: *(weakly, in a delirium)* Yes. Laius. Laius. Don't go. Don't go.

MAIDSERVANT: *(grimly)* The queen is not well. She has lost much blood. She may not survive this night.

NARRATOR: The king looked to his feeble wife—his joy washing away.

LAIUS: *(softly)* You cannot die, my wife. You've just brought our happiness into the world. You must live—live to see this blessing of ours grow into a—*(startling boom of thunder)*

NARRATOR: Laius stopped in mid-speech. A flash of lightning had silhouetted a dark form standing near the doorway—a new arrival to the birthing chamber.

JOCASTA: *(frightened)* Laius!

LAIUS: *(angrily)* Who's there? How dare you enter our royal quarters! Explain yourself at once!

NARRATOR: The wiry frame of a man stood forward. In a smooth motion he threw his muddy traveling cloak back from his shoulders. Darkness shrouded him once again.

LAIUS: *(enraged)* Speak, spy! What is your purpose here? Speak! Or, we will burn the words out of you. What have you seen?

NARRATOR: Yet another flash from the skies lit the face of the stranger. Overflowing their sockets were two bulging eyes, a milky glaze across pale irises.

TIRESIAS: *(coyly)* See? I see nothing in this world, my king. But, in the next, I see much.

NARRATOR: The king and his young wife stared in horror. The child let out a shriek.

(wail of a child)

TIRESIAS: Silence that child. I am sent from my master with a message for you.

LAIUS: You will make no orders here. What master would you have higher than me? I am the king, and there can be no higher.

TIRESIAS: Not so. I serve Lord Apollo, your majesty.

NARRATOR: These words caught Laius by the throat. Olympus had sent this man with the news of Apollo, God of Prophecy, upon his lips.

LAIUS: *(nervously)* Forgive me. Your master is surely higher than I. What news do you have for me? Will my wife die from this birth?

TIRESIAS: Do not forget your place in the world, king. The gods see and direct all. *(pause)* Your wife *will* die because of the birth of your son—but not for many years hence.

JOCASTA: *(terrified)* Laius, what does he mean?

TIRESIAS: *(angrily)* Were you not warned about this child? Were you not told what an abomination he would be to your country?

LAIUS: *(hesitantly)* Warned? Well, yes. But, that was years ago. I am a king—I must have a son! Who will rule after me?

TIRESIAS: The jackals and the dark creatures of night will rule after you, Laius King. The Oracle spoke then, and the Oracle speaks now. If Laius shall have a son, that son will slay him.

JOCASTA: No!

TIRESIAS: But, I have said only half, my lady. If Jocasta shall bear a son from Laius, that son will come to share her bed—in unholy love.

NARRATOR: The queen cried out in fright and fell back upon her bed in a swoon.

LAIUS: *(yelling)* Silence! Do not speak those words! I forbid it!

TIRESIAS: I speak as I am commanded. These words have been spoken before, but you chose not to listen. They fly from my lips once again—one final warning against this child.

LAIUS: *(forcefully)* Leave immediately, or I will have you gutted—your head stuck on a pole.

TIRESIAS: I am quite safe from your threats. Lord Apollo keeps me close to his side. You have heard his words. Heed them.

NARRATOR: A lightning bolt—one much bigger than the others—shook the walls of the chamber. When the flashing subsided, the blind man was gone—vanished without a trace. The serving women rushed to the queen, while the king looked at the wriggling child in his arms.

JOCASTA: *(reviving)* What can we do? What can we do? Our baby—our baby.

NARRATOR: Laius rounded angrily upon the servants.

LAIUS: *(determined)* Leave us at once! Forget what you have seen and heard here this night, or I shall put out your eyes and cut your ears from your heads.

NARRATOR: The serving women fled terrified. They had witnessed the cruelty of Laius before. As she darted past, the king caught the final maidservant by the arm and pulled her close.

LAIUS: *(hissing)* Fetch me the shepherd. Tell him it is time to prove his loyalty to his king.

MAIDSERVANT: *(stammering)* Yes—yes—my lord.

NARRATOR: Freed from his grip, the woman dashed into the corridor. Laius turned and lowered his newborn son into his wife's pleading hands. Frantically, Jocasta searched the face of her husband.

JOCASTA: *(frantically)* Is it true? What can we do?

LAIUS: *(angrily)* Quiet, woman! I'm trying to think!

JOCASTA: *(whimper)*

NARRATOR: Gritting his teeth, Laius clinched his hair within two fists. He turned, quickly, and ripped a dagger from his belt.

LAIUS: *(sternly)* Now, do exactly as I command. Hold up the child!

JOCASTA: *(crying out)* Laius! No!

LAIUS: *(loudly)* Do as I say!

NARRATOR: The frightened girl raised her child up into the air. The king moved closer—dagger in hand.

LAIUS: *(ceremoniously)* Child born on this hateful night, you are no longer the heir of Thebes. *I* curse you as the gods have cursed you. You are no son of mine.

NARRATOR: Spitting upon the infant, he seized its two tiny, kicking feet and pushed the point of the dagger through each. Blood gushed forth, and the child wailed. *(wailing child)*

LAIUS: He will show these scars forever. They will show that he was born a commoner, an illegitimate—no son of the king. The king shall have no son.

NARRATOR: In the darkness the royal shepherd entered, panting and frightened.

SHEPHERD: *(out of breath)* You sent for me, your majesty?

NARRATOR: The king turned—the wailing, bloodstained child in his arms.

LAIUS: Take this boy into the wilderness and leave him on the mountain of Kithairon to die.

NARRATOR: Horrified, the servant looked up to his master.

SHEPHERD: *(stammering)* But—but—your majesty. Who is this child?

LAIUS: You need know nothing more. Do as I say—or you will find your neck stretched by the executioner's rope.

NARRATOR: The shepherd took the screaming infant into his arms and backed slowly from the chamber. The queen began to weep, and the king held his head to hers.

LAIUS: *(whispering)* Shh. Forget that child. He died in the womb. Stillborn. Forget him. His memory will fade soon enough.

NARRATOR: And so, in the midst of a tempest as the Earth had never seen, the baby was carried into the wilderness by loyal hands. The kind shepherd had known as soon as he had taken the bundle into his arms that he would not be able to leave it to die. And, as he pushed through the battering rain into the wilderness, he had been formulating a plan. The night sky lit up like noon for a moment. The jagged peak of Kithairon towered above.

SHEPHERD: *(to the baby)* Tonight, the gods are angered. But, you do not fear them, little one. The heavens have crashed, but you haven't made a sound.

NARRATOR: The rough man stopped and looked down into the bundle he shielded from the rain.

SHEPHERD: If you do not fear the gods, why should I fear a king? We'll find you a home and tell your wicked parents that you have died. It will be our little secret.

NARRATOR: Soon the storm subsided, and the thin glow of dawn broke the horizon. On one of the many mountain paths, the shepherd happened upon a traveler.

SHEPHERD: Which way are you headed, brother?

SERVANT: I return to Corinth. I serve the king there.

SHEPHERD: Take this child for me. Thebes is no place for him. Find him a good home. Living with me in the wilderness is no fate for such a child.

NARRATOR: The traveling servant saw the shepherd's urgency, and he agreed to take the child.

SHEPHERD: I cannot thank you enough. *(to the child)* Goodbye, little one. I wish you all the happiness in the world.

NARRATOR: The Corinthian servant bore the child back to his homeland. Upon his return, he was greeted with horrific news. A sudden plague had taken the life of the newborn prince. The King of Corinth, the servant's master, sat brooding and mourning the loss of his son.

SERVANT: *(meekly)* Sire, I know your loss is great, but I believe the gods have given you a second chance. A stranger in the wilderness gave me this child, an orphan, and told me to find it a good home. Will you take it as your own and forget your grief?

NARRATOR: King Polybus marveled at such a coincidence and at once declared the intervention of Olympus. He accepted the baby as his own son and named him prince of the realm.

POLYBUS: But, his feet have been wounded. What trials this child has already suffered. We shall call him Oedipus for his swollen feet. Relax, Little Oedipus, your troubles are over.

NARRATOR: Years passed. The child Oedipus experienced the happiest of days that any child could. He was kept completely ignorant of the royal adoption that had so changed his fate. The child with the swollen feet soon grew into a young man, and when he reached 18 years of age, he prepared for the ancient ritual of manhood.

OEDIPUS: *(confidently)* Father, I am ready.

POLYBUS: To do what, my son?

OEDIPUS: To go to Delphi, of course, to visit the Oracle.

POLYBUS: It's a long road. Are you sure you're up to it? You can always go next year, you know.

OEDIPUS: I'm ready to hear my fate and become a man.

POLYBUS: Your mother and I will miss you terribly. I remember my own journey to the Oracle, you know. Be careful, and hurry home.

OEDIPUS: I will.

NARRATOR: The journey from Corinth to Delphi proved uneventful. Excitement fueled each and every one of Oedipus' steps. When he at last climbed the crooked mountain that housed the Oracle's cave, his heart beat in furious anticipation.

OEDIPUS: *(cautiously)* Hello? Is anyone in there?

NARRATOR: Inside the cave turned into a cavern, and Oedipus cautiously made his way into its mouth. The air soon became cool, and hissing mist rose from the cracked floor.

ORACLE: *(booming voice)* Enter, young man.

NARRATOR: A young woman was seated on a tall, metal stool ahead in the darkness.

OEDIPUS: *(nervously)* It is I, Oedipus.

NARRATOR: He winced at his own words.

ORACLE: *(quiet laugh)* Swollen foot. I know your name—and its meaning.

OEDIPUS: I am the Prince of Corinth. I've come to hear my fortune.

ORACLE: *(slyly)* Fortune would be an odd word for a future such as yours.

OEDIPUS: *(scared)* What do you mean?

ORACLE: *(grimly)* All ahead is darkness—darkness of mind—darkness of thought.

OEDIPUS: *(nervously)* For me? Are you serious? This is *Oedipus.*

ORACLE: *(dry laugh)* Everyone always expects happiness. Not everyone can be happy. I don't deal in lies—only truth. Now listen closely. Once it is said, I will speak no more. *(pause)* Oedipus, you are destined by high Olympus to commit two horrible sins. You shall murder your father—and marry your mother.

NARRATOR: The heart of the young man went cold.

OEDIPUS: *(weakly)* No. No. There must be some mistake. *(pleading)* It's—it's only a prophecy. It can be changed—right? Oh, please tell me it can be changed.

NARRATOR: Robed priests appeared from nowhere and seized Oedipus by either arm. As they pulled him toward the cave mouth, he continued to cry out.

OEDIPUS: *(yelling)* Tell me it can be changed! Tell me, please!

NARRATOR: But, the Oracle only closed her eyes and bowed her head. She had spoken.

It was hours before the boy moved again. He lay upon the mountain, stunned, listening to the wind rip through the crags. When he did finally rise, he did so completely against his will. Gasping for breath, he turned and vomited among the bushes. He turned his red-rimmed eyes heavenward.

OEDIPUS: *(decidedly)* If this truly is my fate, I will undo it.

NARRATOR: With weary, halting steps, he descended the mountain. At its base, two paths stretched out before him. One led to a home that he could no longer return to; the other—into the wild, the unknown.

OEDIPUS: Goodbye, father. Goodbye, mother. You won't understand, but at least you will be saved from your wretched son.

NARRATOR: Oedipus struck out—down the unknown path—fleeing fate with the words of the Oracle burning in his mind. Slow steps broke into a run, and at last he fought back tears. He ran and ran until his sides ached as if they would split open. Then, he lay down in the dirt and remained still. The hot summer sun beat down upon him, and the bright, white light consumed his mind until he knew nothing else.

OLD MAN: *(yelling)* Halt! What is going on here? Stop! Stop!

NARRATOR: Oedipus opened his weary eyes. Through the swirling dust, he saw an old man on a horse snarling down at him. The boy sat up.

OLD MAN: *(angrily)* Get out of the road, you miserable peasant!

NARRATOR: Oedipus rose as the old man glared at him fiercely. Behind him there followed a group of servants.

OLD MAN: *(sarcastically)* Sorry to interrupt your nap. It's hard enough to get our caravan down this road without riffraff lying across it.

NARRATOR: Heat rushed to Oedipus' face.

OEDIPUS: *(dangerously)* Watch it, old man. You're dealing with someone who is cursed—a murderer.

NARRATOR: The old man roared with laughter.

OLD MAN: *(loud laugh)* We are certainly frightened. We should have ridden over you when we had the chance. *(forcefully)* Now, trash, move—or we will move you ourselves.

NARRATOR: Immediately, anger thrilled through every vein of the boy's body.

OEDIPUS: *(roaring)* I will not!

OLD MAN: *(coldly)* Very well.

NARRATOR: The man pulled a knotted whip from his satchel, raised it up into the air, and brought it swiftly down toward Oedipus' face. *(cry of pain, whip-crack)* The boy ran forward, avoiding the blow. Seeing nothing beyond his own rage, he barreled into the side of the old man's horse. *(neigh of a horse)*

OLD MAN: *(crying out)* Ah!

NARRATOR: The force of the blow knocked the old man from his mount. Flailing his arms madly, he fell—pitching to the side—landing hard upon his neck.

OEDIPUS: *(yelling in a frenzy)* Ha! Who controls the road now, you old buzzard!

NARRATOR: Oedipus seized the abandoned whip from the man's limp hand and turned upon the servants.

OEDIPUS: *(yelling)* Who's next?

NARRATOR: Terrified, the remaining travelers fled.

OEDIPUS: *(yelling)* That's right! Run, cowards! Run from the cursed one!

NARRATOR: Oedipus seethed with satisfaction as he saw the last of them disappear down the road.

OEDIPUS: Your *friends* have abandoned you, old man.

NARRATOR: The boy turned back to the fallen form. It remained motionless—its head turned at an odd angle. The riderless horse nuzzled its master.

OEDIPUS: *(breathlessly)* Gods. I killed him. *I* killed him.

NARRATOR: He stared at the whip in his hand and then threw it to the ground.

OEDIPUS: She was right. If I'm capable of this—I'm a monster.

NARRATOR: A sudden fear burned inside of him—fear of himself, fear of the deed done by his own hand. He did all he knew how to do: He fled. Oedipus traveled for days, haunted by his dreams and hunted by phantoms. He took no notice of where his feet led him. Landscapes rose and fell. So, it was no surprise that he did not happen to see that the roadside fields soon became barren, and he met no more travelers. Even the shining whiteness of the bones that littered the roadway escaped his notice. It took the towering form of a sphinx to stir his attention.

SPHINX: *(otherworldly)* Halt, mortal.

NARRATOR: Oedipus looked up from his daze, but his eyes remained bleary. The most bizarre creature he had ever seen was seated beside the road. The head of a woman was gazing imperiously down at him. That is where the creature's human form ended. The body and furry haunches of a lion drew the various parts together—the wings of an eagle and the tail of a snake. The sphinx was leisurely licking her paw upon her bed of bones.

SPHINX: You're awfully calm for being in the presence of a monster.

OEDIPUS: *(daze-like)* I could say the same for you.

SPHINX: I have killed a hundred men. Their bones litter the roadways. Do you not fear me?

OEDIPUS: *(numbly)* I fear only myself.

NARRATOR: A smile of intrigue passed over the sphinx's womanly face.

SPHINX: Perhaps you wish to die. Is that why you've sought me out?

OEDIPUS: Kill me if you must. Rid the world of the cancer you see before you.

SPHINX: Don't be too hasty, mortal man. I don't kill for the sake of killing. I'm actually a very civilized creature. I believe in giving everyone a sporting chance.

OEDIPUS: *(sarcastic)* How noble—a civilized monster.

SPHINX: I will give you the same chance I have given everyone else who happened to pass this way: The chance to solve my riddle.

OEDIPUS: Riddles are for children. What if I refuse to play?

NARRATOR: The sphinx smiled at him.

SPHINX: *(beastlike)* Then I shall eat you—slowly—one end at a time.

OEDIPUS: I'll play your little game. At least if I lose, my misery will come to an end.

SPHINX: *(happily)* That's the spirit. I'm also very fair. If on the off chance you actually win, I will voluntarily forfeit my own life. Here is my riddle:

NARRATOR: The sphinx cleared her throat and spoke in a resonating boom.

SPHINX: What creature walks on four legs in the morning, two legs at noon, and three legs in the evening?

NARRATOR: The wind lazily whipped up the dirt around them.

OEDIPUS: How much time do I have to answer the question?

SPHINX: As long as my patience holds out.

NARRATOR: Though he did not will it, Oedipus' mind began to move and click.

OEDIPUS: *(absentmindedly)* Perhaps she does not mean only one day. There is a morning and an evening to life.

SPHINX: *(growing impatient)* Your time is running out.

OEDIPUS: Life changes many creatures. Many creatures walk on two legs, and many creatures walk on four legs. But, three legs—there is the riddle.

SPHINX: *(screaming)* Enough of your babbling! Do you know the answer or not?

OEDIPUS: Of course, that's it.

SPHINX: *(angrily)* My patience is growing thin!

OEDIPUS: Man. The answer is man. We crawl in the morning of our lives, we walk on two legs in our prime, and when we are old we walk with a cane.

NARRATOR: Oedipus smiled in spite of himself, and he looked almost surprised to see the sphinx still standing beside him. A bizarre light had come into her eyes, and she shrieked. *(hellish shriek)* With huge swoops of her wings and a gust that pushed Oedipus to the ground, she took to the air, howling and wailing. She didn't fly long, but climbed high and then fell, down into the faraway sea—extinguishing her own life.

OEDIPUS: *(understated)* Huh. I guess she was a civilized monster after all.

NARRATOR: A sudden corner was turned in Oedipus' mind. He felt his spirits revive. He still held the power to put the past behind him. As he continued on the path, he noticed for the first time that nothing was growing for miles around. The sphinx had brought a curse upon the land. At last a set of shining city walls gleamed in the distance. They shone out like hope—a new start. When Oedipus neared the massive gate, he found it bolted against him.

GUARD: *(shouting)* Who's there?

OEDIPUS: *(shouting)* A traveler!

GUARD: There have been no travelers on this road for months! The sphinx has killed them all.

OEDIPUS: Let me in! I have killed the sphinx.

NARRATOR: The guard looked down at the boy in shock. He turned to his fellow guards and conversed in hushed tones.

GUARD: *(hesitantly)* Very well. Come inside. We shall take you to Creon, and he will decide what to do with you.

NARRATOR: The gigantic doors opened. Oedipus was taken roughly by either arm and escorted into the city.

OEDIPUS: Everyone seems a bit on edge here. What city is this?

GUARD: You are in Thebes, stranger. You have come at our darkest hour.

NARRATOR: Soon Oedipus found himself in the royal hearing hall. The Creon they had spoken of was a thin, serious man wrapped in a black robe. He looked at Oedipus distrustfully.

CREON: *(suspicious)* Are you a spy? Tell only the truth.

OEDIPUS: No, sir. As I told the guards, I am a traveler.

CREON: If you are a traveler, where did you come from?

OEDIPUS: I came here from Delphi.

CREON: *(snorting)* Impossible! There is a monster that kills any who travel on that road!

OEDIPUS: Not anymore. I have destroyed it.

CREON: *(disbelief)* You? How?

OEDIPUS: I solved its riddle.

CREON: Since when do man-eating beasts ask riddles?

OEDIPUS: This one did, and it threw itself into the sea when I won its game.

CREON: A foolish claim to make, young man. We will be able to confirm your story soon enough. If we find that you are lying, we will put you to death.

OEDIPUS: Has the monster caused all this paranoia?

NARRATOR: Creon looked at Oedipus coldly.

CREON: *(slowly)* Our king is dead, killed by roadside thieves.

OEDIPUS: He must have been a foolish man to travel with such a creature at large.

CREON: *(coldly)* He went by a secret path that rejoins the road to Delphi. He was seeking the oracle. But, I owe you no explanations. What is done is done. Until we have checked out your little story, you shall be a prisoner.

OEDIPUS: *(angrily)* What right do you have to keep me prisoner?

CREON: *I* am in charge here now. The queen is my sister, and I rule until a new king shall be chosen. Take him away.

NARRATOR: Oedipus spent many days in the Theban jail. Creon dispatched men to verify his tale. No trace of the creature could be found. The news spread through the city that the mysterious stranger had slain the monster. Creon himself came to free Oedipus from his cell.

CREON: I have to apologize for doubting you, young man.

OEDIPUS: I understand your doubt. I can hardly believe it myself.

CREON: The people are overjoyed. They sing your praises. I have also been charged to tell you that they wish to make you their king.

OEDIPUS: *(shocked)* Me? Why?

CREON: You have saved us. I am the people's humble servant. If they wish *you* to rule them, I will not stand in their way.

NARRATOR: Oedipus could barely believe it. Was this truly his *good* fortune? Had he escaped his destiny at last?

OEDIPUS: *(happily)* I accept.

CREON: There is one thing you should know. In order to legitimize your claim to the throne, we ask that you marry our queen. Her time of mourning for her husband has ended, and she is still young enough in years.

OEDIPUS: May I meet her first?

CREON: Certainly.

NARRATOR: The queen pleased Oedipus. He was surprised at her beauty. True, she was some years older, but she had worn her years well. There was still life and love within her. Oedipus became the King of Thebes, and it seemed that he had in fact escaped the foul prophecy of his past. With Jocasta, his new wife, he was exceedingly happy. And, once again the years passed by like a breeze. Together they raised a royal family, two boys and two girls, each with the vibrant glow of life in their eyes. Oedipus all but forgot his past, and the darkness that had threatened to consume it. Thebes loved their king, and it seemed that a happy ending would be had after all.

Then came the drought. The skies refused to give up their rain, crops failed, and the people began to starve. Only the gods could be the source of such a misfortune.

OEDIPUS: Send a man to Delphi at once. Ask the Oracle what must be done to remedy this problem.

NARRATOR: It was strange, but Oedipus barely remembered the words the Oracle had spoken to him so long ago. All he knew was that they had been spoken in error. He had proved them false. A messenger was dispatched and returned in haste. The Oracle had spoken: The murderer of the old king must be found and brought to justice. Then, and only then, the skies would give forth rain once again.

JOCASTA: *(joyfully)* Thank the gods! They are crying out for justice at last!

OEDIPUS: I was told of Laius' death when I came here. I'll send out the soldiers to search the highways. Any bandits there must be put to death—then we will have rain.

NARRATOR: This news relieved Oedipus. It seemed an easy solution. He called for Creon.

OEDIPUS: Creon, brother-in-law. Do the men who traveled with Laius when he was murdered still live?

CREON: I am sure they do, my lord. If you remember, it happened shortly before you arrived here in Thebes.

OEDIPUS: Do you remember their names? May we question them?

CREON: They were servants and slaves. They barely understood what they saw happening.

OEDIPUS: *(angrily)* There must be some way of solving this riddle! The gods would not leave us without a way out.

CREON: There is man who wanders near Thebes—a blind man, who is said to have the sight of the gods.

JOCASTA: *(excitedly)* Tiresias! Of course. He will tell us what we need to know.

OEDIPUS: Summon him. Let us put an end to this mess.

NARRATOR: Word was sent out through Thebes: Tiresias must be brought before the king. The old blind man came soon enough and stood proudly before the throne.

TIRESIAS: *(old voice)* What does King Oedipus wish to know of the gods?

OEDIPUS: Tiresias, Delphi has sent us a message: Thebes must find the man who murdered Laius the former king. Only then will our land be healed.

TIRESIAS: This land will never be healed while you sit upon the throne, my lord.

OEDIPUS: *(in shock)* What did he say?

JOCASTA: *(angrily)* How dare you speak to the king in such a way?

NARRATOR: The old man began to laugh a cruel laugh.

TIRESIAS: *(mockingly)* You fools. Do you not see?

CREON: *(angrily)* Do you mock your king?

TIRESIAS: I mock those who deserve it.

NARRATOR: The old man turned to go.

JOCASTA: *(loudly)* Stop! Tell us what we want to know!

NARRATOR: The old man stopped and turned.

TIRESIAS: What can the past hold but sadness? Why dig up things long buried? Let your kingdom die and perhaps you will live.

OEDIPUS: *(coldly)* Tell us, or I will have you put to death.

TIRESIAS: *(slowly)* I do not fear you, but do you not fear my words?

OEDIPUS: *(firmly)* Nothing you say can shake us.

TIRESIAS: Very well. I know the man whom you seek, king. He is *here* in this very room.

(loud gasping)

OEDIPUS: *(yelling)* Where, Tiresias? Where?

TIRESIAS: The man you seek is *yourself.* You yourself killed the king—or do you not remember?

NARRATOR: They all froze, and Jocasta was the first to break the silence.

JOCASTA: *(laugh)* The old fool! I see his game now! He's making a joke.

CREON: *(angrily)* Lies! Oedipus never met Laius! Who has bribed you to say such treachery?

TIRESIAS: *(sadly)* I expected as much. Fools refuse to see the truth.

OEDIPUS: *(slowly)* I can assure you, noble seer—I have never killed anyone.

NARRATOR: Tiresias smiled.

TIRESIAS: You tried to run—and now you try to lie. But, nothing can save you. Do you forget so soon, an old traveler, who attempted to break you with his whip?

NARRATOR: The stomach of Oedipus sank into his feet.

OEDIPUS: *(stunned)* But—but—that man was no king. He was a dusty traveler on the road to Delphi.

TIRESIAS: Would a king wear his crown on such a journey?

CREON: *(figuring it out)* That's true. He was going to see the Oracle.

OEDIPUS: *(numbly)* But, I didn't know.

TIRESIAS: You still fail to see the whole picture, my lord.

JOCASTA: *(angrily)* What do you mean? What other treason would you dare utter here, you madman?

TIRESIAS: My lady, you of all people should have seen the similarities. You should have looked at Oedipus and seen him for what he truly is—your and Laius' son.

NARRATOR: The queen laughed a strange laugh—half snort, half shriek. Oedipus turned pale.

JOCASTA: *(ranting)* Impossible! Our child was cast into the wilderness. Laius pierced his feet to mark him for death.

NARRATOR: Tiresias nodded grimly.

TIRESIAS: I remember the night very well, my lady. Perhaps we should ask the king. Sir, what marks do you bear upon your feet?

OEDIPUS: *(numbly)* Two scars. *(realizing)* But, my father was the King of Corinth.

TIRESIAS: The shepherd who was sent with you into the wilderness took pity on you. If only he had killed you as he had planned. His mercy has cursed you.

CREON: *(angrily)* You lie!

TIRESIAS: I expected such disbelief. I have sent for the shepherd. He dwells near the mountain still. He will be here soon enough to verify my story.

OEDIPUS: But, I was no shepherd's son! I was raised as a prince! How do you explain that?

TIRESIAS: That kind shepherd gave you to a passing traveler to take into Corinth. That man presented you to his lord, the king of Corinth, who adopted you as his son.

NARRATOR: Immediate grief washed over Oedipus' face as the truth broke in upon him. Jocasta stared at him in wordless horror.

OEDIPUS: *(in disbelief)* How could I have known? How could I have known?

JOCASTA: *(softly)* Then it was true. Our child did murder his father—and—and—married—

NARRATOR: She looked to Oedipus with white, trembling lips.

JOCASTA: *(whispering)* Forgive me. *(yelling)* Gods! What have I done?

NARRATOR: Crying to the heavens and tearing her gown, Jocasta rushed from the room.

OEDIPUS: *(crying out)* Jocasta, no!

TIRESIAS: *(loudly)* You can fight it no more. You have fought it since you were born. Accept it—accept your curse!

OEDIPUS: *(screaming)* No! No!

NARRATOR: Oedipus dashed after his fleeing wife, grasping blindly at her flowing robes. She rushed into her chambers, and the door slammed in his face.

OEDIPUS: *(yelling)* Jocasta!

NARRATOR: He began to throw himself against the door—a madman—attacking it with all his might.

OEDIPUS: *(wailing)* Open the door! Open the door!

NARRATOR: When at last the door splintered and he broke through, he immediately hid his eyes in horror. Dangling from the ceiling from a twirling rope was the body of his queen. Her eyes were pale and looked heavenward.

OEDIPUS: *(weakly)* No—no—no. Why have you done this to me?

NARRATOR: He stumbled forward and fell to the floor beneath her suspended feet. His hand grasped something cold. It was a brooch pin, fallen from her now broken neck.

OEDIPUS: *(angrily, insane)* Why? Why? Why should a man live in such a world? Why should I see such a monstrosity? My wife and mother dead before my very eyes? And, all because of me. I have been blind—blind! Now, I will be blind forever.

NARRATOR: Releasing the point of the pin, he drove it sharply into each of his eyes. Blood poured down his cheeks, and sobs racked his body. Rushing up on the grisly scene, Creon appeared in the doorway and gasped at the horror before him.

CREON: *(calling out)* Tiresias! Oh gods! Tiresias! Come and tell me what I should do! The queen is dead, and the king has gone mad.

NARRATOR: The blind man was already there—placing a calm hand on Creon's shoulders.

TIRESIAS: Pick him up, wash him, and send him away. Thebes is yours again. Let it be healed.

NARRATOR: Creon turned to the prophet in confusion.

CREON: This man is my brother-in-law. Surely I owe him more than that.

TIRESIAS: You have asked, and I have told you. Listen to the will of the gods.

CREON: But, his children . . .

TIRESIAS: His daughters will go to him and care for him when they are older and ready to accept their parents' sin. Until then, Oedipus will roam the countryside—blind and forgotten.

CREON: I don't know.

TIRESIAS: *He* did not listen to the gods. Will you ignore their commands as well?

NARRATOR: Creon paused.

CREON: Very well. I will send him into the desert.

TIRESIAS: It is what must be done.

NARRATOR: The servants were sent for, and they came timidly into the horror of that place. They took down the body of the queen and bandaged the wounds of the king.

CREON: *(sadly)* I mourn for such a wretched man.

TIRESIAS: *(quietly)* Do not mourn too loudly, King Creon. Sadness will be no stranger to your own home. Farewell—until our next meeting.

NARRATOR: And so, the stooped and bandaged form of Oedipus was led away and left again to the will of the wild. He walked blindly now with broken steps, running his fingers over parched lips, trying to remember his former life. He would wander alone for many years, cursed and eternally spurned by the gods—until they finally took pity and allowed him to pass beneath the Earth, where his wearied soul at last could find rest.

DISCUSS

- How is the story of Oedipus a warning about attempting to escape your fate?
- The gods, the ones responsible for Oedipus' doom, never make a direct appearance. They insinuate themselves through their earthly messengers (the oracle, Tiresias). Why is this so?
- After reading this story, have your opinions on fate changed? Why or why not?

Fickle Fate

Here's a scenario. Let's just say that your Magic Eight Ball™ developed a minor malfunction. It developed the ability to *actually* tell the future. Not just those one-word catch-alls either, but specific, complete-sentence answers. You now have a chance most people just dream about: You can know the future.

So, you ask it the question that haunts most people, "How will I die?" It takes a second to answer. The blue bubbles swirl around as your answer appears. *You will be struck by a car and die.* There it is, your ultimate demise, spelled out. What now?

Knowing how you will die gives you an advantage. You're *supposed* to die that way, but what if you happened to cheat death? If you know your exact cause of death, there's a good chance you can avoid it. You want to live, so you'll just have to avoid being struck by a car. Cars in motion are usually found outdoors (near streets), so the only surefire way to avoid your death is to stay indoors. You decide this is a good plan.

You have all the necessities of life within your grasp: water-on-tap, television, take-out food. So, you live your life completely indoors. Your skin begins to turn white, then yellowish, and then slightly transparent like a cavefish. All of your relationships deteriorate. Yet, every time you hear the growl of an engine or the screech of a tire, you smile, thinking of the hideous fate you've avoided. Eat that, fate.

Ten years go by like this. Then one day, unbeknownst to you, a little old lady is driving down your street in her Cadillac. A kitten steps out into the road. The little old lady's vision is just good enough to make out the kitten, so she swerves to miss it. Unfortunately, her focus on the kitten prevents her from seeing the curb or the yard she's plowing through. Meanwhile, you've just begun another morning of not leaving the house, when a Cadillac breaks through the wall and crushes you under its front tires. The little old lady puts on her left blinker.

Who wouldn't love to be the reporter who happened upon this story? *Man Learns Future, Attempts to Escape Own Death, Killed by Car, Dead Just as Predicted.* The article would practically write itself. And, for the perfect headline: *A Simple Twist of Fate.*

Fate is good at twisting.

What *would* happen if you attempted to change the future, cheat death, or alter your fate? There was a film made a few years, that asked this question. A group of teenagers didn't die as they were supposed to. Then Death (the Grim Reaper himself) started picking them off one by one in gruesome ways, reclaiming the souls that were rightfully his. In the end, the question the film asked turned out to be more interesting than the film itself. Can you escape your fate?

The best questions are the ones that refuse to be answered. Fate (and its sister, free will) have been batted back and forth from one great mind to another. Is a human's fate set in stone (predestined)? To what degree do we have a say in what happens to us? Or, do we just *think* we're in control? Are we actually forced down a certain path like a train on a track? Are some people just doomed?

Our word *fate* comes from Greek mythology. The Three Fates, supernatural sisters who worked a cosmic spinning spool, spun the thread of each mortal's life, measured out its length, and then snipped it loose when the time came to die. It's an emotionally detached concept. The Fates don't hate you; they're just doing their job. When it's your time, it's your time. It would be pointless to beg and plead. The *fatal* shears are coming for us. Ask not for whom the shears snip.

Even though the sisters are an interesting metaphor for how fate works, it still doesn't answer the question. Perhaps that's why Sophocles, an Athenian playwright, chose to dramatize the myth that dealt most closely with fate, Oedipus Tyrannos or Oedipus Rex (both meaning "Oedipus the King"). It's almost as if the Delphic Oracle and, more importantly, the gods had it out for him. Oedipus did what most people with a grim fate from a prophecy (or malfunctioning Eight Ball) would do—he tried to escape it. Maybe his story will help you decide what you believe about fate. Is it possible for people to foresee their fate? If there were, would there be any way to change it? Is the future a mystery for a reason?

DISCUSS
- Does everything happen for a reason?
- If you knew your future and were not happy with it, would you attempt to change it? Explain.
- How is fate different than luck?

RESEARCH
Research what famous philosophers believe on the subject of free will vs. predestination. Present your findings to your classmates.

The Most Famous Fortune-Teller of Them All

Out of all the prophets, seers, and oracles that populate Greek Mythology, Tiresias is the most prominent. He even beats out the age-old Oracle of Delphi. Although not all who heard the sage's advice chose to follow it, his wisdom was always in hot demand. Even after his death, Tiresias still couldn't rest as a famous adventurer called his spirit up from the Underworld to get one final bit of information.

Some are born great, some achieve greatness, and some bumble into it. Tiresias was not born blind or omniscient. The events behind his transformation into famed blind prophet are interesting (and unusual). One day, the young Tiresias was walking along a mountain path when he spied two large serpents copulating in the middle of the path. The last thing the world needs is more snakes, so the young man struck the two serpents with his walking stick. There was a flash, and the snakes disappeared. To his surprise Tiresias found himself transformed—into a woman.

If you better understood the mystical importance that ancient cultures placed on serpents, this event wouldn't be so surprising. The snake's shedding of its skin showed the Greeks that the creature was capable of supernatural rebirth. The serpent was said to have magical powers, including healing. On Hermes' mystical staff, the caduceus, two golden snakes curl around the handle as a sign of its power. But, all this superstition did Tiresias no good. He had already struck his sex-changing blow.

So, Tiresias, taking careful consideration of the situation, decided that there was little he could do. He would just have to make the best of it. Having all of the experiences that went with his new gender, Tiresias lived the next 7 years of his life as a woman. Some say he even gave birth to a daughter. In the eighth year after his transformation, he was walking up the same mountain path. There again, the two enormous serpents were coupling. He knew what he had to do. He walked quickly forward and gave them a good rap with his stick. When the blinding light receded, he was a man again. Although interesting in itself, this story doesn't explain Tiresias' blindness or his powers. They came later. Years after this gender-bending episode, Zeus and Hera were having a PG-13 conversation. They were arguing over sex. Who derives more pleasure from intercourse? The man or the woman? Naturally, Zeus thought the woman did, and Hera, the man. It seemed like the two would rail on at each other forever, until Zeus proposed that they get a third party's opinion. Tiresias, he said, would know. He'd been around the block a few times—as a man *and* a woman.

Apollo: (Roman Name: Phoebus Apollo)

God of Light, Truth, Poetry, Health, Prophecy, and Music
From all of the important titles laid at Apollo's feet, you can see the Greeks thought very highly of him. He is called the "most Greek" of all the gods. He, above all others, represented the ideal man—handsome, athletic, intelligent, talented, and good. His twin sister is Artemis, Goddess of the Moon. Over time, Apollo came to replace the Greek god Helios as God of the Sun as well. The lyre is Apollo's instrument, as he is the master musician. Apollo's tree is the laurel. A wreath of laurels was awarded in Greece to those who won a contest of poetry. Apollo's oracle in Delphi was the most reliable and the most popular.

Tiresias grew nervous when he saw the shapes of the god and goddess solidify before him. Situations involving divine arguments never ended well. Zeus and Hera posed their question to the man and asked him to resolve their dispute. Tiresias realized there was no way to win. Whichever side he chose, he would receive the anger of the other. Whether he spoke truthfully or lied to please the god, we do not know, but he declared that Zeus was right. Women *do* derive the most pleasure.

Zeus laughed to himself, while Hera hurled a curse at the cringing mortal and disappeared. Tiresias rolled upon the ground in pain, feeling his now-blinded eyes. A tiny bit of guilt started to well up in Zeus' heart. His argument *had* ruined this man's life. Maybe he should at least try to make it better. Zeus raised Tiresias to his feet. He told him that he could not undo his wife's curse, but he could give to him the gift of prophecy. In addition Zeus would grant him the ability to live for seven lifetimes, and by the end of his career, the prophet would be renowned far and wide for his god-given wisdom.

Tiresias could never again see the world of man, but would forever peer into the world of the gods.

DISCUSS

- Do you know any other cultures that place a mystical importance on snakes?
- In another version of Tiresias' transformation tale, he sees Athena bathing, and she strikes him with blindness. After she calms down, she feels bad for her actions and gives him the ability to hear bird speech. Augury (the mystical interpretation of bird flight and speech) was a popular way of telling the future in the ancient world. Which version of the story do you prefer? Explain.

The Greek Theatre

You may not be a theatre person. You may not enjoy dramas, comedies, one-acts, or musicals. Maybe you haven't even seen a staged play before, but you surely enjoy the theatre's modern-day descendants. Movies and TV owe *everything* to theatre. They're just fancier, flashier versions. And, theatre? Theatre owes *everything* to the Greeks.

The Classical Greeks understood that people need entertainment. People have problems, people have cares, and people need a way to forget about them—just for a while. They need a way to be temporarily transported from their world to a different one. There they can watch fictional characters battle fictional problems and detach themselves from their own. Although there were other ancient cultures that invented their own mass entertainment (like the Romans, who liked nothing better than seeing gladiators rip one another limb from limb—an ancient, better-acted version of Wrestlemania), the Greeks were more intellectual and understood that carnage, while exciting, isn't soul cleansing.

It's been a long journey from the drama of the Greeks to modern films. Greek plays would bore most modern audiences stiff. They had no gory death scenes (all of the carnage occurs off-stage), no sex, and no special effects (unless you count lowering someone in on a rope). If the plays were missing all this, did anyone come to see them? They did *en masse*. The *theatron* (hillside theatre) in Athens, which seated 14,000 spectators, was frequently filled to capacity—an impressive crowd even by our standards.

There were no sound guys in ancient Greece. Actors were required to have massive lungs in order to reach "the cheap seats." Their costuming did give them a bit of help. All actors wore masks, usually with exaggerated features (those at the top needed to be able to make them out), and the mouthpiece cut into each mask acted as a megaphone, projecting the actors' voices even further than they could on their own.

The masks also helped for those problematic female roles, because women were not allowed to participate in the theatre. An actor wearing a feminine mask with blonde tresses attached played the female roles. (Even 1,500 years later in Shakespeare's time, women were still forbidden to act.) Some parts required actors to wear padded robes and raised boots to increase their size. Acting (as we know it) would be nearly impossible in this get-up. While modern actors rely on facial expression, Greek actors had to rely on hand gestures and voice inflection. Because of the limitations put on acting, the playwright's words gained optimum importance.

The chorus was an integral part of every Greek play. As the name suggests, the chorus was a group of 12 to 15 men who sang and danced in response to the actor's words and actions. During the events of the play, they were the voice of the people and public opinion. The democratic Athenians would want to know, "What do Oedipus' subjects think of his actions? What do the people of Thebes think?" In fact, the very first plays were probably just a chorus, relating all of the events of a story solely through song and dance. Thespis, a legendary playwright, allegedly first came up with the idea of adding a speaking part, or an actor who was not a part of the chorus. This revolutionary idea is why actors are now called *thespians.*

Before drama really hit its peak, only one speaking character inhabited the stage at a time. Because characters didn't interact and were differentiated by masks, one actor could play all parts. Just imagine a movie made up entirely of monologues—not the most interesting way to tell a story. Modern audiences want to see how characters interact, but the Greeks were so used to the old way, they never dreamed it could be improved upon.

When the playwright Aeschylus came up with the idea of adding a second character to the stage, it again revolutionized the industry. Now there was the interaction the audience never knew it was missing. Of course, once this innovation hit the scene, no one thought the two-actor approach could be topped until Sophocles wowed them again by introducing a *third* character to the stage. In this period of rapid innovation, drama was truly born.

As I mentioned before, what we would consider special effects were almost nonexistent. They had effects, but they weren't very special. The only device that could remotely qualify was a crane called the *mekhane*, which allowed gods or magical characters to "fly" out from behind the *skene* (painted backdrop) and give the audience a shock. Characters committed their grisly murders, suicides, or eye-pluckings entirely off-stage, leaving it to their servants to run back in and recount what happened in full detail. In *Oedipus Rex*, Oedipus leaves the stage to see the dead body of his wife for himself. A servant re-enters and tells how Oedipus took up Jocasta's brooch to put out his kingly eyes. Only then does Oedipus re-enter—with fake blood running from the eye-sockets of his mask.

The Greeks drama offered catharsis, an emotional purging. By going through the suffering of Oedipus with him, the audience felt pity and sadness, ridding themselves of these negative emotions. When the play was finished, even though the events of the play were depressing, the audience would actually be *happier* than when they came. In a simpler way: Next to Oedipus' problems, everyone else's looked pretty minor.

The Greeks perfected the art of tragedy, retelling ancient myths like that of Oedipus to reflect modern concerns. Through these continued

Pythia

The Oracle at Delphi was established shortly after the god Apollo slew a mighty serpent that was terrorizing the countryside there. With the monster, known as the Python, slain, Apollo sought to establish an oracle for himself on the slopes of Mt. Parnassus. The priestess he chose was called Pythia in honor of his conquest. The oracle sat upon a golden tripod over a crack in the ground. Strange fumes (some said these were from the decomposing body of the Python in the ground below) wafted up from the cleft, and in a trance-like state, caused by the fumes, the oracle would receive the words of Apollo. Some stories report the oracle speaking clearly, but others say that she babbled incoherently while another priest or priestess translated. It was not only in the myths that the oracle was consulted. The city-states of ancient Greece consulted the Delphic Oracle before all major decisions. The last prophecy uttered by the Delphic Oracle was in 393 A.D. when the Roman Emperor declared all activity in pagan temples to cease.

DISCUSS

- What was Oedipus' tragic flaw?
- Horrific acts of violence were committed offstage in Greek theatre. When is keeping violence hidden more effective than showing it?
- As a society, do we prefer tragedy or comedy? Why?
- Have the formulas for comedy and tragedy changed since ancient Greece? Explain.

successes, the idea of the *tragic hero* was formed. This is the character placed at the center of the play's tragic events. He is typically a king or nobleman who undergoes a fall. Sometimes this fall concludes with his death, or in Oedipus' case, abject misery. This breakdown is caused by the hero's *tragic flaw*, an imperfection in his character. All of his decisions are influenced by this flaw, and before the end of the play, he has locked himself into a series of events from which there is no escape. The most common flaw selected by the Greek tragedians was *hubris* (overweening pride, which placed one on level with the gods).

The Athenian festival of Dionysus meant a full day of plays, a kind of ancient movie marathon. Playwrights were chosen to compete for the prize of tragedy. The three tragedy playwrights (only three were selected to participate in a single festival) presented four works: three original tragedies and a satyr play. A satyr play was a crude parody of a famous myth, presented with a chorus of anatomically correct satyrs who humorously participated in the actions. Satyrs were half-men, half-goat creatures associated with the god Dionysus, the patron of the festival. After all that emotional purging (not to mention hours sitting in the sun), the audience needed something light and raunchy to wrap things up and lift their spirits before the long walk back to their homes.

The Greeks may have adored their soul-cleansing tragedy, but they enjoyed comedy too. Comedies were presented at the Dionysia, and playwrights fought for the prize of comedy. While tragedies and satyr plays often used the old myths as their source, comedies were contemporary jabs at daily life in Athens. The comedic playwrights took shots at everything from philosophers to the city assembly to their fellow playwrights. And, for all their intellectual superiority, the Greeks weren't above crude humor. The "fart joke" is much older than most people think, with the Greek comedies using flatulence to its full potential.

Today we are merely adding more bells and whistles to what the Greeks started long ago. Television and film may seem far removed from those humble beginnings, but beneath it all, the goal is still the same: to trigger human emotion (whether it be gasps, screams, tears, or laughter) and give the mind a temporary escape.

Sophocles and the Theban Trilogy

Sophocles lived from 496–406 B.C. and enjoyed a very full career. At the age of 27, he first competed for the prize of tragedy at the festival of Dionysus and won, beating out Aeschylus, the most famous playwright of the time. It was an impressive victory for the young writer. It would be the first of many successes over his 63-year career. Unfortunately, out of the 120 tragedies he wrote, only 7 have survived to modern day.

Dionysus (Roman Name: Bacchus)

God of the Vine and Wine, Patron God of the Theatre

Dionysus was a latecomer to Mt. Olympus. He is the only god to have a mortal parent. Dionysus is a two-sided god. On one side, he is the gentle planter of the vine. On the other, he is a wild drinker, inspiring his followers to commit terrible acts through their intoxication. Satyrs, half-men half-goat creatures, were said to be the companions of Dionysus, along with his fanatical female followers (the maenads). Followers of Dionysus gathered in the wilderness and drank themselves into a wild frenzy. More often than not their gatherings ended with violence. In many stories, kings, who do not approve of the new god or the behavior he promotes, forbid his worship. This probably reflects Greek society's displeasure with the worshippers of Dionysus, whom many viewed as hedonistic drunks. Despite his late addition to the gods and his initial opposition from men, Dionysus became one of the most popular additions to the Greek pantheon. Athens dedicated its springtime drama festival to the god, solidifying his place as patron of the theatre.

Stories work best in threes. It's the tried and true formula, as the Greeks discovered. *Oedipus Rex* was only one part of a three-part saga concerning Oedipus and his children. *Oedipus at Colonus* tells of Oedipus' journey into the wilderness accompanied by his two daughters, seeking forgiveness for his sins. At the end of the play, Oedipus is at last allowed to die in peace. In *Antigone*, the final play of the trilogy, Antigone, Oedipus' teenage daughter, returns home to find Thebes at war. Her brothers have killed one another on the battlefield over the right to rule. Her calculating uncle Creon has taken control of the city-state. Creon refuses to bury the brother who started the war and, according to him, betrayed Thebes. Creon goes one step further and decrees that anyone who dares bury the body of Polyneices will be put to death. Antigone, enraged by this decree, defies the order and buries her brother's body. (The Greeks believed that the soul could not enter the Underworld until the body was properly buried.) When this "crime" is discovered, Creon stays true to his word and has Antigone arrested. Thus begins the king's dilemma: Does he go back on his declaration to save the life of his niece? Ismene, (Antigone's sister), Haemon (Creon's own son, betrothed to Antigone), and Tiresias all appeal to the king to see reason. Before Creon finally relents and agrees to release Antigone, a violent chain of events has already been set in motion, resulting in the suicides of those dearest to him. The end of the play finds him a broken and repentant man, lamenting his overweening pride.

Critics regard *Oedipus Rex* as the greatest drama Greece ever produced. As mentioned earlier, the Greek playwrights frequently took ancient stories and restaged them with themes relevant to their day and age. On the surface *Oedipus Rex* seems to have little to do with life in ancient Athens. Oedipus is King of Thebes. What relevance could his story have to the Athenian democracy?

As the age of Classical Greece emerged, people started to question the gods. Because the gods themselves were unavailable for comment, the scrutiny fell on their earthly mouthpieces—their priests and oracles. If the gods didn't really exist, where were the "servants of the gods" getting their prophecies? The Oracle at Delphi had so much influence, she was a Pope-like presence. Consulted before any war or major event, her opinion could make or break a major decision. Needless to say, with this political power came corruption. Her words were supposed to come from the God of Truth, but many began to question what was talking louder: Apollo or money?

Amid this controversy, Sophocles produces *Oedipus Rex,* which has at its center a controversial prophecy. Oedipus doubts the words of the oracle, believes he can undo them, and because of this, is led into ruin. The Athenians had already heard the tale of Oedipus. They knew the ending and all the stops along the way. What Sophocles did was infuse it with relevance, as any good storyteller does. His message was read loud and clear: Don't mess with the gods. They're bigger than you are.

DISCUSS
- What are some other examples of old stories that find modern significance?
- What are some other examples of famous trilogies? Why do these stories work best in three parts?

READ

Read *Antigone* (either the Robert Fitzgerald or Seamus Heaney translation). How are the themes of *Antigone* and *Oedipus Rex* similar?

Sigmund Says

Dr. Sigmund Freud, the Austrian physician known for his major contributions to the field of psychology, named one of his most interesting complexes after Oedipus. The Oedipus complex is the sexual desire a child feels for the parent of the opposite sex, accompanied by a hatred for the parent of the same sex. Freud believed this to occur in children between the ages of 3 and 5. He viewed it as a natural process for establishing gender roles. In his original theory, both boys *and* girls felt the same love for the mother and hatred of the father.

Carl Jung, another psychiatric giant, later voiced the opinion that Freud's theory was wrong in respect to girls. According to Jung, girls did not have the same feelings as boys, but a reversal of them, feeling jealous of their mother and wishing for the love of their father. He called this tendency the Electra complex, named for another character from Greek mythology. Electra, the daughter of Agamemnon, brings about the death of her mother.

WATCH
Watch the *Star Wars* trilogy (1977–1983) created by George Lucas. What does this film series have in common with the story of Oedipus? How was Lucas influenced by Sigmund Freud?

Oedipus! The Musical Version of Sophocles' Tragedy

Why You Hate Your Job

As a Hollywood director, you're often called upon to create movies that you absolutely loathe. This is one of those cases. Hollywood has been trying to come out with a new musical every year, and some big-shot idiot (one of your many bosses) has decided that *Oedipus Rex* will be the newest subject of a Hollywood makeover. And, the guy's wife has had the brilliant idea of making it a musical. You're stuck with it, because the bad news is that the last few films you've made have been stink bombs as well. You better make this one as good as you can, or it's back to filming infomercials.

Casting

Your first job is to round out your cast with Hollywood's hottest actors. If your boss has plenty of one thing, it's money, so he's sparing no expense. Of course, you have to rationalize your choices. Write your choice of actors to play the following characters along with a rationale.

- *Oedipus*: Oedipus should be confident, reasonably young, and good-looking. The audience is supposed to sympathize with him. This actor will have to carry the film, so make sure you choose someone with a bit of experience.
- *Jocasta*: Jocasta is a *bit* older (hint, hint) but still attractive. Oedipus and Jocasta should have some chemistry (as disturbing as that is). The actor you chose for this part should have some dramatic capability. She will have to go mad at the end of the movie.
- *Tiresias*: Tiresias is very old and mysterious and should be played by a veteran actor.

- *Shepherd*: If there's any room for comic relief in this production, it would come from the shepherd. Choosing someone with some comedic ability will make the movie appeal more to modern audiences.
- *Creon*: Creon is a very serious and duty-bound man. He also will be the ruler of Thebes after Oedipus. Keep this in mind when you are casting.

Musical Numbers

This is the part you've been dreading. How can you add musical numbers to something as depressing as *Oedipus Rex*? Well, you aren't the composer, but you do have to come up with some titles of songs. Then you can give them to the composer, and he'll work out all of the details. Come up with song titles to match the situations, and write them in the boxes on the following page. Remember: When people have a problem in their soul, what do they do? They sing!

Publicity (choose ONE of the following)
- *Soundtrack*: To boost publicity for the movie, the film company is going to release a CD of the songs your composer has written. Design a colorful cover that represents something from *Oedipus!* with your song titles listed on the back.
- *Movie Poster*: Create a movie poster depicting a few key scenes from the movie. You may include your actors' and actresses' names. Make it colorful, and put the title on it as well.

SITUATION	SONG TITLE
A bizarre plague is killing off the people of Thebes	
Oedipus remembers his experience with the sphinx	
Creon tells Oedipus that they must find the murderer of Laius	
Jocasta and Oedipus laugh at Tiresias' words	
The shepherd tells his part of the story	
Oedipus accepts the truth	
Jocasta hangs herself	
Oedipus pokes out his eyes	
Oedipus is led away, blind and broken	

CHAPTER 4

Beauty: The Eye of the Beholder

THE JUDGEMENT OF PARIS

Cast

Eris *(Mischievous goddess of discord)*

Paris *(Exiled prince of Troy)*

Aphrodite *(Goddess of love)*

Hera *(Queen of the gods)*

Athena *(Goddess of wisdom)*

Zeus *(Ruler of the gods)*

NARRATOR: On the great mountain of Olympus, nothing was a more exciting event than a wedding. This day a great crowd had gathered from around the world (and beneath it) for the union between Thetis, a sea nymph, and Peleus, a mortal. Thetis had been the desire of many a god, but none had ever taken her as their bride, for a terrible prophecy haunted the one whom she married: A child of hers was destined to be greater than his father. Zeus had greatly desired this nymph, but did not wish a son to be born greater than he. It was the same with Poseidon, Ares, Apollo, and the rest. So, it was decided that she should marry a mortal and be done with it.

ZEUS: Greetings, guests—gods, goddesses, nymphs, dryads, naiads, centaurs, and the like. We are gathered here today to witness a grand ceremony. The son of these two will be legendary. I have foreseen it. So, let us drink to the happy couple.

(cheers from the crowd)

NARRATOR: Although this was a happy occasion, not everyone in attendance was pleased to be there. Eris, the goddess of discord, was up to no good. She loved nothing more than to cause trouble.

ERIS: Fools. Happy for nothing. Let's see them sort this one out.

NARRATOR: As the guests laughed and capered, Eris pulled forth from her pocket a golden apple. Engraved upon it were the words:

ERIS: For the Fairest. *(laughs)* This should get them going.

NARRATOR: Careful not to draw attention to herself, she placed the apple among the gifts for the newly wedded couple. It did not take long for Aphrodite to notice it there.

APHRODITE: *(cooing)* What a marvelous apple! It was apples much like this one that I gave to Atalanta's young love. And look, it's engraved: *(reading)* For the Fairest. Someone has obviously placed this gift here for me.

ATHENA: How can you be so sure?

APHRODITE: *(snidely)* Well, it's obviously not here for you.

ATHENA: *(angrily)* Why wouldn't it be?

APHRODITE: *(giggling)* Beauty is not commonly associated with manliness.

ATHENA: I ought to box your ears.

HERA: Ladies, ladies, I have a simple solution to this problem: I am the queen of heaven, so, therefore, the apple would naturally be for me.

APHRODITE: Oh, please. This is foolishness. The apple is mine.

HERA: Kindly unhand that apple. You're tarnishing it.

ATHENA: There's no telling where you've been.

HERA: Under the nearest man surely.

APHRODITE: The fact that you despise me for my own advantages with men should be proof enough that I am the fairest. Do not blame me, Hera, that your husband finds you undesirable. And, Athena, what man would want to spend time with you unless he loved his own gender?

ATHENA: Why you—

(sounds of female squabbling)

NARRATOR: Now, because this was going to be no easy discussion and the guests started to feel a bit awkward, the wedding disbanded. The wedded couple left, their day ruined. Eris laughed to herself. Her plan had worked perfectly. Time to the gods is but the blink of an eye, and as the goddesses argued, much time passed. Thetis and Peleus conceived a son. He truly was to be greater than his father—the greatest warrior Greece had ever seen. To ensure his safety, Thetis took the boy into the dark Underworld, where the Styx twists like a dark snake.

There, holding him by the heel, she dipped him into the waters. This river had magical powers. It would bestow upon the boy invulnerability. No sword or spear would ever pierce his blessed skin. But, foolish Thetis forgot to dip the heel by which she held him, and through this, her son, Achilles, was doomed. Back on Olympus, impervious to the constraints of time, the argument was still raging. Zeus had had enough.

ZEUS: *(angrily)* Ladies! This bickering must stop! The apple belongs to no one! My head will split open if you do not stop.

ATHENA: Oh, father, I have been insulted. What is a headache to my pride?

ZEUS: Silence! I would not take my headaches so lightly if I were you. It was from one of their kind that you were born. And, my wife, you are the queen of heaven—start acting like it!

HERA: And, you are a husband. Perhaps you should start acting like one.

ZEUS: Do not make me angry. You shall regret it. And, sister—born of the sea foam—this argument does not flatter you. Where is the love in this?

APHRODITE: *(coyly)* Brother, don't speak of things you know nothing about.

ZEUS: *(yelling)* I have had enough! This fighting must cease!

HERA: Then, husband, you must choose between us. You must decide who is the fairest: The wife, the sister, or the daughter?

ATHENA: I agree.

APHRODITE: You are a good judge of beauty, brother.

HERA: *(hatefully)* A little too good at times . . .

ZEUS: I will do no such thing. How could I choose between you? You are my wife, my sister, and my daughter. Such a choice would anger two and please only one. I cannot win.

ATHENA: Then find us a judge or we shall come to blows, and all the Earth shall feel our conflict.

ZEUS: *(sighing)* I will do what you ask.

HERA: Good—now be off!

ZEUS: Hmph. Women.

NARRATOR: Zeus looked down upon the Earth. Where would he find a suitable judge? This contest must be fair. Three of the mightiest goddesses were involved. Only the most adept connoisseur would appease them. There was a kingdom that was dear to Zeus' heart—

the great kingdom of Troy. Wise king Priam lived there, and he had amassed great wealth through wise ruling, but he was old, and his heart no longer pulsed with life as young ones did. He had 50 children—among them many strapping sons. Foremost of all was the great Hector. But, to Zeus, he seemed too serious—and married. What do married men know of love? Zeus' eye peered into the Trojan countryside. One son of Priam lived apart. As a baby, this boy had been prophesied to bring about the destruction of Troy. Because he was a good man, Priam did not have the heart to put the boy to death—and sent him into exile instead. Here his young son, Paris, lived as a shepherd. He was a great lover—a fond playmate of the river nymphs who lived nearby.

ZEUS: He will be my judge. *(clearing his throat)* Ladies!

HERA: Have you found us a judge, husband?

ZEUS: I have chosen Paris, Prince of Troy.

ATHENA: Does he know his women?

ZEUS: He is a great lover. He has loved many of the local river nymphs.

HERA: A man after your own heart.

APHRODITE: Let us go to him at once.

ZEUS: Take care. I love this land of Troy. Do nothing to harm it—do not poison it with your jealousy.

NARRATOR: The three goddesses disappeared in a cloud of smoke. In Troy, Paris sat on a rock, humming softly to his sheep. There was a loud clap of thunder *(clap of thunder)*, and the three goddesses stood before him.

ATHENA: Mortal prince, do not fear. We are goddesses from Olympus, come with a task for your noble mind.

NARRATOR: Terror-stricken, Paris fell to his face.

PARIS: I will do whatever you wish.

HERA: We have been having a bit of a disagreement, young Trojan. We wish you to settle it.

PARIS: What do I know?

APHRODITE: Beauty, silly.

ATHENA: Judge between us. We will each present ourselves in our best light, and you, Paris, will decide once and for all who is the fairest between us.

PARIS: I will try.

NARRATOR: Paris was frightened but sat himself back on the rock and waited for his next order.

HERA: I am queen of heaven. I shall go first.

NARRATOR: There was a flash, and Hera reappeared—furs dripping from her naked shoulders. Her skin was milky white and her eyes piercing. She was stunning. She drew forward to Paris and leaned in. She smelled of fine wine.

HERA: *(quietly)* Young prince, choose me in this contest, and I will make it worth your while. I will make you a lord of Europe and Asia—power beyond your wildest dreams. I know power, and I know how to get it. Choose me if you are wise.

APHRODITE: What are you saying up there?

ATHENA: You have had time enough.

HERA: I am finished.

NARRATOR: She backed away from Paris—her eyes never leaving his.

ATHENA: Now, it is my turn.

NARRATOR: There was a fluttering sound in the air. Gray-eyed Athena appeared, as she never had before. Her helmet was gone. Her hair was piled into great amber mounds on top of her head—a shining robe clothed her lithe body—her virgin beauty shone forth. Paris was speechless. She, too, advanced toward him and leaned in. She smelled of a grassy meadow—fresh and breathtaking.

ATHENA: Trojan prince, choose me in this contest. I will offer you victory—victory over the Greeks. They have envied your treasures. What can prevent them from taking them? Think of your family. I am the goddess of war. It is in my power. Glory comes to the victorious warrior.

HERA: What lies are you telling the boy?

APHRODITE: Your time is up. It is my turn now.

ATHENA: I am finished.

NARRATOR: She retreated, her lips parted in a celestial smile. The fragrance of nectar drew Paris' gaze. Aphrodite was advancing. Flowers were dancing through her hair. She wore a gossamer gown that shifted and flowed as if it were weightless. Her face was the most glorious thing Paris had ever seen. Truly, she was the goddess of love. She advanced and leaned in, her cherry lips whispering in his ear.

APHRODITE: Don't be fooled by the others. They are dried up and foolish. I can see what you truly want. What else would any young, handsome boy such as you want? Love. It's what I do. Gorgeous prince, if you chose me, I shall give you the hand of the most beautiful woman in the world. I swear it by the Styx.

NARRATOR: Paris' heart stopped. His desire did not rest with glory or power—but with love.

Aphrodite felt this, and she smiled smartly as she backed away.

ATHENA: I hope you did not promise something that you cannot deliver.

APHRODITE: On the contrary.

NARRATOR: Excited—forgetting that he was in the presence of immortality—Paris jumped up.

PARIS: I have made my decision.

HERA: Remember, boy, we are powerful—to offend us would have great consequences.

NARRATOR: But, it did not matter to the Trojan Prince. He had found the desire of his heart.

PARIS: I choose Aphrodite, goddess of love.

ATHENA: (angry) Fool! I knew you were worthless! I will remember this when you call upon my name! May your kingdom crumble!

NARRATOR: With that, Athena disappeared in a huff.

HERA: I curse your marriage, Trojan whelp. Whatever future you have, I will do all in my power to make it a sad one.

NARRATOR: Hera, too, was gone in the blink of an eye. Only Aphrodite was left, holding a golden apple—a smile of triumph on her face.

APHRODITE: You have made a wise choice, Paris of Troy, and I will bestow my reward on you. Prepare yourself. I will return momentarily to tell you how to claim your prize.

PARIS: Thank you! Thank you!

NARRATOR: As swiftly as she could, Aphrodite flew back to Mt. Olympus to announce her victory to Zeus. But, he had already heard.

ZEUS: Aphrodite, I hear from my infuriated wife and daughter that you have won the competition.

APHRODITE: (beaming) I have!

ZEUS: Hopefully, you did not promise the boy something out of your means.

APHRODITE: No, no. It was a stroke of brilliance really. What else would a great lover want than the most beautiful woman in the world?

ZEUS: (pausing) Oh, foolish Aphrodite. Tell me you did not.

APHRODITE: Why? What harm is there in that?

ZEUS: Do you know who this girl is?

APHRODITE: Not offhand . . .

ZEUS: She is my daughter, Helen—Helen of Sparta.

APHRODITE: So?

ZEUS: (annoyed) Aphrodite, she is already married.

APHRODITE: I don't see the big problem with this. Affairs happen all the time. *You* should know that. Don't be so uptight.

ZEUS: Her husband is King of Sparta. He does not take sharing his wife lightly.

APHRODITE: (flippantly) The affairs of mortals do not trouble me. What do I care? I must keep my promise.

ZEUS: I will not let you keep this promise. It will start a war.

APHRODITE: (confused) I have sworn by the Styx . . .

ZEUS: Fool! *(sigh)* Go! Carry out your brainless errand. I fear I have doomed this boy and his kingdom with this burden.

APHRODITE: Remember, brother, love conquers all.

ZEUS: No, it doesn't.

NARRATOR: Aphrodite reappeared in the Trojan countryside. Paris jumped up from the perch where he had been anxiously waiting.

PARIS: I thought maybe you weren't coming back.

APHRODITE: Don't be silly. Now, come to me. Hold on.

NARRATOR: A great cloud started to envelope the world around them—the sun was blotted out—and Paris got the sensation he was flying.

APHRODITE: Have you ever heard of Helen of Sparta? She's Zeus' daughter. *(whispering)* He took her mother in the shape of a swan.

PARIS: If she is half as beautiful as you, I shall be pleased.

NARRATOR: The world materialized about them. They were in an ornately decorated sleeping chamber. A beautiful woman was asleep on the bed—golden hair, rubious lips. She was everything promised. Paris was overcome with passion.

APHRODITE: We are in Sparta, in Greece. There is Helen—asleep. Her husband, Menelaus—

PARIS: She's married?

APHRODITE: Don't worry. She's terribly unhappy. Her husband, Menelaus, is an ugly, hulking man—very undesirable. You will have no trouble wooing her—handsome as you are!

PARIS: But . . .

APHRODITE: I'll take you back to Troy now. Go to your father, King Priam, and reconcile with him. I'll put the idea into his head to send you to Sparta.

PARIS: On a mission of peace! Then when Menelaus isn't looking, I'll steal his wife away.

APHRODITE: Perfect. Now, let's go, before anyone sees you. I have fulfilled my promise.

NARRATOR: As Aphrodite returned her prince to Troy and ascended to Olympus, the gods watched with dissatisfaction.

ATHENA: Brainless! Do you not know what you have started?

APHRODITE: *(defensively)* All's fair in love and war.

ATHENA: Exactly. Once Paris returns to Troy with Helen, Priam will have no choice but to protect his son.

APHRODITE: I can protect his son.

HERA: Can you? We shall see about that. You and your twittish ways have angered me against these Trojans. I will send all of Greece after your two lovers.

ATHENA: As will I. It is not right what you have done!

APHRODITE: You two don't frighten me. Paris is brave and beautiful. He will fight for Helen.

HERA: He will die for her, and I shall laugh as the crows pick his bones.

APHRODITE: Are you so sure? Do not forget that the god of war shares my bed.

ATHENA: Among many others—but you will be outmatched. All of Olympus will soon be in an uproar.

HERA: This time you have bitten off more than you can chew.

APHRODITE: We'll just see about that.

HERA: *(playfully)* What do you think, Athena? Will the Mighty Aphrodite be remembered as the fairest of them all or the destroyer of many?

ATHENA: The goddess of death, I say.

HERA: Let the battle begin then. I am ready.

NARRATOR: And so, the chain of events was set into motion. The greatest war of man was about to begin. The face that would launch a thousand ships had been taken, the fairest city ever built would soon be under attack, and thousands would die.

ATHENA: And to think, it all began with a simple apple.

DISCUSS
- What do you think would have happened if Zeus had chosen between the three goddesses? Why do you think this?
- What is the male author of this story saying about female jealousy? Is it a fair assertion?
- What does Achilles' single spot of invulnerability tell us about human nature?

The Price of Beauty

The new kid walks into the lunchroom. Immediately, all eyes are on him. He looks completely normal, except for his head, which is so pointed that it's shaped like a traffic cone. The lunchroom goes dead quiet. Everyone's in shock. This is the best looking guy the school has ever seen. In the next 6 months, the new kid goes on a steady string of dates. All of the other guys are jealous, wishing their heads were pointy like his. The new kid has quickly become the most popular boy in the school.

What's wrong with this picture? If this new kid came to your school, would he receive the same reaction? Probably not. That's because in our culture, a pointed head is not a sign of attractiveness. But, in another time and another culture, it was. *Beauty is in the eye of the beholder.*

The culture you were born into is responsible for the way you view almost everything, and beauty is no exception. Remember the cone-headed new kid? In many cultures from ancient Egyptians to Native Americans, the shape of a man's head showed his handsomeness and intelligence. To achieve the desired shape, a male infant's head, when it was in its most moldable state, would be bound tightly with rags. Some cultures' technique gave the skull a flat-topped look, while others elongated and pointed it, resulting in a conehead. If his head had the right shape, *he* was an attractive guy.

And, what about the girls? The culture of feudal China thought the sexiest part of a woman was her feet. Incredibly tiny feet (called *lotus feet*) were what most Chinese women (and their prospective husbands) desired. This feature could occur naturally, but most often it occurred by having the girl's feet cruelly and tightly bound with rags during her childhood. Some went so far as to break the foot arches before they bound them. With constricted growth, the feet became miniature deformities. The result was the desired "beautiful" feet, but a lifetime of walking agony.

You might be glad that you weren't born into either of these cultures. You might like your rounded head and normal-sized feet, but our culture and media have their own stipulations on what it takes to be beautiful. Most magazines set a clever trap. On the cover, there's a picture of beautiful person who probably looks 10 times better than you do. You say to yourself, "Man, I wish I could look like that." Luckily, you notice that the magazine features articles that tell how *you* can look like this too. You buy it immediately. The magazine has played its trick.

Our culture may not be in the business of deforming babies, but people today are obsessed with conforming to a concept of beauty. All across the nation, the young and old are injecting toxic chemicals under their skin, sacks of liquid into their chests, and harmful steroids into their bloodstreams. They're letting dangerous rays tan and simultaneously damage their skin. Girls are starving themselves to get thin, while boys are ingesting three times the amount of required protein to build muscle. For the right price, skin can be tightened, hair replanted, bodies reconstructed, and fat sucked out. Are any of these things actually *good* for the body? We shouldn't laugh at the coneheads just yet. We're not too far off.

Yes, our culture is obsessed with appearances, but haven't most other cultures been too? Is it wrong to want to be beautiful? No, it's a natural human desire. No one wants to be thought of as unattractive. But, when people sacrifice their health and happiness on the altar of beauty, they end up missing the true pursuits of life. There's another saying about physical beauty that sheds light on the subject. It comes from the poet Wallace Stevens. He said, "Death is the mother of Beauty." At first, it may sound strange. *Death* is something we associate with being old, while *beauty* is something we associate with being young. How could the two be related?

Hera (Roman Name: Juno)

Goddess of Marriage, Queen of Olympus

Hera usually is shown as a crafty schemer and jealous wife. She is the mother of a few of the second-generation gods: Ares, Hephaestus, and Hebe. Zeus and his frequent affairs are enough to keep her busy, punishing his many lovers and cursing his illegitimate children. Hera is labeled as the protector of marriage, even though she cannot protect her own. Wives with unfaithful husbands could definitely sympathize with her. Hera has a fiery temper and enough venomous anger to last centuries. Her beast is the cow, and her bird is the peacock. The Romans named June, the season for marriage, after Juno.

The poet's point was this: Beauty is temporary. But, at the same time, *that* is exactly what makes it beautiful. One day, beautiful eyes will dim, beautiful faces will wrinkle, and beautiful bodies will sag. If people were always young, would we still consider them beautiful? If flowers were always in bloom, would we still notice their springtime colors? Without the night, how could we appreciate the day? These questions raise bigger questions. If beauty is such a fickle creature, one that changes with time,

DISCUSS
- How do modern men and women sacrifice their comfort and sometimes even health in the name of beauty?
- In modern society, are the pressures of beauty harder on men or women? Explain.
- Diamonds are rare jewels. Gold is a rare metal. Natural blondes make up roughly 5% of the American population. What part does rarity play in beauty?
- Describe a time when your concept of beauty was different from another person's.

place, and season, why do we continue to pursue it? Should beauty be the main goal of your life?

Our society places young people in a pressure cooker of differentiated demands. Magazines, television, and film all try dictate how you should look, act, and feel. Beauty and image figure heavily into self-perception, and self-perception controls self-esteem. It's easy to say, "Just don't listen to society," but it's a hard message to block out. Let's consider a few things though. Beautiful people are no happier than those who are not. Physical beauty, by itself, adds no value to life. Beauty is impossible to keep forever. The old cliché is right: *Looks aren't everything.*

The Greeks were definitely concerned with the outward appearance. Their gods (except for Hephaestus, of course) appeared as physically perfect humans. But, as much as they prized their beauty, they knew that the exterior wasn't an accurate gauge of the interior. The gods and goddesses, although perfect on the outside, were deeply flawed on the inside. Locked in a constant struggle to stay superior, the gods destroyed mortals whose looks started to rival their own. Their Olympian beauty provided only a skin-deep covering for what was truly beneath.

Think about how important attractiveness is to you. If you focus too much on your outside, what can happen to the inside? The Greek gods just might hold the answer.

Understanding Helen

Sparta had always been Helen's home. The high walls of the citadel were her protection and her prison. From the day of her birth, her looks were legendary. Her royal parents, King Tyndareus and Queen Leda, knowing and fearing her reputation, took it upon themselves to shield her from the outside world. She was kept in virtual isolation. Her handmaids and serving women hated her for her perfect beauty, and the few men she encountered simply stared with grasping desire. She had become the object of all Greece's attention, but in spite of that, she felt painfully invisible.

One evening, when the princess was down in the kitchens stealing a secret snack, she heard the cooks speaking her name.

"Curse that beautiful Helen and her head-turning looks!" one was saying. "Too bad you or I weren't born a daughter of *Zeus*!"

Hiding in her corner, Helen's heart leapt.

"Rubbish! She's no god-daughter," the other cook replied. "Don't tell me you believe that lie!"

"No, it is true. I was there the day it happened. The queen was going for a stroll. I was her maidservant. All of a sudden, a swan, as big as a man, burst out of the woods. We all saw the strange look in the bird's black eyes, and the queen began to run. The rest of us stood as if in a trance, powerless to help her!"

Aphrodite (Roman Name: Venus)

Goddess of Love and Beauty

Aphrodite was so lovely that the Greeks couldn't imagine her being born in the usual way. Instead she sprang from the white beauty of the sea foam. In an odd arrangement, this most beautiful goddess was married to the only ugly Olympian, Hephaestus, the deformed forge god. Some said that Zeus forced her into the marriage; others, that she chose him herself. Either way, her vows did not stop her from having many affairs. Gods and mortal men found her charms simply irresistible. Whenever on business abroad, Aphrodite is pulled through the sky by a swan-drawn cart. The swan and the dove are both symbols of her grace. In Greece her worship was popular, although the temple priestesses were rumored to be prostitutes. Our word aphrodisiac, a passion-inducing substance, is derived from her name.

"That's ridiculous! A swan attacked the queen? Unbelievable!"

"It is true. It is true. When we found her, she was beside herself, crying for her husband. She said that it had been Zeus that had visited her."

"I don't believe a word of it!"

"Well, doubter, hear this: I was there the night when Princess Helen was born, and she was not born in any natural way."

"What do you mean?"

"She was hatched from an egg. I swear it to Zeus himself. We kept it in the royal bedchamber for weeks. And, when it hatched, out came the princess."

"The king would raise a child that isn't his?"

"Who says he knows? Since I left that birthing chamber, I've been sworn to secrecy."

"And, you're doing a good job of keeping it a secret, I see."

The two cooks laughed.

When the voices had faded away, Helen wept. Her whole life had been a lie. She was an outcast, the unwanted daughter of a god. From that day forward, she gave up any hope of ever being a part of the world around her.

Shortly after her 14th birthday, the news came that it was time for her to be wedded. Helen was prepared, suitably numbed. She knew that every king in Greece would want her for his personal trophy. Ego could clash against ego. It would be war.

Almost every king and noble in Greece vied for her hand, showing off their riches, their land, and their power. Her one relief was that the decision was not hers to make. King Tyndareus faced the problem alone. He must choose, but his decision was bound to start a conflict. At last he resolved on a shrewd compromise. To ensure that war did not break out between the city-states, he made each of the suitors swear an oath. No matter whom he picked, the rest would protect the honor of the man he chose. If any suitor tried to take Helen by force, he would be locked into a war against the rest of Greece.

When the day came for his choice to be announced, King Tyndareus presented Helen on the walls of the city. She was adorned in the richest jewels, and her skin had been soaked in perfumes for days. She was as glorious as the goddesses of Olympus. To the spectators she had never appeared more vibrant and alive, yet in her own mind, she was already dead.

Her suitors waited below, young and old, skinny and fat. Despite their differences, she saw the same look in their eyes. It was the same look, she imagined, that her mother had seen in the swan's eyes long ago.

When her father breathlessly announced that mighty King Menelaus of Mycenae would be her betrothed, she did not falter and forced a smile from her lips. Below the walls, she saw the fire-haired king raise his arms in triumph and rush toward the steps. She was already resolved. She would go and be the wife of a man she did not love. She would become a doll, stunning on the outside and perfectly preserved, but inside only stuffing, an empty space where *Helen* had never been given a chance to exist.

DISCUSS

- Name some ways in which Helen is more fortunate than most Greek women. In what ways she is less fortunate?
- What type of modern person is similar to Helen, someone who feels eternally trapped?
- If you were trapped like Helen and had a chance to escape, would you take it? What would the consequences be?

Description of Helen From *Doctor Faustus*

The poet Christopher Marlowe (1564–1593), a contemporary of Shakespeare, penned the most famous description of the power Helen holds over men's hearts.

Was this the face that launched a thousand ships,
And burnt the topless towers of Ilium?
Sweet Helen, make me immortal with a kiss:
Her lips sucks forth my soul, see where it flies!
Come Helen, come, give me my soul again.
Here will I dwell, for heaven be in these lips,
And all is dross that is not Helena! (Marlowe, 1604/2001, p. 488)

DISCUSS
- Does Marlowe effectively capture the essence of Helen's beauty? Explain.
- Is love a good reason to fight a war? Or, does hate provide a better one?

Odysseus the Draft-Dodger and Achilles the Drag Queen

War had broken out in Greece. The honor of Menelaus, King of Sparta, had been slighted, his wife stolen away by an impertinent Trojan prince. Menelaus was not equipped to command the forces of united Greece, so he asked his brother Agamemnon, ruler of powerful Mycenae, to champion his cause. Agamemnon heartily agreed and called upon the kings of Greece to remember their sworn oath. He ordered them to bring their armies to Mycenae at once. Any who denied the call of war was a traitor and a coward.

Odysseus, the king of the tiny island Ithaca, heard this news, and his heart grew heavy. He was no warrior. He was a simple man—one who enjoyed working his fields side by side with his subjects. Although he had competed for the hand of Helen with the rest of the Greek kings, he'd since found a beautiful wife, who had borne him a son. The Odysseus who'd made that ridiculous oath was a different person now, a man with a family. He thought of the long voyage across the seas to Troy. He thought of the death and the destruction he would encounter there. What if he did not return? Would his son ever know his father? The thought of it made him almost want to weep.

But, he also knew what a bully Agamemnon was. If Odysseus refused his call to war, Agamemnon could and *would* force the deal. The only way to escape would be through a trick. Odysseus, his mind filled with twists and turns, started to formulate a plan. A month later, a company of Agamemnon's soldiers rode into Ithaca looking for Odysseus. He hadn't reported to Mycenae as commanded. When they asked where he could be found, the peasants pointed sadly toward the fields. "Look how he sows his crops. He has gone mad."

The soldiers looked toward where the peasants pointed and gasped at the sight. There was Odysseus. He was almost naked, his clothes ripped to shreds, red scratches running down his face. He was plowing his fields, but not in any normal way. The oxen were charging this way and that, zigzagging across the soil. With his eyes rolling back and forth, Odysseus manned the plow, muttering to himself.

"What is that he's throwing on the ground?" one soldier asked.

"Salt. That field will never give crop again," the sorrowful peasants replied. Odysseus *had* gone mad.

As the soldiers turned to carry this news back to Mycenae, their shrewd captain stopped them. He looked thoughtfully at the mad king of Ithaca.

"Bring me the son of Odysseus," he said in a low voice, "or we will burn his place to the ground."

Iris

Goddess of the Rainbow, Messenger of the Gods

Second only to the godly messenger Hermes, Iris delivers the divine decrees of Olympus. The Greeks saw the rainbow beginning at a distant point and touching down at the opposite end of the horizon. To their ancient minds, this multicolored trail could only be one thing: The path left by a goddess as she made her way through the heavens. In the modern world, the colorful part of the eye is named for this goddess. The plant iris also is named after her for its variety of colorful flowers.

The peasant stared at him in shock.

"Do it at once!"

They scurried to comply and soon returned with the infant Telemachus.

"Now," the captain said coldly, "place him before the plow. We shall see how crazy your lord really is."

The Mycenaean soldiers drew their swords, and the peasants reluctantly laid the child in the path of the plow. If Odysseus were truly mad, the child would be crushed under the hooves of the stampeding oxen. As the plow grew nearer and nearer to his son, Odysseus knew he could no longer continue his trick. At the last second, he pulled fiercely on the reins, driving the oxen aside and stopping their charge. He hung his head in shame.

The captain reprimanded Odysseus for his feeble attempt to escape his duty. "Agamemnon will not be pleased when he hears of your cowardice. If you value your life or the life of your family, I suggest you come and aid us *willingly*."

"I will do what you ask," said the defeated Odysseus.

Ithaca had only been the soldiers' first stop. Achilles, the greatest warrior in Greece, had gone missing. None of the Greek kings dared fight a war without their best soldier. If he wanted Agamemnon's forgiveness, the captain informed Odysseus, he would help them track down Achilles. With a reluctant heart, Odysseus held his family in his arms for possibly the last time.

The mother of Achilles was Thetis the sea nymph, and although her young son had bristled at the thought of war, she had other plans. An oracle had told her at Troy he would win himself worldwide glory but lose his life. This was not a price she was willing to pay. Against her son's wishes, she spirited him away to the island of Scyros and disguised him as a maiden-in-waiting among the daughters of King Lycomedes. There, she thought he would remain undetected until the Greek ships were far away.

Achilles was not very subtle though. His disguise soon wore thin. When one of King Lycomedes' daughters became pregnant, rumors began to circulate about a certain disguised warrior living in his court. These rumors reached the ear of Odysseus and the Mycenaean soldiers. They made their way to Scyros, and once again, Odysseus hatched a brilliant plan. He took the guise of a merchant peddling his wares and set up a small stand in the city marketplace. His stand included many things that would interest women—perfumes, scarves, and rare oils—but amid the pile, he placed a shining sword.

For days, he watched wealthy women pass by his stand. They all picked through the daintier items and ignored the weapon. Then one morning, Odysseus saw a brawny hand reach out and grasp the sword. He looked up and beheld the manliest woman he had ever seen. It was Achilles. Odysseus reached out, grabbed the large wrist, and uttered one simple phrase: "You are caught, my friend."

Sacrifice at Aulis

With Odysseus and Achilles, the two wayward warriors, back in hand, Agamemnon commanded all troops to convene at the port of Aulis. From there they would launch their "thousand ships" for Troy. As the companies

DISCUSS
- Was Odysseus wrong for not wanting to go to Troy? Explain.
- During the Vietnam conflict, draft-dodgers were those who attempted to avoid the wartime draft. Many of them did not agree with the reasons for the conflict. Critics called their bravery and patriotism into question. Should you fight in a war you do not believe in? Explain.

DISCUSS

- What is especially tragic about Iphigenia's death?
- Think about Odysseus and Agamemnon. Both were placed in similar predicaments. If Odysseus had run over his young son, Telemachus, with the plow, he could have avoided the Trojan War and saved himself 20 years of grief. How is Odysseus different from Agamemnon?
- The Classical Greeks were appalled by this record of human sacrifice in their past. In their day several alternate versions of the story had been circulated. One claimed that a moment before the Greek kings put the knife to Iphigenia's throat, Artemis replaced her with a deer and spirited the maiden far away. What does this change about the story? Which version do you like better?

marched to the sea, a seemingly unimportant event happened. A family of rabbits, trying to dart in between the feet of the marching troops, was trampled to death. When the armies arrived at Aulis, they boarded their ships, chanting for victory, and waited for the contrary winds to change direction. But, for days the winds continued to blow against them, keeping them firmly in place. Their hopes began to sour. These winds could mean only one thing: The gods were unhappy.

Calchas, a prophet Agamemnon had brought to interpret the will of the gods, beseeched Olympus, asking what must be done to satisfy whomever they had angered. Artemis, the goddess of the moon and wild things, answered him. The Greeks troops had thoughtlessly murdered a family of rabbits and shown no remorse for their actions. Therefore, she would not allow the winds to blow until Agamemnon, the leader of the armies, agreed to sacrifice a member of his own family, his daughter, Iphigenia.

Agamemnon was flabbergasted. As he stood upon the brink of the greatest military campaign in Greek history, the gods ask him to murder his own flesh and blood. The prophet's word quickly spread through the warriors and kings. They watched their leader expectantly. Would he disband the army he had worked so hard to organize? Would he risk mutiny and possibly his own death for such a cowardly act? Or, would he allow his daughter to die?

At last he decided that the gods must be appeased. Iphigenia was the apple of his wife's eye, and he knew she would never willingly let her go. Therefore, he devised a trick. He sent word to Clytemnestra, his wife and queen, to prepare Iphigenia for a long journey to the sea. The handsome Achilles has requested her hand in marriage, he said, in return for his allegiance to the cause. Reaching Mycenae, the news thrilled Clytemnestra, who eagerly prepared Iphigenia for her seaside wedding. The army had been camped at Aulis for weeks when they finally saw the wedding procession approaching. Iphigenia, flowers pinned into her hair, rode within the marriage cart, smiling broadly at the happy prospect of her future. When she came close enough to see the faces of the soldiers, they did not reflect her joy. Something was wrong, she told herself. When she finally beheld her father, he looked far older than she remembered. More importantly, he refused to meet her gaze.

As she stepped from the cart, Iphigenia felt forceful arms grab her at either side. They pulled her to the top of a rocky hill, where a makeshift altar had been prepared. The princess began to sob. Throwing her down upon the damp stones, she heard the dim voice of her father, "Behold, Artemis. Take your sacrifice, and let come the winds of war."

Iphigenia's Lament

DISCUSS

- A death is tragic when it is unexpected or undeserved. What is another tragic death that you might write a poem about?

The Victorian poet Alfred, Lord Tennyson (1809–1892) found the death of Iphigenia to be especially tragic, and he chose it as the subject of one of his most compelling poems. Iphigenia's story is told in Tennyson's poem "Dream of Fair Women," included below:

> I was cut off from hope in that sad place,
>   Which yet to name my spirit loathes and fears;
> My father held his hand upon his face;
>   I, blinded by my tears,
>
> Still strove to speak; my voice was thick with sighs,
>   As in a dream. Dimly I could descry
> The stern black-bearded kings, with wolfish eyes,
>   Waiting to see me die.
>
> The tall masts quivered as they lay afloat,
>   The temples and the people and the shore;
> One drew a sharp knife through my tender throat
>   Slowly, and—nothing more. (Bulfinch, 1855/1998, p. 199)

Nymphs

The Female Spirits of Nature

Nymphs lived in springs, pools, grottoes, meadows, mountains, forests, rivers, and oceans. They were the personification of the natural beauty these places radiated. In their physical form, nymphs appeared as lovely maidens and frequently were targets of amorous gods and mortals. Naiads were fresh water nymphs, Dryads were tree nymphs, and Oceanids were salt water nymphs. Satyrs (half-man, half-goat creatures) were the companion creatures to these nymphs. Both types of creatures were associated with excessive sexual desire. Because of this connection, *nymphomaniac* is a modern psychological term for a female with excessive sexual desire.

CHAPTER 5

War: The *Iliad* and the Trojan War

THE *ILIAD:* THE TROJAN WAR, PART I

Cast

Zeus *(Ruler of the gods)*

Thetis *(Sea nymph, mother of Achilles)*

Achilles *(Greatest warrior for the Greeks)*

Agamemnon *(Leader of the Greek army)*

Menelaus *(Husband of Helen)*

Paris *(Prince of Troy)*

Priam *(King of Troy)*

Hector *(Greatest prince of Troy)*

Hera *(Queen of the gods)*

Athena *(Goddess of wisdom)*

Helen *(Wife of Menelaus)*

Aphrodite *(Goddess of love)*

Calchas *(Greek prophet)*

NARRATOR: The Trojan War had been raging for 9 long years. Many Greeks and Trojans had met unflinching deaths on the plains of Troy. Achilles, the mightiest warrior for the Greeks, had fought fiercely for King Agamemnon, the leader of the united Greek chieftains. But, there was trouble in the camp.

ACHILLES: *(roaring)* AGAMEMNON! AGAMEMNON!

NARRATOR: A sickness had spread though the Greek troops while they were entrenched on the coast. Men had fallen dead, struck down by the arrows of an unseen god. Calchas, the prophet, had come to speak to Agamemnon. He feared his news would anger the king, and cowered behind the powerful Achilles for protection. His tidings were simple, but dangerous: Apollo, the Archer of Olympus, was offended—by Agamemnon himself.

CALCHAS: *(frightened)* The Trojan girl, Chryseis! She is the reason for the plague—for the sickness among the men.

ACHILLES: The girl we captured in the countryside, remember? She shares your bed, doesn't she, Agamemnon?

NARRATOR: The king calmly stroked his beard.

AGAMEMNON: Yes. But, why is Apollo concerned with her? We've stolen plenty of women. Even Achilles here has one in his tent.

CALCHAS: Chryseis is different! The father you stole her from was a priest to that god.

ACHILLES: Give her back to her father, or the god will strike us down.

NARRATOR: The king scowled. He did not enjoy taking orders from warriors or prophets.

AGAMEMNON: Are you *sure* this is the reason for the sickness among the men?

ACHILLES: *(angrily)* How many more men must die before you listen to reason? The gods have spoken!

AGAMEMNON: *(coldly)* Very well. Return the girl to her father.

NARRATOR: The warrior and the prophet turned to go.

AGAMEMNON: But, Achilles, don't think this is the end of the issue . . .

NARRATOR: Achilles was so selfless with other men's women, but what about his own? While the army battled on the plains, Agamemnon ordered his guards to retrieve Briseis, the concubine of Achilles, from the warrior's tent. When the swift-footed Achilles returned, wearied from battle, he found his lodge empty.

ACHILLES: *(roaring)* AGAMEMNON! AGAMEMNON!

MENELAUS: Brother! Achilles has returned! He has learned what you have done.

AGAMEMNON: Allow him to enter—and let me remind him of his place in this army!

NARRATOR: But Achilles, powerful as he was, needed no permission to enter. He tore past Agamemnon's guards and into the king's presence. The nobles paused in their business to hear the words of the enraged Greek.

ACHILLES: WHERE IS SHE?

AGAMEMNON: *(loudly)* Remember whom you are talking to, Achilles! I am a king! What are you?

ACHILLES: Me? I am the one who will cut your throat if you do not tell me where she is!

AGAMEMNON: She is here in my tent. What does it matter?

ACHILLES: *(growling)* She's mine!

AGAMEMNON: Possessions, possessions. You asked me to give up my prize, and I did. I have taken yours in her place. It's a fair trade. *(pause)* And, you would be wise to watch your tone.

ACHILLES: You would be wise to not shake that finger at me—unless you wish to lose it.

AGAMEMNON: Ha! What can *you* do to me?

ACHILLES: *(to the others)* I will fight no more for this man. You have my word. He is a thief and a dog. He is not worthy of Greece. *(spits)* See how well your precious war goes without *me* leading the charges!

NARRATOR: With his honor slighted, Achilles stormed back to his tent. His failure infuriated him. In spite of his power—power given to him by the gods—he could not get what he desired.

Back in his tent, he sat sulking, wiping his eyes over the lost Briseis. It was here that his mother, the silver-footed sea nymph Thetis, found him.

THETIS: *(softly)* Achilles.

ACHILLES: Briseis?

THETIS: No, dear, it's your mother. Thank heavens you got rid of that awful girl.

ACHILLES: Mother! What do you know? Briseis was so beautiful. She was—she was—beautiful—

THETIS: Oh, Achilles. You never were good at words, were you? Why couldn't my son have been a poet, I say to myself. Warriors have such dangerous lives. Poets would always be safe and sound at home.

ACHILLES: Mother, I am strong. I am fierce. This is my destiny.

THETIS: Oh, destiny. If destiny had anything to do with it, dipping you in the River Styx wouldn't have worked the wonders that it has.

ACHILLES: Mother, that has nothing to do with it. Bravery has made me great.

THETIS: Yes, and bravery will get you killed. Now, listen—I've conveniently overheard you and King What's-His-Name arguing.

ACHILLES: I declared I would no longer fight for a man like him!

THETIS: No, I should think not.

ACHILLES: The Greeks will see. Without me, they are nothing. They will come to me and beg me to lead them.

With me as their true leader, we'll crush Troy—once and for all!

THETIS: Errr—that's nice, dear. *(excitedly)* I know what would really show Agamemnon you mean business!

ACHILLES: And, what would that be?

THETIS: If you went home—back to Greece—right now. That would certainly give him a taste of his own medicine. He would be red with fury. Why I think—

ACHILLES: Mother, I won't run away like a coward.

THETIS: Coward is such a strong word. "Intelligent young man"—that's what I would say.

ACHILLES: No! That's my final answer.

THETIS: *(sadly)* I see—but think about it, my son . . .

ACHILLES: *(to himself)* I will stay here until Troy has been destroyed.

THETIS: *(to herself, sadly)* And, you along with it.

NARRATOR: But, Thetis was not so easily defeated. She had done so much to save the life of her doomed son. Yet, there was still one more card to play. She flew upward—through the darkness of the night sky—to Olympus. She would go right to the top—to the god in charge. She appeared to the royal Zeus.

THETIS: *(grandly)* Zeus, wide-seeing lord of the sky. It is I, lowly Thetis.

ZEUS: *(kindly)* No need for formalities, Thetis dear. What is it that you want?

THETIS: Great Zeus, it was you who gave me my wonderful son. You said he would be great, but now his life is in danger!

ZEUS: He will be great. His life will be glorious, but short. So it goes with mortals.

THETIS: Yes, but here is what I ask. This war has raged for 9 long years. My son still stands as the greatest among them . . .

ZEUS: How could he not be with such a cunning mother?

THETIS: Thank you, but I wish for a speedy end to this war. Achilles says that he will no longer fight for Agamemnon. If the Greeks were to attack without Achilles, they would be defeated once and for all.

ZEUS: Yes, but they are not stupid enough to attack without their finest warrior.

THETIS: No, not yet. But, if you—greatest of gods—appeared to them, telling them to strike—

ZEUS: Ah. But, I have sworn not to interfere. My brother, Poseidon, my wife, Hera, and daughter, Athena, all favor the Greeks. My sons, Apollo and Ares, my daughter, Artemis, and my dear sister, Aphrodite, all fight for the Trojans. Someone must stay neutral.

NARRATOR: At this, Thetis dropped her robe. Underneath she was dressed in a gown made from the shells of the sea. They shimmered in the dim light of the Olympian hall. She knew that time had not paled her beauty.

THETIS: *(seductively)* Zeus, O Zeus. You are such a strong, powerful god. Surely, you could do this one, tiny favor.

ZEUS: Well—I—

NARRATOR: She leaned in close to the god—her lips almost touching his.

THETIS: *(seductively)* I would be most grateful.

ZEUS: *(resisting)* I—I—I need to think—leave me!

THETIS: Yes, Zeus, make your decision. I shall be waiting.

NARRATOR: Once Thetis had disappeared, Zeus sat alone in his throne room. Dare he get involved in this mortal war? Thetis was definitely persuasive, and in his heart, he loved Troy more than any city on the face of the Earth. Every other god and goddess had certainly meddled enough in this affair. Why shouldn't he?

ZEUS: I have decided.

NARRATOR: He descended through the atmosphere into the very mind of Agamemnon, where he interrupted a very pleasant dream the Greek commander was having.

ZEUS: *(booming)* Agamemnon! Agamemnon!

AGAMEMNON: *(in shock)* Ah! This can't be! Zeus Almighty!

ZEUS: I am speaking to you through a dream, wide-ruling Agamemnon. I come with an important message for you and my Greeks.

AGAMEMNON: Yes, cloud-gatherer!

ZEUS: You must attack immediately. Troy is weak. Strike tomorrow, and you shall win the war.

AGAMEMNON: *(shocked)* Attack without Achilles? It would be suicide!

ZEUS: *(booming)* Do I lie? Am I not the Lord of the Gods? Do not question me, mortal, unless you wish to be a smear upon the sand. This is your message. Do with it what you will.

NARRATOR: And so, the glory of Zeus left the mind of Agamemnon. The king awoke and ran from his tent, yelling at the troops.

AGAMEMNON: *(shouting)* To arms! To arms! We attack at dawn!

MENELAUS: *(confused)* Brother! Have you gone mad?

AGAMEMNON: Zeus has come to me in a dream!

MENELAUS: *(sarcastically)* That answers my question.

AGAMEMNON: Silence! *I* command this army. We strike at dawn. Ready the men.

NARRATOR: With the frenzy of Agamemnon spurring them on, the Greeks made ready to attack at daybreak. The king acted like one possessed. He ran around his troops gleefully shouting and throwing his arms toward Olympus.

AGAMEMNON: *(shouting)* Glory to Zeus! Glory to Zeus!

NARRATOR: Meanwhile, the actions of the Greeks did not go unnoticed by Trojan spies. They brought their report back to Ilium, where Priam waited in the throne room with his eldest son, Hector.

HECTOR: Father, the spies have reported that the Greeks are preparing for an offensive.

PRIAM: *(feebly)* I see. Many more men will die tomorrow.

HECTOR: We need to end this war. I love my brother, but I grow tired of defending his vanity with the blood of our countrymen.

PRIAM: I have wronged your brother enough, Hector. Because of fear, I sent him away. When he returned, I knew that the gods had reunited us for a reason.

HECTOR: *(angrily)* So that our city could be destroyed?

PRIAM: Our destiny is not our own to decide. We will continue to fight.

HECTOR: *(sigh)* All for a woman.

PRIAM: I would have started such a war for your mother, son. Helen has captured us all in her spell. Men's hearts are mighty things.

HECTOR: Mine is not. It has grown cold with death. Father, what if there were some way to end this war *without* any more senseless bloodshed?

PRIAM: If it were honorable, I would call it a good plan. What is your idea?

HECTOR: We rest the fate of the war on two men—the two whom it most concerns. Menelaus, the husband of Helen, has brought all of Greece to our doorstep. He must face off against . . .

PRIAM: *(shocked)* Paris?

HECTOR: Do not let your love of your son cloud your judgment, Father. What about your love for your people?

PRIAM: Paris is not a fighter. You do not understand. He is not strong and valiant like you.

HECTOR: I can teach him what he needs to know. Menelaus is no Achilles.

PRIAM: I do not like it, but it will be for your brother to decide. Summon him.

NARRATOR: Paris was sent for, and soon, he entered with the lovely haired Helen walking by his side. When the men-at-arms beheld her, their mouths went slack. Truly, she was the most beautiful creature in the world. This woman alone was worth a thousand years of war.

PRIAM: *(kindly)* Paris, my son. Helen, beautiful Helen.

HECTOR: The Greeks will attack once again tomorrow, Paris.

PARIS: Troy's walls will hold.

HECTOR: *(angrily)* And, how do you know that? Perhaps you would care to join us on the field of battle once in a while? Instead of bathing in the sun with your beauty! We are growing short in number—protecting *your* interests.

PARIS: I am not a coward. But, I am no warrior. I would only bring shame on my family.

HECTOR: *(spitefully)* You have done enough of that already.

PRIAM: Hector! *(softly)* Paris, we have an idea of how to end this conflict, but it would require your permission and cooperation.

PARIS: I will do whatever you ask, father.

HECTOR: Menelaus has come for Helen. Nothing else. I say you two must fight it out. Winner takes the spoils.

HELEN: Nobody need die for me.

HECTOR: Too late. Perhaps you should have thought of that before you so easily left your husband!

PARIS: *(angrily)* Don't you talk to her that way!

PRIAM: My sons! Helen, I beg your forgiveness. Hector feels only for his people. You are our guest, my adopted daughter. Troy has offered you its protection. It was given freely. Feel no guilt.

HELEN: Thank you, but—

PARIS: I will fight him.

HELEN: *(shocked)* Paris!

PARIS: I can do it! It's my fault anyway—this whole mess.

HECTOR: I will teach you. You have much to learn.

PARIS: I can learn quickly.

HECTOR: See that you do. You face him tomorrow.

HELEN: Tomorrow? *(crying)*

PRIAM: Paris, you have made me very proud, my son. You have lived up to the name of Prince of Troy. May the gods smile upon you. You will succeed. I feel it in my heart.

NARRATOR: Hector quickly took Paris to be trained. There was no time to lose. He had to learn how to find the chinks in armor, how to wind a large adversary, how to throw a heavy spear—all in one night. Helen was left weeping in the throne room. It was her lot in life to weep. She was made beautiful, yes, but eternally sad. Night tore on, and the morning broke. At the first sight of the sun, the Greek troops began to march across the Trojan plain to the high walls of Troy. Achilles watched as they scurried like ants across the dirt. His own men, the Myrmidons, had stayed behind. If their leader did not fight, neither would they.

ACHILLES: Look at them. Sheep following a fool! Go! Fail without the Great Achilles. I will be here when you return—to hear you begging.

NARRATOR: Priam and Helen watched from the height of the Trojan walls as the great army finally came to a halt far beneath them.

AGAMEMNON: *(shouting)* Trojans! Beg for mercy! Zeus has smiled upon his Greeks!

NARRATOR: As if in response, the Trojan gates opened, and Hector, Paris, and a troop of men issued slowly forth—holding the banner of truce above their head. Agamemnon and Menelaus came forward to meet them.

AGAMEMNON: *(boasting)* Ah, so I see you have come to grovel! How pleasing!

HECTOR: *(sternly)* Hold your tongue, Greek. We have come to suggest a solution to this bloodshed.

AGAMEMNON: A solution is at hand. Zeus has promised *us* victory.

HECTOR: *(sarcastically)* Yes, I'm sure he has. But, I do not come to speak to you, but to your brother. Tell me, Menelaus, do you like being the laughing stock of the whole world?

MENELAUS: *(angrily)* Why you!

HECTOR: My brother, Paris, has made fool of you. He has stolen your pretty wife. Wouldn't you like his insolent head on a platter?

PARIS: *(whispering)* I don't think he needs any persuading.

MENELAUS: *(angrily)* Yes! I should have known that was you, you miserable whelp. Hiding behind your walls!

We have missed you in the battle! Have you been hiding with the women?

HECTOR: Enough. I've come to give you a chance to exact your revenge on my dear brother.

AGAMEMNON: What do you propose?

HECTOR: A man-to-man battle.

MENELAUS: (excited) To the death!

HECTOR: Exactly. Agamemnon, if your eager brother here wins, we will give you what you have come for—Helen of Troy. Or, should I say Sparta?

PARIS: (forcefully) Troy.

HECTOR: And, if my love-struck brother should win, we keep Helen, and you may all go home. We will even give you enough gold to make your vacation here worthwhile.

AGAMEMNON: Brother, may I speak to you a moment?

NARRATOR: Agamemnon and Menelaus withdrew from the others.

AGAMEMNON: Zeus has promised victory. It doesn't matter how—great armies or man-to-man. You must fight this boy.

MENELAUS: Gladly! He has insulted me! His very face is a mockery to me! I will cut it open.

AGAMEMNON: Good. (loudly) Trojan princes, we agree to your terms. My brother is ready. Is yours?

HECTOR: Yes.

NARRATOR: And so, the two crowds parted, making way for the combatants. High above on the walls of the city, Helen held the hand of King Priam crying softly. Higher still, other spectators—of the immortal variety—were watching with even greater interest. Hera and Athena, who both had been furiously trying to bring about the defeat of the Trojans, sat on the chairs of Olympus peering down on these events.

HERA: Ha! The little wispy prince is going to fight the mighty Greek king. Come, Athena, let us watch him be skewered.

ATHENA: He looks like a woman in that armor. Pathetic.

HERA: No wonder he was such a terrible judge of beauty. No manliness in him at all.

NARRATOR: From across the marble hall in which they sat, Aphrodite floated into view. She, too, had come to watch this battle.

ATHENA: (disappointedly) Ugh. Don't look now.

HERA: Aphrodite, how nice. We were just starting to watch your darling Trojan Prince be filleted by a hulking Greek.

ATHENA: I bet he cries—begging for mercy before the end.

APHRODITE: (shocked) Paris, no!

NARRATOR: Below them, the battle was beginning. Athena had been right. Paris' armor dwarfed him. He held his sword as if he had never done so before. In fact, he almost hadn't. What did he know of fighting? He had been raised as a shepherd. Menelaus was a redheaded giant, rippling with power. His great frame held his weapon and shield aloft with majesty. All could see that Paris was no match for him.

AGAMEMNON: (shouting) Fight!

MENELAUS: Hopefully, you have kissed my wife goodbye. This will be the last time you see her.

PARIS: I doubt that.

NARRATOR: Menelaus hurled his spear forth with all his might against Paris' shield. (CLANG) The shield clattered to the ground. Menelaus roared with laughter.

MENELAUS: Boy, I plan to gouge your eyes out and then send you into Hades blinded.

PARIS: We'll see!

NARRATOR: Menelaus drew his sword and sliced, but Paris was too fast. He swooped beneath it and brought his own sword up against Menelaus' breastplate.

(CLANG)

MENELAUS: I grow tired of this, Trojan. I had hoped to pierce your pretty little head on the first throw.

PARIS: Sorry to keep you waiting.

NARRATOR: Moving swiftly, Paris brought his sword about. It flashed through the air and met Menelaus' with a crash of sound. *(CLANG)* The force of the blow knocked the sword from Paris' hand, and he fell backward into the dirt.

MENELAUS: *(laughing)* These weapons are for *men*! Not for pretty things such as yourself!

HECTOR: *(shouting)* Get up, Paris! Get up!

AGAMEMNON: *(shouting)* Finish him!

NARRATOR: From her viewpoint in the clouds, Aphrodite saw him fall. In the flash of an eye, she was gone—flying toward the Earth to save her darling Paris.

ATHENA: *(angrily)* Cheat! How dare she interfere! After her!

HERA: *(calmly)* Patience, Athena. This should be interesting. Let us watch the Trojan Prince be protected by the goddess of *love*. *(snotty laugh)*

ATHENA: *(laughing)* I never thought of that. How embarrassing to be saved by that creampuff!

NARRATOR: Menelaus reached down into the dust and grabbed Paris by the horsehair crest of his helmet. He began to drag him. The Greeks started to cheer. *(loud cheering)*

MENELAUS: Troy! Look at your beautiful *princess*! I drag *her* through the dirt! Have you no *men* to send to fight me?

NARRATOR: He turned to drive his sword through Paris' throat. But, Aphrodite was there—invisible to all. She broke the strap on Paris' helmet, and he was free.

APHRODITE: *(shouting)* Run, Paris, Run!

MENELAUS: Coward! Have you not shamed your country enough?

HECTOR: *(disappointed)* Oh, Paris.

NARRATOR: As Paris ran, Aphrodite shrouded him in a giant cloud. When the smoke cleared, he was gone. He had been taken back safely into the walls of Troy. Aphrodite's move had been played. Now, it was Hera's turn.

HERA: Athena, let us descend.

NARRATOR: The Greeks were in an uproar. Never before had they seen such a display of cowardice.

AGAMEMNON: Trojans, is this the best you can do? You have forfeited your prize. Bring her forward so that we may go home—in Zeus' victory!

NARRATOR: On the walls of Troy, Priam hung his head in shame. Helen began to sob.

HELEN: *(crying)* Is there nothing that can be done?

PRIAM: I am sorry, my dear. We have agreed to the terms.

NARRATOR: With an invisible gush of wind, Hera and Athena settled to the Earth quietly behind the Greek ranks.

ATHENA: *(angrily)* This is ridiculous! The war can't be over! Troy is still standing!

HERA: Do not worry. We shall see it burn yet. They will not get off so easily.

MENELAUS: *(shouting)* My wife! My wife! Bring forward my wife!

HERA: That young Trojan archer—with the brown eyes. Do you see him?

ATHENA: I do. Do you have a plan?

HERA: Of course. Go to him. Whisper in his ear. Persuade him to fire his weapon and break this truce. If Helen is returned to Menelaus, we will see this war end too soon!

ATHENA: Lovely. A carefully placed arrow would be the perfect thing to get this battle back to fever pitch. You are full of good ideas.

HERA: Naturally.

NARRATOR: As the Trojans prepared to re-enter the city and present the Greeks with Helen, Athena moved silently behind Pandarus, a young Trojan archer.

ATHENA: *(forcefully)* Pandarus, look at that evil man—Menelaus. He has won unjustly today. He has mocked your country—your king. He will not leave Troy so lightly. He will not stop until he has burned it to the ground—killing your children—taking your wife as his own. End his life now, before he ends yours!

NARRATOR: And Pandarus, barely knowing what he was doing, turned—bow in hand—and fired an arrow into the shoulder of Menelaus. *(cry of pain)* Pandemonium ensued. Menelaus was wounded but not killed. The Greeks brandished their swords. The Trojans turned—confused—and rushed to meet them. The battle was thick once again. On the walls, Priam groaned.

PRIAM: Well, my dear, it seems that you shall not have to go—but I fear many more Trojans will die.

HELEN: *(sadly)* All for me.

NARRATOR: Though none could see them through the rush of bodies, the clashing of metal, and the dirt of battle, two Olympian forms sauntered as if out for a summer's stroll.

HERA: Not, bad, dear. Not bad.

NARRATOR: Athena was pulling her bloody spear from the quivering body of a Trojan youth.

ATHENA: All in all, I say it's not a bad day's work.

NARRATOR: In the midst of the surrounding chaos, a silvery cloud began to form in front of them.

HERA: Aphrodite, darling, have you delivered your weakling prince?

APHRODITE: *(seething)* Oooh! You two do not play fair!

ATHENA: What do you call swooping down to save your Trojan pet?

APHRODITE: I am not the only god who will be caught up in this! I have powerful allies! Many gods who are close to me!

HERA: Yes, and we have some idea *how* close.

ATHENA: We're terrified. Really.

NARRATOR: Aphrodite's cloud disappeared with a cry of disgust.

HERA: She is rather unattractive when she's angry.

ATHENA: True.

HERA: I don't know about you, goddess of war, but I think this conflict has only just begun.

ATHENA: As do I.

HERA: Soon, we will be dancing over ravaging flames. We shall hear their women wailing—lamenting the dead. Smoke will rise from the walls—billows of smoke from the burning of Troy, Aphrodite's precious city. What a day that will be!

ATHENA: Amen.

DISCUSS

- How are Paris and Hector typical brothers?
- Judging by Homer's portrayal of the gods' actions, do you think he actually believed in them? Explain.
- Homer begins the *Iliad* with a reference to the "rage of Achilles." How will Achilles' rage affect the other characters in the story?
- The *Iliad* could have ended after the duel of Paris and Menelaus. Would this have been a satisfactory ending? Why or why not?
- Remember this is a Greek story. Does Homer present the Trojans, the enemy, in a favorable light? Explain.

WRITE

Write a dialogue between two Trojan soldiers discussing the predicament of Troy. What do they think of their country's situation? Perform your dialogue for the class.

THE *ILIAD:* THE TROJAN WAR, PART II

Cast

Zeus *(Ruler of the gods)*

Athena *(Goddess of wisdom)*

Ares *(God of war)*

Artemis *(Goddess of the hunt)*

Apollo *(God of light)*

Hera *(Queen of heaven)*

Diomedes *(Mighty Greek warrior)*

Aeneas *(Trojan warrior, son of Aphrodite)*

Aphrodite *(Goddess of love)*

Hector *(Greatest prince of Troy)*

Paris *(Prince of Troy)*

Priam *(Old king of Troy)*

Helen *(Captive Greek)*

Andromache *(Wife of Hector)*

Thetis *(Mother of Achilles)*

Achilles *(Greatest Greek warrior)*

Patroclus *(Achilles' best friend)*

NARRATOR: An eagle soared above the plains of Troy. Far below, it could see tiny bodies rushing at one another through the fog of war. Its eyes were the eyes of Zeus.

ZEUS: *(sigh)* This battle will never end, I fear.

NARRATOR: Not only men, but also the gods fought in hand-to-hand combat. The war had become personal, and they warred in the midst of the mortals—god against god. The eye of the eagle focused in.

ATHENA: How dare you, you little worm!

ARTEMIS: *Ooof! (choking) (sounds of scuffling)*

NARRATOR: Amid the fray, Athena had taken Artemis' bow from her hands and was lashing her across her face with it. Aphrodite rushed in to rescue her.

APHRODITE: Take this, you cheating cow!

NARRATOR: The goddess of love swung her fist with all her might into the gut of her niece.

ATHENA: Ugh. You call that a punch?

NARRATOR: Blazing like the sun, Apollo swooped in from nowhere driving his golden chariot and waving his arms frantically.

APOLLO: Artemis! Ladies! You are goddesses of Olympus! You should not be fighting amongst the mortals!

NARRATOR: Hera drove her spear into the spokes of Apollo's chariot wheel, and it shattered immediately. The god of truth was thrown violently to the ground.

ARTEMIS: Polly! Why you—Nobody picks on my brother!

NARRATOR: Artemis cried out and jumped onto Hera's back—taking handfuls of pampered locks between her fingers.

HERA: *(cries in pain)* Hair-pulling! Typical of a weakling.

NARRATOR: Artemis yanked Hera's head back fiercely and reclaimed her bow from the queen of heaven's hands.

ARTEMIS: I'll show you a weakling, you old bag!

NARRATOR: The gods continued to struggle.

ZEUS: *(sigh)* Show me the mortal realm.

NARRATOR: The view blurred and changed. In between the gods, now the humans could be seen—fighting just as fiercely. Achilles still refused to re-enter the battle, and in his absence, the mighty Greek Diomedes had gained acclaim. By his prowess alone, he had brought down many noble Trojans. At the moment, he was working on one more. He had cornered Aeneas, the Trojan son of Aphrodite. A cruel smile spread upon his lips.

DIOMEDES: Filthy Trojan! I have slit the throats of many of your countrymen. Now, I have come for yours.

AENEAS: Go home, fool, or I shall send you to Hades.

NARRATOR: Diomedes cried and lunged forward. Aeneas faltered and came under the mercy of the vicious Greek. Diomedes raised his spear to skewer his Trojan enemy. But, Aphrodite had seen her darling son at the point of death. She turned from her own battle to come to his rescue.

APHRODITE: Aeneas!

NARRATOR: She shot forward—between him and the cruel weapon of the Greek—reaching her beautiful arms out to grasp Aeneas and carry him away. Gazing through the dust of battle, Diomedes blinked. Inches in front of him, he thought he saw a beautiful form appear around Aeneas—a goddess! He paused with his spear in midair.

DIOMEDES: *(in awe)* A goddess!

NARRATOR: And, as the otherworldly arms encircled her son to carry him away, a new thought crossed Diomedes' mind.

DIOMEDES: Why should I fear Olympus? This is war!

NARRATOR: With a cry, he drove the point of his weapon into the soft flesh of Aphrodite's hand.

APHRODITE: Ahhhhhhhhhhhh! My hand! *(cries of pain)*

NARRATOR: She grabbed her wound—dropping Aeneas back into the dirt.

DIOMEDES: *(yelling)* Goddess of love, do not forget Greece! She has stung you!

NARRATOR: Aphrodite flew toward Olympus—holding her injured hand—wailing and moaning as she went.

APHRODITE: *(shrieking)* A mortal! I've been wounded by a stinking mortal!

NARRATOR: Diomedes rushed forward to once again take the Trojan life he had coveted. But Apollo, in his goodness, saw Aeneas where his mother had abandoned him and enveloped him in a golden cloud—transporting him back behind the walls of Troy to safety.

APOLLO: Go, son of Troy. You are no match for this bloodthirsty Greek. I will send Hector his way and see how he fares against a prince.

NARRATOR: Meanwhile, Aphrodite made a noisy entrance into the echoing colonnades of Olympus. There her cries had stirred the attention of Zeus. He turned from the eyes of his eagle.

ZEUS: What is this noise, woman?

APHRODITE: *(enraged, whining)* Brother, a disgusting Greek stuck his sword into me! How dare he cause a goddess to feel pain! I want to know what you're going to do about it!

ZEUS: *(laughing)* Nothing. Now you know how mortals feel. Perhaps that will teach you not to interfere in their affairs.

APHRODITE: *(hatefully)* Maybe you should get off your high horse and put an end to all this!

ZEUS: *(seriously)* Look at them, Aphrodite. Dying for what they believe in: Honor, valor, even love. They all look to us for guidance. What guidance do we give them if we are just as petty as they are?

APHRODITE: *(angrily)* I wouldn't expect *you* to understand!

ZEUS: *(sigh)* Aphrodite, leave me. Return to your battle. You have made your bed—now you must lie in it.

HERA: Ah, but, husband, she is far better at lying in other people's.

NARRATOR: Hera, her face dirty and clothes torn, had appeared in the hallway—glaring at Aphrodite.

HERA: Remove yourself at once, or I will do it for you.

NARRATOR: With a final whimper, Aphrodite was gone.

ZEUS: Has there ever been a greater battle than this one? The gods even feel the pain of it. *(sigh)* What do *you* want?

HERA: This Greek, Diomedes, has proved himself most capable in Achilles' absence. He is fighting Hector, the Prince of Troy, as we speak.

ZEUS: So? I grow weary of bloodshed. Let them kill until they have had their fill.

HERA: You're not listening. Alone Hector is no match for Diomedes, but Ares fights alongside the Trojan Prince, filling him with the power to hack Greeks down left and right. Our swine-headed son has chosen to side with Aphrodite.

ZEUS: And, your point? I'm sure *your* hand has been in plenty of Greek victories.

HERA: I do not wish to give Diomedes an advantage necessarily. I just want to even the playing field. Aphrodite has been wounded. Let me cause Diomedes to see beyond his own world and behold the great god of war! Let the god feel the sting of mortal steel!

ZEUS: *(can't believe it)* Our son? You wish to do this to our son?

HERA: He is no son of ours. He is a tumor, a blight on our glorious mountain. We must cut him out. But, he will not die—only taste my anger.

ZEUS: *(sigh)* I know you. You will not let me rest until you have had your way. Do as you will. I wish all the gods could feel pain. Then perhaps we would not be so quick to give it to others.

HERA: A very wise decision. I go at once.

ZEUS: *(to himself)* Where will it all end?

NARRATOR: Settling back to Earth, Hera neared where Diomedes and Hector furiously battled. Ares was there behind the Trojan prince, guiding his arm. Diomedes was soon to fail under the onslaught of the duo.

ARES: Ah, mother. Come to see my latest kill?

HERA: *(shouting)* Son, do not be too quick to forget your brain and leave all decisions to the loins! You should not have sided with Aphrodite!

ARES: *(angrily, growling voice)* Mother, you don't know anything about war! I love to see death—Greek or Trojan it matters not.

HERA: You are no son of mine, you cur. Prepare to know my hatred.

NARRATOR: Waving her arms, Hera pulled back the veil of the mortal world. Into Diomedes' view came the towering form of Ares, red skinned, and clad in black, shining armor. Once again his lust for glory drove his arm, and he hurled his spear—not at Hector—but into the chest of that terrible god. Ares let out a bellow—one that knocked every mortal from their feet and caused every Olympian to freeze in mid-strike.

ARES: *(screams)* Ahhh! Zeus shall hear of this, wench!

NARRATOR: Shooting straight up into the air, Ares cursed his mother, and Hector was left alone amid the fray.

ARES: *(screaming)* FATHER! FATHER!

ZEUS: *(exasperated)* What is it now?

ARES: Hera has allowed a mortal to wound me—ME—the god of war!

ZEUS: Ares, please, don't take yourself so seriously.

ARES: Father, I have put up with this as long as I can. She is *your* wife. You must control her. If you do not have the backbone to stand up to her—then you are not fit to sit on that throne!

ZEUS: *(yelling)* Silence, insolent pup! Don't forget who wields the mighty thunderbolt! It was my generation that defeated the Titans, not you sniveling brats!

NARRATOR: Zeus rose from his throne—his figure growing, filling the room. Ares shrunk back in fear.

ZEUS: I rule the universe! Let all the gods together fix a chain to me! You will not drag down Zeus! I have given you a home! I have given you power! I have given you life! Yet, I hear nothing but complaints day after day! I am sick of it! Enough!

NARRATOR: He cupped his hands into a divine megaphone.

ZEUS: *(shouting)* Olympians, return immediately or face my wrath!

NARRATOR: On the battlefield below, every god and goddess stopped in his or her tracks. They had heard the cry of Zeus. He meant business.

ZEUS: There will be a meeting at once!

NARRATOR: In the blink of an eye, every immortal was in the great hall—nervously tapping their fingers and avoiding eye contact. Only Hera seemed unbothered by Zeus' seething anger and strolled among the others like a lioness.

ZEUS: *(yelling)* This nonsense will stop! My sisters! My brothers! My sons! My daughters! Fighting! Like common men amongst ourselves! We are gods! We should start acting like it! We do not let petty jealousy divide us! From this moment on, *I* shall direct this war. No one else.

HERA: She started it!

NARRATOR: Hera pointed an accusing finger at Aphrodite.

ZEUS: And, *I* am going to end it!

HERA: I hardly think that's fair!

ZEUS: Silence, woman, or you will feel more than sharp words.

NARRATOR: Hera scowled—but stayed silent. Zeus stalked angrily among them.

ZEUS: No one is to leave the halls of Olympus. Greece and Troy are dead to you. Your glory is no longer theirs. Your interference is done. Now, I have said my piece. You may go.

NARRATOR: Sulking—the gods and goddesses milled out of the great hall. Zeus slunk down into his throne, sighed, and covered his head with his hand. He heard soft footsteps approaching him. He groaned.

ZEUS: *(half-groaning)* Yes?

THETIS: Zeus!

NARRATOR: He slowly looked up. It was Thetis, the immortal mother of Achilles.

ZEUS: Yes, Thetis. What is it?

THETIS: Surely you have not forgotten your promise. The Greeks haven't failed yet. I have seen the future. My son will soon re-enter the battle, if you do not intervene.

ZEUS: I have removed all interferences. No god or goddess will give his or her support to either side.

THETIS: Here on Olympus maybe. But, what about mighty Poseidon? Who will watch him? How do you know that he will not slink out of the sea and aide the Greeks?

ZEUS: Do not try to turn me against my brother Poseidon. I have agreed to help you, and I will. I will give my support to the Trojans—but only slightly. I will not determine the course of this war. It is for men to decide.

THETIS: That is all that I ask. Thank you, Zeus.

ZEUS: *(sigh)*

NARRATOR: With the support of Zeus and the removal of the Olympians, the tide turned in favor of the Trojans. They drove the Greeks back to their camp beside the hollow ships. Victory was almost at hand. In his lodge, Achilles heard the fight raging just over the top of the hill. He felt soft footsteps in the gloom behind him.

ACHILLES: I see that you have been busy, Mother.

THETIS: Yes, there isn't anything I wouldn't do to save my darling boy.

ACHILLES: Like slaughtering a thousand Greeks.

THETIS: Achilles! I only do this because I love you.

ACHILLES: Uh-huh.

THETIS: Now, stay here with your men. I will warn you when the fighting is closer. Then, you and your Myrmidons can board your ships and return home.

ACHILLES: Yes, mother.

NARRATOR: He felt a rustle of wind, and Thetis was gone. Running footsteps beat their way up to the flap of the tent. His dearest friend, Patroclus, burst inside—out of breath.

PATROCLUS: Achilles, the Trojans have nearly topped the hill! If they break through the walls, we're finished!

ACHILLES: This is not our fight, Patroclus.

PATROCLUS: You have to do something! How long can your stubbornness hold out? The Myrmidons will follow you into battle! Lead them!

ACHILLES: I will not fight for Agamemnon!

PATROCLUS: Odysseus says that Agamemnon has agreed to give Briseis back to you—and—and gold—if you'll only fight!

ACHILLES: The girl? This isn't about a girl. And gold? He could offer me all the gold in Egypt. I would die before I helped him.

PATROCLUS: (somberly) Then, we really are doomed.

ACHILLES: Not *we*, Patroclus—*them*.

PATROCLUS: No. We are all Greeks. I, for one, will not sit by and let my brothers be slaughtered. Let *me* wear your armor. Let *me* lead the Myrmidons.

NARRATOR: Achilles paused and stared into the eyes of his friend.

ACHILLES: If you think this is your fight, I will give you my blessing. But, do not ask me to go against my heart.

PATROCLUS: Thank you!

NARRATOR: The swift-footed warrior placed his hand on Patroclus' noble shoulder.

ACHILLES: We were raised as brothers, Patroclus. I could bear the loss of all others—but not you. I promised father I'd return you safely home. Take my armor. Drive the Trojans back. Save the Greeks—for today. But, stay away from stallion-breaking Hector.

NARRATOR: His comrade took up the glistening armor and turned to go.

ACHILLES: Patroclus.

PATROCLUS: Yes?

ACHILLES: Return safely.

NARRATOR: When Patroclus topped the hill, disguised as Achilles, the Myrmidons rose from where they had been sitting for days and cheered.

PATROCLUS: (shouting) Men! It is time to fight! Let us see Troy in ruins!

NARRATOR: Thinking that their leader had finally come to his senses, the men grabbed their weapons and charged after him. Achilles was back! The Greeks were sure to conquer now! When Hector—fighting among the dunes—saw the armor of Achilles top the hill, his heart sank. The shining backs of the Myrmidons began to plow through the Trojan ranks.

HECTOR: Father Zeus protect us.

NARRATOR: Zeus viewed this all from above. Something monumental was about to happen. He would need to—

HERA: (soothingly) Husband . . .

NARRATOR: He turned. Hera was there—but she was different—dressed in a radiant gown—the same gown in which she had appeared to Paris. Zeus' heart leapt. Somewhere deep down he remembered why he had chosen her as his bride.

HERA: (sing-song voice) Husband, worrying has become your hobby, has it not?

ZEUS: (confused) Yes, it has. No thanks to you and your posse.

HERA: (cutely) I know, I know, darling. That's why I've come. I've come to apologize—for my behavior.

ZEUS: Apologize? That is a bit odd for you.

HERA: But, definitely deserved. I was a fool. I let my jealousy get the best of me.

ZEUS: And, your blasted temper!

HERA: Oh, yes, a terrible temper. How do you ever put up with me? (seductively) Come here, husband, let me rub your shoulders.

ZEUS: Well, that would be nice.

HERA: Greeks—Trojans—forget about them—I have—just relax—

NARRATOR: She began to hum softly—weaving her spell.

HERA: Sleep, Zeus—sleep—forget the world—forget Troy.

ZEUS: Well—I—certainly—am—feeling—a bit—sleepy—*(snoring)*

HERA: *(hatefully)* Ha! Dumb oaf.

NARRATOR: She left his side and ran quickly through the deserted halls of Olympus. Reaching the east edge of the palace, she leaned over, looking down to the ocean far below.

HERA: *(yelling)* Brother Poseidon! I have put the great Zeus to sleep! I have worked my spell! Now, let's make these Trojans bleed!

NARRATOR: Poseidon heard her cry and from beneath the sea his mighty hands surged forth.

The Greeks felt his power move through them. Not only had the fearsome Achilles returned, but now, the gods once again favored them. The Trojan troops were driven back even further from the beaches. Patroclus, as Achilles, pushed forward, cutting Trojan heads from Trojan bodies. Many fled before him, but one stood his ground—the brave Hector. The Prince of Troy loomed through the clouds of dust and came face to face with the mighty opponent he had not yet faced.

HECTOR: At last, Achilles, we two meet. It is here that this war will be decided—with our blood.

PATROCLUS: Correction—your blood!

NARRATOR: Patroclus let out a war cry and rushed forward. Wearing Achilles' armor had perhaps given him too much confidence. It was a clumsy attack, and Patroclus exposed his weakness. Hector sidestepped Patroclus effortlessly and brought his spear up beneath the golden shield. The Greek felt the Trojan's spear enter his stomach. The force of his run drove it in deeper. Hector removed Patroclus' helmet, and the gathered men gasped. This was an imposter.

HECTOR: What is the meaning of this?

NARRATOR: There was no reply as the spirit of the young Greek slipped from his body and sank into the Underworld. Slumbering loudly on his throne, Zeus had missed this fateful battle. Aphrodite, who had been furiously pacing about the palace, suddenly appeared in the doorway of the great hall.

APHRODITE: *(screaming)* Zeus! What are you doing?

ZEUS: *(waking up)* Huh, what?

APHRODITE: Sleeping? The fate of the known world is at stake, and you're sleeping?

ZEUS: Sleeping? But I—*(roaring)* HEEEERA!

NARRATOR: Below on the battlefield, Hector had removed the golden armor of Achilles from Patroclus. This was his prize now. Its true master would soon be there to reclaim it. Until then, Hector would wear it. He fell back to where his men had retreated—below the walls of Troy. In camp, Achilles learned of what had befallen his friend. Blinded by tears of rage, he jumped into his chariot—sword in hand—and whipped the horses into a frenzy. He was out for blood! He would slaughter the man who had slain Patroclus!

ACHILLES: *(screaming)* Hector! Hector!

NARRATOR: Achilles tore down the plains toward Troy. The land was a blur beside him as he sped, but in the smeared flashes of color, he saw his mother flying alongside him.

THETIS: *(frantically)* Achilles! No! All that I have worked for! Don't risk your life for this man!

ACHILLES: *(crazy)* He has killed Patroclus! I will kill him and everyone he loves!

THETIS: Son! He may kill *you*!

ACHILLES: I will not die. It will be his flesh that the birds will feast on.

THETIS: *(crying)* Son, you have no armor! Please, this is madness.

ACHILLES: I will fight him with my fists if I have to, mother. *(screaming)* Hector!

THETIS: *(frantically)* There! In your chariot, I had hoped not to use it. I had Hephaestus make you almighty armor in his forge! It will protect you! Please, promise you will take it!

ACHILLES: I don't need magic to protect me! I'm not a weakling! I am Achilles! *(screaming)* Hector!

THETIS: *(softly)* Please, son, for your mother—

ACHILLES: *(quietly)* I will, mother, but your meddling is done. My fate is my fate. Whatever will be, will be.

THETIS: But, Achilles—

ACHILLES: Goodbye, mother. *(yelling)* Hector! Hector!

NARRATOR: His chariot was now in sight of the Trojan walls. Hector stood inside Troy's open gates watching the trail of dust make its way across the plain—his face grim.

HECTOR: This man will be the death of me.

NARRATOR: His wife, Andromache, came to stand with him one last time. In her white arms, she held their infant son, Astyanax.

ANDROMACHE: *(crying)* Be careful, my husband. I have heard stories of this Greek's brutality.

HECTOR: *(soothingly)* Hush now.

ANDROMACHE: What will I do? What will our son do if you should die?

HECTOR: Troy will always live on—no matter what happens to me. He is our future. Astyanax, did you hear that? You are our future.

NARRATOR: He took his child and kissed its head. Then he took his wife and kissed her one final time.

HECTOR: Now, I must go. Troy will not fall this day.

ANDROMACHE: *(crying)* See that *you* do not.

ACHILLES: *(bellowing)* HECTOR! HECTOR!

NARRATOR: Without looking back, Hector stepped through the gates of Troy. They closed behind him as Achilles' chariot skidded to a stop yards before him. In the distance, large groups of Greeks could be seen making their way toward the city. They were coming to see the fight.

Achilles jumped quickly out of the chariot and started to buckle on his shining armor.

ACHILLES: *(violently)* Hector! You and I! No one else. You have killed my friend. Now, I return the favor!

HECTOR: I only did what I had to do. You would have done no less.

ACHILLES: Do not speak to me, you piece of filth!

HECTOR: I will fight you, but I ask one thing—

ACHILLES: Do not ask me for anything! I give murderers no favors! Wolves make no pacts with lambs!

HECTOR: Are you not an honorable man? If I die in this battle, give my body back to my family, so that I may have a godly burial.

ACHILLES: You deserve nothing! What do you know of honor? Whose armor do you wear now, you vomiting dog?

HECTOR: Yours—but I see that you have gotten a fine replacement—from the gods no doubt.

ACHILLES: Enough! I will cut your body to pieces, and it shall lie in the sun until the birds pick it clean.

HECTOR: So be it.

NARRATOR: The two faced off under the heat of the blazing Trojan sun. Swift-footed Achilles began to dance, crouching and springing. The long fight had been building up within him. Hector stood his ground, strong and regal, worthy of a Trojan prince. They started to circle one another. From the walls, Paris watched with shame.

PARIS: This is all because of me.

HELEN: No—me.

ACHILLES: Time to die, Trojan.

NARRATOR: Achilles darted forward—spinning as he came. His spear hummed as it cut the air. *(CLANG)* Hector blocked the blow, but it had been close.

HECTOR: *(sarcastically)* Perhaps *I* would be a better warrior if *I* had the powers of the Styx protecting *me*.

ACHILLES: Perhaps I will use your guts as a sash.

NARRATOR: Achilles charged again, but this time, Hector brought up his spear. Achilles faltered for a moment, but changed direction and gripped the spear—ripping it from Hector's grasp.

HECTOR: *(grunt)* Not to worry. I have other ways of defending myself.

NARRATOR: Hector pulled out his sword. He steadied himself—waiting for the next advance.

ACHILLES: Skewered by his own spear—how fitting!

NARRATOR: Achilles pummeled forward once again—sword and spear in hand. Hector blocked the sword with his shield, but the spear Achilles drove deep within the soft flesh at his neck.

HECTOR: *(cries out)* *(choking)*

ANDROMACHE: Noooooo!

NARRATOR: Hector fell on the battlefield. The world stood still for a moment. Achilles knelt over the body and pushed the spear in deeper for good measure. A black pool of blood started to spread out over the sands. Wailing was heard from the walls of Troy.

PARIS: Hector! I must save him—

ANDROMACHE: *(weeping)* Too late. You had your chance!

PARIS: I—I—Hector.

ANDROMACHE: Don't say his name. You are not worthy enough to speak it. He has died for your stupidity. Now, leave him be.

NARRATOR: The triumphant Greek spectators cheered, and rushing forward from the ring they had formed, began to kick the lifeless body and drive their own swords into its flesh.

ACHILLES: Trojans! See what I have done to your dishonorable prince! Who is next? I will kill you all for the grief that you have given me.

NARRATOR: From his high viewpoint, Priam clutched his chest. His most beloved son now lay in the dirt.

PRIAM: *(weeping)* My son—gods above—give me back my son.

NARRATOR: But Hector was gone. In his madness, Achilles shooed away the soldiers, rolled the corpse over and spat in its face. Taking the point of his sword, he drove it through the dead man's feet. Through these holes he fed leather thongs, and he lashed them to his chariot.

ACHILLES: Now see how the Greeks honor fools!

NARRATOR: He spurred his horse forward. The chariot rocked into motion—the body of Hector being dragged behind. Achilles started to scream.

ACHILLES: *(screaming)* Fear me, Trojans, the mighty Achilles! See your dead Hector! See how his skin rips from his body! How low is your precious prince now?

NARRATOR: He drug the body around the walls of Troy. Andromache turned away in grief—Paris could not look away. Priam buried his head in his hands.

NARRATOR: On Olympus, Zeus watched with disapproval. The champion of his favorite city was being dragged through the dirt like a dead animal.

ZEUS: *(booming)* Thetis! Thetis!

NARRATOR: Thetis appeared in a shimmering wave of color.

THETIS: *(innocently)* Yes, Zeus?

ZEUS: Your son is shaming Greece.

THETIS: *(groveling)* Oh, Zeus, please. I told him not to. He won't listen.

ZEUS: You must make him listen, or he will anger me.

THETIS: Yes, Zeus.

ZEUS: Destroying the body of the Trojan prince is shameful. He must give it back to the father or face the consequences.

THETIS: But, Zeus, he's so hardheaded. He never listens.

ZEUS: You will make him listen, or he shall be destroyed.

THETIS: I will.

NARRATOR: The sun began to set on the grisly scene. Achilles had pulled the body until it was almost unrecognizable—round and round the city—and finally, he had stopped. With one final battle cry, he turned his back on the Trojan walls and headed to camp—the body kicking up dust behind him. That night, Zeus sent Iris to the old king Priam. She informed him that he must claim the body of his dead son. Zeus would ensure that no harm would come to him.

PRIAM: Honor will once again come to my household.

NARRATOR: Hermes himself guided Priam through the night, undetected into the Greek camp.

As a younger man, his anger would have cried out for the death of the Greek warrior, but he was tired of death. He only wanted his son. In the blackness of night, he slipped into Achilles' tent.

ACHILLES: Who's there?

PRIAM: An old man—an old father.

ACHILLES: You! How did you get here?

PRIAM: Please, do not sound an alarm. I come in peace.

ACHILLES: No one could sneak in here.

PRIAM: The gods have sent me. No man deserves the punishment you have dealt my son.

ACHILLES: You do not know what your son has done.

PRIAM: Yes, he has killed many. But, tell me, Achilles, how many have you killed?

ACHILLES: It's not the same!

PRIAM: How many friends? How many husbands? How many sons?

ACHILLES: (weakly) I will not hear this! I will call the guards!

PRIAM: No, you will not, because surely you remember *your* old father, and you know how he would feel if he were to lose you as I have lost my son.

ACHILLES: No.

PRIAM: As I held Hector, he held you in his arms on the day of your birth. Sons are precious things. *My* son is a precious thing. Please, let me take him and bury him. Give him one last shred of honor. You have proven your point.

NARRATOR: Achilles was silent for a moment. The old king knelt to the ground, and took the warrior's bloodstained hand and kissed it.

PRIAM: (slowly) There. I have done what no father has ever done before. I have kissed the hand of the murderer of my own son.

NARRATOR: Achilles pulled his hands from the grip of the old man and brought them to his face. Hot tears welled up—for his own father, for Patroclus, for the father who knelt before him. When he cleared his own eyes, he saw tears upon Priam's cheeks as well.

ACHILLES: I will give you your son.

NARRATOR: He took the old man by the hand.

ACHILLES: Had we met under different circumstances, we might have been friends, old king. I will hold back the Greeks until you have mourned your son.

PRIAM: Eleven days is all we ask. To wash him, bury him, and celebrate his life.

ACHILLES: Then, I am your enemy once again, but tonight, I give you leave.

PRIAM: Thank you—my son.

NARRATOR: Priam was gone. Achilles sat silently in his tent. He began to weep once again. He did not know why. For Patroclus? For Hector? For himself? Many days later when he entered the morning air, Achilles could see the silhouetted walls of Troy far away. Smoke billowed up between the rosy fingers of the dawn. It was the funeral pyre of Hector—burning on the walls of Troy. Its greatest prince was fading away—his death preceding the death of his great city.

ACHILLES: Goodbye, Hector. We shall see each other again soon, I think—but not in this world. We were both built too glorious to be long on this plane. Years from now, people will remember us—in stories, in song. Greek and Trojan children alike will say, "Tell us of the great city of Troy." Our names and deeds will live not but for a time—but for an eternity.

NARRATOR: And so, the Trojans buried Hector, breaker of horses.

DISCUSS

- Has Achilles changed during the course of the war?
- The Greeks and the Trojans both worship the same gods. Why does this make the fact that the gods have chosen sides more interesting?
- Why is it almost impossible for the gods to truly understand war?
- If you had the choice between a long, uninteresting life and a brief life filled with fame, which would you chose? Why?
- In Homer's time, it was not considered unmanly for a warrior to weep. How has this concept changed? Explain.

DRAW

Create a trading card based on a character from the *Iliad*. There should be a picture of the character on one side and information about the character on the other. Make sure to list your character's "stats." After you are finished, show your card to your classmates.

War! What Is It Good For?

History is taught in schools with this idea in mind: If the present generation learns about the mistakes of the past, they will not repeat them in the future. Whether or not you've paid a lot of attention in history class, you should know that the past is filled with mistakes. When people make mistakes, it creates problems, but when countries make mistakes, it makes war. Some try to categorize past wars into "good wars" and "bad wars." They typically place conflicts that were fought for noble causes into the "good war" category. For most, World War II fits here. One look at the heartless and inhuman reign of Hitler, and you can see what the world would have been like if Nazi Germany had taken control. Most agree that Hitler needed to be stopped, and, luckily, he was.

World War I is a different story. It started with a political assassination, which triggered a chain reaction. Alliance upon alliance forced country after country to fight for a cause that was not their own. The result? Twenty million people died worldwide. It is horrible when any life is lost in war, but especially senseless for a cause that meant so little to so many.

Benjamin Franklin, a man who saw his beloved America born from a war, said, "There has never been a good war or a bad peace" (Franklin & Sargent, 1855, p. 462). The cause does not change the fact that war is a terrible, grasping place, filled with the horrors of death. The tragedy of all wars is that they happen in the first place.

With World War II a terrifying new weapon entered the world. The threat of nuclear warfare forces us to consider our motives more than ever. A single war could mean the end of the world as we know it. Instead of planning how to win a war, the countries of Earth are faced with a new problem: How do you keep war from ever happening again?

You may not have an opinion about war, but it's time to develop one. Not too long from now, you will be able to elect your representatives. Those representatives will decide whether or not your country goes to war. War is a part of our past, war is a part of our present—but does it have to be a part of our future?

War might have changed since the ancient world, but it's never been pretty. In ancient Greece, defeat by an enemy city-state meant total annihilation—death for the able-bodied men, a life of rape and servitude for the women, and slavery for the young. In spite of their advanced learning, the Greeks still hadn't solved the problem of war. The Greek city-states were locked into eternal combat. Neighbors became enemies, enemies became allies, and allies became enemies once again. In their eyes war was simply a necessary evil, a problem that could never be remedied. The

Classical Greek philosopher Aristotle put it bluntly, "We . . . war that we may be at peace" (335/1891, p. 339). Writing more than 2,000 years ago, he realized that war and peace form a paradox.

The *Iliad*, Homer's account of the Trojan War, was a reference point for the Greeks. Yes, Homer told them, war destroys lives, but it also produces heroes. The heroes of the Trojan War were the epitome of manly virtues—poetic warriors who spoke, fought, loved, wept, took and spared life in the legendary past of Greece. Although war brings out the worst in some, it brings out the best in others. As much as he glorified it, Homer never simplified war. Death is the high price paid for glory. His characters don't die gracefully; they suffer agonizing, horrific deaths.

The *Iliad* shaped how the Greeks thought about war *and* peace. It gave them their only guide for how a noble man should live and die. Its influence was so great that Alexander the Great, the man who would finally conquer and unite the city-states of Greece, slept with a copy of the poem under his pillow. What can the *Iliad* teach *you*?

The *Iliad* and Homer

The Trojan War spanned 10 years. It was fought between the city-states of Greece and the city-state of Troy. Most books on the subject refer to one side as the "Greeks," although this term was not in use at the time. Homer calls his people *Achaeans*, *Danaans*, or *Argives*. The Greek city-states were not a unified nation and wouldn't be for many centuries. Instead of fighting in the name of Greece, warriors fought for the honor of their home city-state.

Troy is the more common name for *Ilion* or *Ilium*, the legendary city in Homer's poem. The *Iliad* means literally "a poem about Ilium." To the Greeks, Ilium existed at the edge of the known world, on the tip of Asia in modern-day Turkey. It was a city of great wealth, known for its horde of gold. Powerful walls, erected through the aid of Poseidon and Apollo, had broken the advances of many armies. The Trojans were revered as horse-lords and formidable opponents in battle. The ruler there was King Priam, the father of 50 sons. Two out of that 50 are the most prominent: Prince Hector, the eldest and most noble, and Paris, the handsome but weak-willed prodigal son.

Much of the 10-year Trojan War is left out of the *Iliad*. Interestingly, Homer chooses only a part of the legend to retell, a few eventful days near the end of the conflict. Because the course of the war was already familiar to his audience, he did not need to tell the complete story.

DISCUSS

- Discuss the following quote by John Stuart Mill (1874):

  The person who has nothing for which he is willing to fight, nothing which is more important than his own personal safety, is a miserable creature, and has no chance of being free unless made or kept so by the exertions of better men than himself. (p. 26)

- Would you classify the Trojan War as a "good war" or "bad war"? Explain.

- Is war a necessary evil? Explain.

READ

Read the short story "There Will Come Soft Rains" by Ray Bradbury. What is the message this story sends about war?

LISTEN

Listen to the song "Imagine" by John Lennon. What does John Lennon think about the causes of war?

RESEARCH

- What are some of the reasons wars begin? Look back at history to support your answer.

- Interview a person who is a veteran of war. Ask about the conflict in which he or she was involved. What were his or her experiences and reactions?

WATCH

Watch *The Bridge on the River Kwai* (1957) directed by David Lean. What does this film have to say about war?

Although it begins 9 years into the war, the *Iliad* ends without a final victory for either side. During this snapshot of time, Homer gives us a monumental look at war, its emotions, its heroes, and its victims. Man after man meets an unflinching death. Every detail of their demise is there—splattering brains, spilling entrails, and severed limbs. Amid this carnage, heroes desperately fight for one cause—glory. "Give our enemy glory or win it for ourselves," one warrior shouts (Homer, 750 B.C./1990, p. 336). Glory is primary; Helen, secondary.

The *Iliad* was and is the epitome of Greek literature. The Greeks themselves quoted it in debates and referenced it in important matters. It has been called the Bible of the Greeks for the reverence and admiration the Greeks themselves placed upon its characters. Homer, the poet who finally recorded the complex oral telling of the Trojan War, lived around 750 B.C. He too struggled with the issues of war: For what reason should a war be waged? What are the casualties of war? What part do the gods play in Earthly conflicts? Through masterful storytelling he brings the Trojan War to life, giving human dimension to famous princes and kings of legend, such as Achilles, Hector, and Odysseus.

Hephaestus (Roman Name: Vulcan)

Smith-God of the Forge, God of Fire

Hephaestus, a peace-loving god, is the patron of practical arts. He is renowned for his metalworking abilities. The unparalleled armor of the gods and heroes come from his forge. His lame leg and grizzled appearance earn him the distinction of being the only ugly god. In fact, when Hera gave birth to such an unattractive son, she hurled him out of heaven, laming his leg. Ironically, Aphrodite, goddess of beauty, is his wife. The Romans pictured the fiery god Vulcan working his forge beneath the mountains, and when they saw a hilltop erupt with flame, they labeled it a volcano.

Although Homer did not invent these characters, he breathed life into them. His technique was one of the earliest examples of "poetic license." Selecting a section of the story he thought would work best, he embellished and transformed it into something that far surpassed its subject matter. The term *historical fiction* applies to this technique today—retelling events of the past in an entertaining fashion. Not only telling an excellent tale, Homer did something else unheard of during his time: He *wrote it down.* Before this, poets had to commit their sagas to memory and recite on command. Homer took advantage of a new invention—the written word. The rest is history, or, actually, mythology.

The *Iliad* was not his only hit. He also wrote the *Odyssey* (the story of Odysseus' 10-year journey home from the war). His second poem never achieved the same status in Greece as his first did. The Greeks were more interested in valiant warriors than wandering tricksters.

Because Homer lived so many years before accurate historical records, very little is known about him. By the time of Classical Greece, several legends had grown up surrounding the *Iliad's* mysterious author. One of the most famous traditions was that he was a blind poet, a wanderer who chanted his tales to those who would chance to listen. For this reason most paintings and sculptures of Homer depict him as blind. Some even show him being led by a young guide. Whether Homer's blindness is merely a romanticized concept or based in fact, this legend has become closely associated with the poet.

Did Homer actually exist? Modern scholars have gone so far as to doubt that Homer was even a real person, arguing that "Homer" was a pseudonym a *group* of writers attached to their work. Proposing a different theory, Samuel Butler, a 19th-century author and translator, suggested that while the *Iliad* might be the poet's work, the *Odyssey* wasn't written by Homer at all, but by a nameless *female* author. Even the dates of Homer's life are subject to controversy. Some place him around 750 B.C. (250 years before Classical Greece), while others claim he lived much closer to the projected dates for the Trojan War (1300–900 B.C.). Was Homer an eyewitness to the Trojan War or merely a person who wrote down the story centuries later?

Homer's era is known as the Dark Age of Greece for a good reason. There will probably never be any concrete information to clear up any of these issues. We may be missing some of the facts about his life, but fortunately we are left with the part of Homer that matters most—his words.

Blind or sighted, eyewitness or recorder of tales, male or female, individual or group, Homer will be eternally ranked with the greatest of poets, Dante, Milton, and Shakespeare—yet, on a more personal level, one of the greatest and most inventive storytellers of all time.

DISCUSS
- Why is it more effective to tell only part of a large story?
- Why is the idea of a blind poet romantic?

Epic Poetry

All poems are short, and they rhyme. This is what most people think. Fortunately, they're wrong. In their defense, most people probably don't know that poetry is the oldest form of written storytelling. Works such as the *Iliad,* the *Odyssey,* and *Beowulf,* even though they fill hundreds of pages, are actually poems.

Before writing was invented, stories were kept alive through oral retellings, chants, or songs without music. Many of the elements of modern music went into these retellings—rhythm, repetition, and other mnemonic devices that triggered the memory of the storyteller. After all, when it comes time for children to learn their ABC's or the number of days in a month, they learn a song to remember the information. Repetition, rhythm, and rhyme all aid the memory. When writing did come along, these memorized stories were written down. Line breaks, meter, and repetition remained embedded within the story.

Epic basically means big, sprawling, or enormous. An epic poem sets out to tell a story that is so large it seems impossible. Almost all epic poems are ancient and mythological in nature. Most tell about larger-than-life heroes, who battle man-eating monsters, gain the favor of gods and goddesses, pass impossible challenges, and in the end win treasures untold. The *Iliad* is one of the oldest and noblest of this genre. Although its scope is much larger than typical poetry, the epic poem still uses vibrant language that appeals to the senses. Below is a descriptive passage from the *Iliad* featuring a situation you've probably not seen described in poetry before.

> But Meriones caught him in full retreat, he let fly
> with a bronze-tipped arrow, hitting his right buttock
> up under the pelvic bone so the lance pierced the bladder.
> He sank on the spot, hunched in his dear companion's arms,
> gasping out his life as he writhed along the ground
> like an earthworm stretched out in death, blood pooling,
> soaking the earth dark red. . . .
> (Homer, 750 B.C./1990, p. 362)

It's War! But, What Will I Wear?

The Trojan War, a study by historian Barry Strauss, treats the Trojan War as an actual historical event, comparing the information presented in the *Iliad* with standard practices of Bronze Age warfare. In the following section he describes the weapons and armor of the day.

> The men in the front lines, especially the champions, had a full set of arms and armor. The complete warrior wore bronze greaves (shin guards), a leather kilt, and a crested helmet. He may have worn a loose-fitting bronze breastplate and back plate, which could be extended with pieces to cover his neck, lower face, shoulders, and thighs. An alternative was a linen tunic with bronze scarves to serve as a breastplate. An elaborate belt, perhaps red or purple and decorated with gold or silver, would be worn over the tunic or breastplate. The front live fighter carried a big, heavy shield, shaped either like a figure-of-eight or a tower, and composed of multiple layers of leather on a bronze rim. It hung from his shoulder on a strap that may have passed diagonally over his torso. The shield was meant to offer full protection, which is why very few warriors in Homer are described as wearing both a metal breastplate and holding a shield. A scabbard, holding a bronze double-edged sword, lay along his right thigh, suspended by a strap from his right shoulder. (Strauss, 2006, p. 23)

As Strauss mentioned, this information only applies to the champions or nobles (kings, princes, wealthy landowners). There were common soldiers involved in the conflict, but they get little mention by Homer. Every major warrior, Trojan and Greek, is noble in some manner and draws his power from this status.

The Greeks were successful in storming the Trojan beach, and there they made their camp. Yet, 9 long years of back-and-forth assault failed to win the war for either side. The Greeks would drive the Trojans back behind their high walls; however, the Trojans would storm out once again and push the Greeks back nearly to their ships.

To support their army, the Greeks constantly raided the coastal Trojan villages. They stole women, riches, and cattle from the looted townships. Despite the precarious position of the Greeks, the Trojans had spent 9 years trying to drive them back over the seas—to no avail.

DISCUSS
- The ancient Greeks connected nobility with fighting ability. In other words, the wealthy were the best fighters. How is this idea flawed?
- How has the art of war changed over time?

READ
Read *The Trojan War* by Barry Strauss. What is successful about this combination of history and mythology? What light does it shed on the *Iliad*?

Cast of the Trojan War

Because the *Iliad* has such a large and intricate cast, it's best to familiarize yourself with a few of the principal players if you choose to read that full version. The gods you know, so we'll just have to deal with the mortals.

Greeks
- Agamemnon: King of Mycenae, Menelaus' brother, and commander of the united Greek forces
- Menelaus: King of Sparta, husband of Helen
- Achilles: Greatest warrior for the Greeks, son of Thetis the sea nymph, trained by Chiron the centaur, dipped in the waters of the River Styx
- Ajax: Blood-thirsty Greek warrior
- Diomedes: Formidable Greek warrior, second only to Achilles
- Odysseus: King of Ithaca, known for his cunning tricks
- Calchas: Prophet, brought to Troy to interpret the will of the gods
- Briseis: Captured Trojan slave-girl
- Chryseis: Captured Trojan slave-girl, her father is a priest of Apollo
- Myrmidons: Fighting men of Achilles
- Patroclus: Achilles' best friend and war comrade

Trojans
- Helen: Menelaus' wife, Paris' lover, daughter of Zeus, most beautiful woman in the world
- Paris: Son of Priam, angered Hera and Athena by presenting Aphrodite with the golden apple
- Priam: King of Troy, father of 50 sons
- Hector: Priam's oldest son, heir to the throne of Troy, Troy's finest warrior
- Andromache: Hector's wife, mother of Astyanax
- Astyanax: Hector's young son
- Hecuba: Queen of Troy, mother of Hector, Cassandra, and Paris
- Cassandra: Hector's sister, given prophetic powers by Apollo in an attempt to seduce her, when she refused his advances the god cursed her prophecies to always be unheeded
- Aeneas: Trojan prince and warrior, second only to Hector, son of Aphrodite

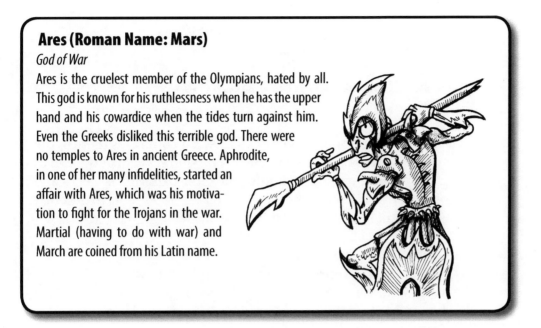

Ares (Roman Name: Mars)

God of War

Ares is the cruelest member of the Olympians, hated by all. This god is known for his ruthlessness when he has the upper hand and his cowardice when the tides turn against him. Even the Greeks disliked this terrible god. There were no temples to Ares in ancient Greece. Aphrodite, in one of her many infidelities, started an affair with Ares, which was his motivation to fight for the Trojans in the war. Martial (having to do with war) and March are coined from his Latin name.

Death! Glorious Death!

The genius of Homer is that he captures the double-sided nature of war. War is filled with glory, but it's also filled with death. Every man-to-man encounter in the *Iliad* ends the same way: one man receives glory, the other receives death. (Unless, of course, he chooses to run away.) Homer gives us two extremes. Achilles, the man built for battle, is so feared that when he appears on the top of a hill midbattle, his armor blazing out like the sun, horses rear and men despair—some even dying on the spot. *That* is glory. Yet, each warrior who meets a gruesome death pulls at our sympathies. They are not faceless henchmen. They're men with families and homes, dying for a cause not their own.

But, these aren't Hollywood death scenes. They're not sentimentalized; they're quick and brutal. The way death in a real war would be. Listen here to the gory demise of Thestor, Trojan charioteer, as he was:

> cowering, crouched in his fine polished chariot,
> crazed with fear, and the reins flew from his grip—
> Patroclus rising beside him stabbed his right jawbone,
> ramming the spearhead square between his teeth so hard
> he hooked him by that spearhead over the chariot-rail,
> hoisted, dragged the Trojan out as an angler perched
> on a jutting rock ledge drags some fish from the sea,
> some noble catch, with line and glittering bronze hook.

So with the spear Patroclus gaffed him off his car,
his mouth gaping round the glittering point
and flipped him down facefirst,
dead as he fell, his life breath blown away. (Homer, 750 B.C./1990,
p. 426)

But, what happens after these noble deaths? What comfort is there in the afterlife? Homer doesn't give much. There is no shining light at the end of a tunnel, beckoning the warriors home. The Greek afterlife is a cold and dark place. Listen to the phrases Homer (750 B.C./1990) uses to describe the final seconds of life.

Hateful darkness seized him. (p. 26)
His life and power slipped away on the wind. (p. 173)
The world went black as night before his eyes. (p. 174)
The dark swirled down his eyes. (p. 423)
Red death came flooding down his eyes. (p. 423)
The mist whirled down his eyes. (p. 423)
Never would he repay his loving parents now for the gift of rearing—his life cut short so soon . . . (p. 452)

Many of these images place us inside the character's head. Here is what death looks like, Homer says. How can we not sympathize with them? On the other hand, Homer's deaths also are designed to entertain. You've probably heard certain adults commenting on violence in television, but if you have healthy imagination, the *Iliad* will have a definite "R" rating, such as the following excerpt:

Idomeneus skewered Erymas straight through the mouth, the merciless brazen spearpoint raking through, up under the brain to split his glistening skull—teeth shattered out, both eyes brimmed to the lids with a gush of blood and both nostrils spurting, mouth gaping, blowing convulsive sprays of blood and death's dark cloud closed down around his corpse. (Homer, 750 B.C./1990, pp. 423–424)

Were the ancient Greeks as entertained by violence as some people are today? Is Homer still presenting the negative side of war with these images, or is he trying to appeal to his audience? Does Homer have an opinion on glory and death—one being worth the other? Well, the answer might not come in the *Iliad*, but there is a passage in the *Odyssey* to consider. When Odysseus travels to the edge of the Underworld, he speaks

DISCUSS
- Why is it dangerous for people to sentimentalize death?
- What elements of the *Iliad* are antiwar? Which are prowar?
- Homer utilizes violent images in the *Iliad*. Is our culture still obsessed with violence?
- Is death too great a price for glory? Explain.

WRITE
Imagine you have traveled to the edge of the Underworld with Odysseus. Write a dialogue between you and a deceased celebrity. Like Achilles, what regrets does he or she have?

with the spirit of Achilles, slain for his glory. What is Achilles' comment on his own life?: "Better to be a slave who sees the sun than to be the greatest king in Hades" (Spivey, 2005, p. 200).

Homeric Epithets

An *epithet* is a descriptive word or phrase that a writer frequently connects to a certain character. For example, Homer often refers to Achilles as "the swift runner" or "swift-footed." This not only adds description but frequently helps the poet complete the syllabic requirement of his line. Below are some other epithets Homer frequently uses. Many of these titles are hyphenated because the original Greek word had a meaning that cannot be expressed by only one English word.

Character	Epithet
Achaeans (Greeks)	long-haired, strong-greaved, bronze-cloaked
Agamemnon	wide-ruling
Ajax	high-hearted
Andromache	white-armed
Apollo	distant deadly archer
Ares	curse of men, sacker of cities
Athena	gray-eyed
Hector	breaker of horses
Helen	lovely-haired
Hera	ox-eyed
Iris	wind-footed
Menelaus	red-haired
Odysseus	great-hearted
Thetis	silver-footed
Trojans	stallion-breaking
Zeus	wide-seeing

DISCUSS
- Do any of these descriptions seem strange? Why do you think this is?

WRITE
- Create a hyphenated epithet for yourself. Share it with your classmates.

Putting the "Fun" in Funeral

When a hero or nobleman dies in Greek mythology, his death is mourned, but his life also is celebrated. Funeral games were a custom in the Dark Age of Greece. This can be seen in the *Iliad*. After the death of Patroclus, the Greeks put the war on hold and arrange contests in honor of the deceased. Achilles, mourning his friend, supplies the prizes for which the contestants compete. There is chariot racing, boxing, archery, wrestling, foot racing, and weight throwing. This may seem like an odd custom to us—especially when the Greeks are in the middle of a war. But, the culture of ancient Greece saw these festivities as an honor. Likewise, Achilles grants Priam 11 days of peace in order for him to bury his son Hector and host the funeral games honoring him.

Even though Greek legend says that Heracles founded the first games at Olympus, many historians believe that funeral games were the actual inspiration for one of the world's oldest traditions, the Olympics.

Poseidon (Roman Name: Neptune)

The Blue-Haired God of the Sea

Next to Zeus, Poseidon is the god the Greeks most feared. As a sea-faring people, they knew the hazards of a stormy sea. The god was known for his mood swings, violent rage one minute, calm the next—just like the waters he controlled. In the Trojan War he favored the Greeks because of their love of shipbuilding, yet legend had it that generations before, he and Apollo had helped build the walls of Ilium.

The Shield of Achilles

Hephaestus, the crippled fire-god, forges a magnificent set of armor for Achilles. Homer goes to great length to describe the gilded scenes depicted on his shield. Remember that Hephaestus is speaking through his art. What is he saying?

First Hephaestus makes a great and massive shield . . .
and across its vast expanse with all his craft and cunning
the god creates a world of gorgeous immortal work. (Homer, 750
B.C./1990, p. 483)

The following scenes are depicted on Achilles' shield: The earth, the sky, the sea, Ocean the great river, and two noble cities. In the first city the people celebrate a marriage, but two men argue over a blood feud. They go before a council of judges to plead their cases. The second city is under siege. The army of the besieged city rushes out and does battle with their attackers. Ares and Athena lead the attack, and many men die.

In a different scene, Hephaestus shows a king's estate with his field-workers bringing in the harvest. The servants prepare a large outdoor banquet to celebrate the bounty. In yet another scene, boys and girls pick grapes from a peaceful vineyard. Among them a young boy plucks his lyre and his music is "so clear it could break the heart with longing, and what he sang was a dirge for the dying year" (Homer, 750 B.C./1990, p. 486). A herd of longhorn cattle graze in another scene. A pair of rampaging lions attacks them. One lion tears into the body of a bull. A gleeful dance, the final scene, shows boys and girls happily interacting.

> **DISCUSS**
> - What is the difference between the two noble cities?
> - Are these a parallel for what is happening in the *Iliad*? Explain.
> - Could any of these scenes be metaphors?
> - Based on his work, is Hephaestus a warrior or a pacifist? Explain.
> - Is it odd for these scenes to appear on a shield, the tool of a warrior? Explain.

Priam's Lament

As Priam sees his most beloved son, Hector, facing down the warrior Achilles, he begins to tear his beard and lament.

"Pity me too!—
still in my senses, true, but a harrowed, broken man
marked out by doom—past the threshold of old age . . .
and Father Zeus will waste me with a hideous fate,
and after I've lived to look on so much horror!
My sons laid low, my daughters dragged away
and the treasure-chambers looted, helpless babies
hurled to the earth in the red barbarity of war . . .
my sons' wives hauled off by the Argives' bloody hands!
And I, I last of all—the dogs before my doors
will eat me raw, once some enemy brings me down
with his sharp bronze sword or spits me with a spear,
wrenching the life out of my body . . .
Ah for a young man
All looks fine and noble if he goes down in war . . .
When an old man's killed
and the dogs go at the gray head and the gray beard . . .
that is the cruelest sight
in all our wretched lives!" (Homer, 750 B.C./1990, p. 543–544)

> **DISCUSS**
> - Priam loves Hector more than all his other sons. What qualities place Hector the highest in his father's eyes?
> - Is it better to die young and glorious than old and helpless? Explain.
> - In the *Iliad*, Andromache does not see the duel between her husband and Achilles. She is weaving in an inside chamber, unaware of what is happening. Why did Homer chose to place her away from the action? Which way is more dramatic?

Hector Says Good-Bye

Before he goes to face the rigors of battle, Hector bids his wife Andromache and his son Astyanax farewell.

> In the same breath, shining Hector reached down
> for his son—but the boy recoiled,
> cringing against his nurse's full breast,
> screaming out at the sight of his own father
> terrified by the flashing bronze, the horsehair crest,
> the great ridge of the helmet nodding, bristling terror—
> so it struck his eyes. And his loving father laughed,
> his mother laughed as well, and glorious Hector,
> quickly lifting the helmet from his head,
> set it down on the ground, fiery in the sunlight,
> and raising his son he kissed him, tossed him in his arms,
> lifting a prayer to Zeus and the other deathless gods:
> "Zeus, all you immortals! Grant this boy, my son,
> may be like me, first in glory among the Trojans,
> strong and brave like me, and rule all Troy in power
> and one day let them say, 'He is a better man than his father!'—
> when he comes from battle bearing the bloody gear
> of the mortal enemy he has killed in war—
> a joy to his mother's heart." (Homer, 750 B.C./1990, p. 211)

DISCUSS

- This episode happens early in the *Iliad*. Now that you know the fate of Hector, what does this knowledge add to his speech?
- Some have argued that this is one of the earliest representations of the modern family unit—a faithful husband and wife, very much in love, who also care for their child. Why would this be rare in the ancient world?

War Wrap-Up

Although the *Iliad* ends with the Trojan War unresolved, the rest of the legend was well known to the Greek people. Shortly after the death of Hector, Achilles is slain. Paris, his arrow guided by the hand of Apollo himself, shoots the mighty Greek warrior in his proverbial heel.

Ajax, a mighty Greek warrior, and Odysseus both lay claim to the god-forged armor of Achilles. To prevent a fight, Agamemnon decides that the armor should go to Odysseus. Ajax fumes. His pride has been insulted. Achilles was *his* cousin after all. The warrior decides that he must revenge himself upon Agamemnon. Ajax plans to sneak into the Greek commander's tent at night and murder him in his sleep. As he sets out to do so, the goddess Athena discovers his trick. She strikes Ajax with madness, and while he believes he is in fact murdering Agamemnon, he has actually made his way to the Greek cattle herds where he begins his plan of slaughter. When Ajax recovers from his madness, he realizes he has massacred cows instead of King Agamemnon. To prevent any further humiliation, he commits suicide.

With Achilles and Ajax dead, the Greeks are at an impasse. They've been at Troy for 10 years. The war must end—and soon. A prophet tells them that they will never succeed until they fight with the bow and arrows of Heracles. When Odysseus hears this news, his memory is jolted. Ten years earlier, as the ships made their way to Troy, the Greeks had abandoned one of their men on an island stop. A snake had bitten Prince Philoctetes (to whom Heracles had entrusted his bow and arrows) when the men went ashore. Rather than deal with his fetid wound, the Greeks had rashly left this prince behind. Now—it seemed—he was exactly who they needed. But, this was only one half of the prophecy. In addition to the bow and arrows, the Greeks also needed the long-lost son of Achilles to join the war at Troy. Then—and only then—they would be victorious.

Odysseus set out at once to secure both necessities. He tracked down Pyrrhus, the nearly grown son of Achilles, and found Prince Philoctetes still living on the island, where they had left him. With his two new comrades in tow, Odysseus returned to the war, and the battle reached fever pitch once again. One day in battle, Paris was slain by the prophetic arrows of Prince Philoctetes. Priam's sons were growing short in number, but the war had one more trick up its sleeve.

Indiana Schliemann?

The *Indiana Jones* films are not based on real events. Their fantasy elements are what make them so exciting. Real archeologists don't use treasure maps or face hostile natives or secretly plunder tombs—or do they?

During his boyhood in 19th century Germany, Heinrich Schliemann became obsessed with the *Iliad*. It is said that this obsession was triggered by a colorful children's book illustration of burning Troy, an image that haunted him the rest of his days (Schuchhardt, 1891). Where was this fabled city? Surely it existed—at some time and some place. Although most people wrote Troy off as a legend, Schliemann made it his lifelong goal to discover this city and prove its existence to the world. The *Iliad* would be his guide and constant object of study. To him it represented a map, a detailed account of how ancient Troy was laid out. Mountains, rivers, beaches, and plains were all described in great detail. Surely, these landmarks could lead him to the long-buried city.

DISCUSS
- Is it odd that Achilles is slain by Paris? Explain.
- What is Ajax's flaw? Explain.

READ
Read *The Cure at Troy*, a translation of Sophocles' *Philoctetes* by Seamus Heaney. In this play the tricky Odysseus must convince Philoctetes to rejoin the war. Philoctetes is reluctant because his countrymen have abandoned him for many years.

Cassandra

She is rarely mentioned in the *Iliad*, but the Trojan princess Cassandra plays an interesting part in the tale. In the days of peace before the war, this daughter of Priam and Hecuba was so beautiful that she even attracted the attention of the gods. Apollo, god of light, came to Troy to woo and seduce her. Cassandra, being a crafty girl, first asked the god what he would offer her in return. He waved his golden hand and conferred the eternal gift of prophecy upon her. Now, she would know the secret thoughts of the gods. He began his advances, but the princess reneged, refusing to give him what he wanted. Apollo waved his hand again, only this time sending out a curse. Cassandra would keep her gift of prophecy (Apollo cannot go back on his word), yet no one would ever heed her wise words.

Such an expedition would require an enormous amount of money, so the young Heinrich set out to make his fortune. He succeeded—twice. Through cunning business tactics, taking advantage of both the California Gold Rush and the Crimean War in Europe, Schliemann amassed two sizeable fortunes by the time he was 40 years old. Now, the dream of his life could be realized.

On his journey to financial success, Schliemann had left two marriages in his wake. He decided that his next wife should be Greek. As he traveled through Greece, he met and married a 17-year-old Greek girl named Sophia, his Helen of Troy (Schuchhardt, 1891).

By carefully studying the clues of the *Iliad*, Schliemann made up his mind that Ilium had in fact existed in the modern country of Turkey, at a site called Hissarlik. Even though he lacked any archeological training, Heinrich organized a dig at once and personally went to the site to attend to the details. Soon his hunch proved to be correct—or at least partially. There *was* a buried city under the hill—a city slightly less epic than the one presented in the *Iliad.* Nevertheless, it was an astounding discovery. He was further rewarded when he discovered what he dubbed "Priam's treasure," a collection of Bronze Age treasures. He decked out his wife Sophia in "the jewels of Helen" and began snapping photographs of his find. He quickly published his results. Needless to say, his discovery shocked the world (Schuchhardt, 1891).

Unfortunately, it also shocked the Turkish government, who immediately revoked his digging permit and demanded a portion of the treasure. Under the cover of night, Schliemann fled from Turkey with the jewels in tow. Convinced he had effectively discovered Troy, Schliemann began other digs, attempting to find Agamemnon's palace at Mycenae. He did discover several artifacts, including a death mask he declared to be the very "Mask of Agamemnon." He also attempted to discover the legendary home of Odysseus, Ithaca.

At last his adventures caught up with him. On one of his expeditions in 1890, Schliemann fell sick and died. He was survived by his wife, Sophia, and their two children, Andromache and Agamemnon Schliemann.

Other archeologists have strongly criticized Schliemann for his lack of technique. There were actually several cities built on Schliemann's "Troy" site. In an effort to reach its deepest and oldest layer, the amateur archaeologist actually destroyed the top layers of the find. Some have also accused him of fraud, claiming Schliemann only *pretended* to find his treasure at the Troy site when he had actually bought the artifacts on the antique market and planted them there. Only Schliemann and Sophia were present at the dig when the treasure was discovered. Other critics also have called Troy's validity into question. What Schliemann discovered was a Bronze Age city, but was it actually the city that inspired the Greek legend? Homer's details in the *Iliad* are too vague, these critics claim, for anyone to be sure they have found the actual Troy.

Regardless of his tactics or his scruples, Schliemann was a fascinating character, a man who believed in the validity of myth and the reality of dreams—probably the closest thing to a real-life Indiana Jones the world will ever see.

> **DISCUSS**
> - Do you think Schliemann actually discovered Troy? Why or why not?
> - Do you agree with Schliemann's tactics? Explain your reasoning.
> - Was Schliemann a real-life Indiana Jones? Why or why not?

The Quotable *Iliad*

As mentioned earlier, the Greeks used the *Iliad* as a Bible of sorts. If they wanted to prove a point, they would select a noble quote from its pages. Below are some of the *Iliad's* famous quotes (Homer, 750 B.C./1990).

"No baby boy still in his mother's belly, not even he will escape, all Ilium blotted out, no tears for their lives, no markers for their graves"—Agamemnon

"Always be the best, my boy, the bravest, and hold your head up high above the others. Never disgrace the generations of your fathers."—Hippolochus to his son Glaucus

"But I, if I should die, my comrades-in-arms will bury me in style!" —Odysseus

"One can achieve his fill of all good things, even of sleep, even of making love . . . But not these Trojans—no one can glut their lust for battle!" —Menelaus

"Well let me die . . . in some great clash of arms that even men to come will hear of down the years!"—Hector

"Die, Trojan, die—till I butcher all the way to sacred Troy." —Achilles

"A man's tongue is a glib and twisty thing . . ." —Aeneas

"Zeus planted a killing doom within us both so even for generations still unborn we will live in song"—Helen to Paris

"You, I hate you the most of all the Olympian gods"—Zeus to his son, Ares

"Take your stand on the rampart here, before you orphan your son and make your wife a widow"—Andromache to Hector

"Why so much grief for me? No man will hurl me down to Death against my fate. And fate? No one alive has ever escaped it, neither brave man nor coward, I tell you—it's born with us the day that we are born"—Hector

"The god of war is impartial: he hands out death to the man who hands out death." —Hector

"It's wrong to have such an iron, ruthless heart. Even the gods themselves can bend and change . . . ."—Phoenix, Achilles' mentor

"Like the generations of leaves, the lives of mortal men. Now the wind scatters the old leaves across the earth, now the living timber bursts with the new buds and spring comes round again. And so with men: as one generation comes to life, another dies away"—Glaucus, Trojan Captain, to Diomedes

"There is nothing alive more agonized than man of all that breathe and crawl across the earth."—Zeus

"Even a fool learns something once it hits him."—Menelaus

"Life breath cannot come back again . . . once it slips through a man's clenched teeth."—Achilles

"Quick, better to live or die, once and for all, than die by inches, slowly crushed to death . . ."—Ajax

"Too many kings can ruin an army"—Odysseus

"There was a world . . . or was it all a dream?"—Helen

"Come—the proof of battle is action, proof of words, debate. No time for speeches now, it's time to fight!" —Patroclus

"Bird-signs! Fight for your country—that is the best, the only omen!"—Hector

"No use to you then, the fine lyre and these, these gifts of Aphrodite, your long flowing locks and your striking looks, not when you roll and couple with the dust."—Hector to Helen

DISCUSS
- Which quote is your personal favorite? Explain.
- Do you think the *Iliad* deserves the acclaim it has received? Why or why not?

CHAPTER 6
National Identity: The *Aeneid*

ESCAPE FROM ILIUM: VIRGIL'S *AENEID*

Cast

Aeneas *(Trojan son of Venus)*

Priam *(Aged king of Troy)*

Hecuba *(Queen of Troy)*

Laocoön *(Trojan priest, son of Priam)*

Sinon *(Greek soldier)*

Creusa *(Wife of Aeneas)*

Anchises *(Elderly father of Aeneas)*

Achates *(Aeneas' loyal servant)*

Juno *(Queen of heaven)*

Venus *(Goddess of love)*

Jupiter *(Ruler of the gods)*

Hector's Ghost *(Ghost of the deceased prince of Troy)*

Iulus *(Young son of Aeneas)*

Pyrrhus *(Warrior son of Achilles)*

Note. *Because Virgil's* Aeneid *was written in Latin, the Roman names for the gods are used here.*

NARRATOR: The remains of the Greek encampment dotted the yellow sands. A perplexed party of Trojan noblemen gathered there, staring at a three-story high wooden structure, pieced together from rough timbers with mud and pitch. Supported by four stout legs, a barrel-shaped body, topped by an equine neck and head, formed the crude shape of a horse. Trojan scouts had spotted the structure earlier in the day. News had spread through the city: The Greeks had fled.

PRIAM: *(overjoyed)* At last! I knew the gods would give us victory.

NARRATOR: Among the gathered men stood Aeneas, a handsome young king. For years he had served Priam and battled his enemies, never questioning his judgment. But, he now spoke up.

AENEAS: My king, there's no way to be sure they're actually gone! The Greeks are tricky.

NARRATOR: Priam shook his head.

PRIAM: Who would go to so much trouble for a simple trick? No. They are gone. I can feel it.

AENEAS: This horse—or whatever it is—what does it mean then?

PRIAM: The Greeks are not barbarians, my friend. They serve the same gods as we do. They have made this structure as an offering for a safe voyage home.

AENEAS: But, look at its midsection. There is enough room in there to hold a troop of men.

(muttering from the assembled men)

NARRATOR: A man with the robes of a priest stepped forward from the assembly.

LAOCOÖN: Father, listen to Aeneas. This isn't some gift of peace. The Greeks have attacked us for 10 years. Why would they pack up and leave so quickly now?

NARRATOR: The priest was Laocoön, one of Priam's many sons.

PRIAM: I say that this is a gift to the gods. There can be no evil in such a thing.

NARRATOR: A cry rose from down the beach. Two soldiers were dragging a haggard man between them. He was wailing piteously.

SINON: (screaming) No! Spare me, noble Trojans! Spare me!

PRIAM: (mockingly) Perhaps you *are* right, Aeneas. The Greeks have not fled. They have left one behind. (chuckle)

NARRATOR: The men threw the sniveling man to the ground. He raised his rodent face and kissed Priam's robes between his hands.

SINON: Oh, Trojan king! I have been wronged! Severely wronged!

AENEAS: (sternly) What *are* you babbling about?

SINON: My countrymen have fled—given up! Oh, this long war has broken their will.

PRIAM: When did they leave?

SINON: Yesterday, my lord.

AENEAS: And, why were you left behind?

SINON: The Fates have cursed me—that's why! It was all the fault of Calchas, that lying rat! He said a sacrifice was needed, and that it should be me. What have I done? I'm only a poor farmer! A farmer who will never see his family again! (weeping)

AENEAS: Why were the Greeks so quick to leave without a warning?

SINON: Oh, my lord. Please do not smite my poor head. But, I have been sworn to secrecy! The gods will strike me down!

AENEAS: Answer me, or *I* will strike you down.

SINON: Since the mighty Achilles fell, our army has been doomed. Agamemnon and Menelaus quarreled like spoiled children. The men threatened to mutiny. Our campaign fell apart. And so, they left me, *me* to be tortured by the enemy! Woe is me! (weeping)

AENEAS: (contemptuously) Ridiculous man.

PRIAM: What is the meaning of this tribute then? Tell us, and we will spare your life.

SINON: Oh, noble king! I weep at your generosity! But, I have given my oath never to tell! Apollo will surely curse me if I do!

LAOCOÖN: Apollo does not curse men for telling the truth. If you are indeed telling the truth, you have nothing to worry about.

SINON: We worked many days on the horse—many days. It was a scheme of Ulysses'. His mind is ever working. He told the kings that such an offering would honor Neptune, and our journey would be a safe one.

AENEAS: Seems a bit large for an offering.

SINON: Here is the craftiness of that man! He told the kings to build it so tall that you noble lords could never fit it inside your glorious walls. If you did so, he said Neptune would bless you instead, and their voyage would become perilous. I am ashamed of this trickery—especially if it harms you generous Trojans—

LAOCOÖN: I don't believe you.

NARRATOR: The rat-faced man recoiled in shock.

SINON: Why would I lie? You have saved me. I only repay my debt with this information.

PRIAM: Laocoön, my son. Don't be so suspicious. Think of how this war has tired *us*. The Greeks have been camped upon this beach for 10 years. Is it so hard to believe they have gone home?

NARRATOR: The priest of Apollo said no more, but he gripped the spear within his hand even tighter.

PRIAM: Greek, thank you for this information. You have served us well.

LAOCOÖN: No, Father! It is a trick! I can feel it. I fear the Greeks even when they bring gifts!

NARRATOR: He turned—flinging his spear toward the towering horse. With a dull thud, it stuck into a plank of the beast's belly.

PRIAM: *(angrily)* Laocoön!

NARRATOR: Before another word could be said, the nearby shallows of the sea began to foam. Springing forward from the brine like a black arrow came a serpentine streak. It coiled its dripping body around the frightened priest, and as quickly as it had came, drug him screaming back into the tide.

LAOCOÖN: *(hideous screaming)*

NARRATOR: Aeneas rushed forward, sword drawn, but the body of Laocoön was lost in the waves. Priam drooped to the ground and clutched his chest.

AENEAS: I—I—he's gone, your majesty.

SINON: *(whimpering)*

NARRATOR: Retainers came to attend the king. None dared argue against the Greek tribute now. The gods had made a violent statement of their loyalty. As the men began to help the feeble Priam back to Ilium, he motioned for Aeneas to come close. Gripping the Trojan's tunic tightly, he hissed his orders.

PRIAM: *(quietly, but forcefully)* They have taken my Hector—my Paris. Now I have lost another. Get this horse within our walls at any cost. Let the Greeks be cursed by the sea and die like the dogs they are.

NARRATOR: Aeneas nodded grimly. The ailing king was led away, and Aeneas attended the task of moving the giant structure. Logs were called for and a troop of men. Priam had spoken. The horse would be within the city by nightfall. Aeneas drove his golden chariot back to Ilium, where he instructed the city gate to be dismantled. The horse was coming, and the way must be made. And, by the time the sun set, the fabled weapon of destruction was securely nestled in the midst of the Trojan square. Wearied and worn, Aeneas made his way home to his city-quarters.

CREUSA: *(eagerly)* Aeneas! Everyone is talking about the Greeks' horse!

NARRATOR: Aeneas' wife, Creusa, greeted him at the door. Servants rushed to rid him of his dusty armor.

AENEAS: *(sigh)* Yes, I know.

CREUSA: What is the news?

AENEAS: *(angrily)* The horse! The horse! I'll speak no more of it! Today I've had the longest day of this miserable war.

CREUSA: *(quieter)* Then, rest. I will have a bath poured. *(pause)* There is dancing in the square tonight—in celebration.

AENEAS: Let them dance and drink to their hearts' content. I will have nothing to do with it. I need rest.

CREUSA: But, my husband, how will they celebrate without their greatest hero?

AENEAS: I'm sure they will find a way.

NARRATOR: He drew his wife to himself and kissed her.

AENEAS: I'm just glad that we have seen the end of all this—all this bloodshed. Now, we can go home—to our own city. Maybe I can focus on being a father now, more than being a hero.

CREUSA: They are one and the same to Iulus. He adores you.

AENEAS: *(sarcastically)* Oh, yes. There's so much to be adored. A young man growing older—tired of the world.

CREUSA: Your father has been telling him stories about your battles.

AENEAS: *(laughs)* Father's up to his old lies, eh?

CREUSA: You are right. Rest is what my husband needs.

NARRATOR: In the streets, the Trojans were celebrating—drinking until they could drink no more. The Greeks were defeated! Tambourines and cymbals clanged late into the night, but at long last, the last stragglers succumbed to a drunken slumber, and silence settled over the city.

Under this cover, Sinon the Greek crept forth. He had been brought back into Ilium as a friend. He had toasted and sang with the men. Now, he shimmied up one of the horse's giant legs and triggered the trap door that had been cleverly hidden within the beast's belly.

SINON: *(hissing)* The city sleeps! They are ours for the taking!

NARRATOR: The dark forms of the hidden Greek soldiers dropped down from the hole one-by-one into the shadows. One ran to the ramparts, and lighting a torch, signaled to the troops waiting across the plain. The Greek fleet had merely hidden itself down the coast and sailed back at dusk. Sinon himself saw that the dismembered gates were wide open for the army's advance. The plan of Ulysses had worked perfectly.

SINON: *(laugh of victory)*

NARRATOR: Aeneas was stirred from sleep by what he thought was a scream. He sat up in bed and listened intently. The scream did not come again. He paused. A cry again—followed by another and another—the clashing of swords. He started to bolt from the bed. In the dim light he realized there was a dripping form standing in the midst of the room.

HECTOR: *(slowly)* Aeneas.

NARRATOR: The head of the darkened figure rose. It was Hector—his beard clotted with gore, his face striped with wounds.

AENEAS: *(breathlessly)* Hector?

HECTOR: Aeneas, there is no time to question. If you doubt who I am, look at my dismembered body, ripped to shreds. Look at my pierced feet where I was hooked to the murderer's chariot.

AENEAS: I do not doubt, Hector! I do not doubt!

HECTOR: Run, goddess born. Run. The Greeks have taken the walls. Ilium will fall this night. But, through you, we will live on. Take our holy gods—our righteous ways—

take them across the sea. Build your own high walls there. Build a new Ilium from the ashes of the old.

AENEAS: *(panicking)* Hector! Tell me more! Can Troy be saved?

HECTOR: I have spoken the words I was sent to speak. Now, I descend.

NARRATOR: The shadows of the room engulfed Troy's greatest prince. Aeneas' heart beat violently within his chest. How had they done it? How had the Greeks made it inside the walls?

He shook Creusa awake.

CREUSA: *(sleepy)* Wha—what is it?

AENEAS: *(urgently)* No time! Get Iulus up! Get father! We're leaving immediately.

CREUSA: What? What do you mean? Our things—

AENEAS: Leave them! Bring only what you need.

NARRATOR: He hurried to his armor and belt and began to strap them on.

CREUSA: Where are you going?

AENEAS: To Pergamos! The citadel! I have to try to save the king!

CREUSA: From whom? I—I—don't understand.

AENEAS: *(angrily)* Do as I say!

NARRATOR: Drawing his sword, Aeneas rushed from his chambers and down the hallway. The servants were gathered near the entrance—clutching each other in fright.

AENEAS: *(shouting)* Bar the door! Let no one enter—even if they say they are friendly!

NARRATOR: The streets were chaotic—fleeing men and women clamoring over one another in escape. Man-to-man battles raged on every corner. Buildings were burning and babies were crying. Hades had come to Earth. Aeneas pushed past all of this as best he could. The mighty Trojan warrior cut down several Greek raiders who tried to oppose him—as he aimed his strides toward the citadel and the royal family held within. The mass of the battle was before its gates. Aeneas threw himself in the melee—hacking wildly, biting like a wild animal at any who stood in his way. At last he gained entrance to the hall within. A band of startled Trojan warriors crouched there.

AENEAS: Trojans! Have any Greeks passed your barrier?

ACHATES: We do not know. We only just fought our own way in here, Lord Aeneas. The Princess Cassandra was *right!* Why did we doubt her?

AENEAS: Come with me! We will fight our way to the peak, and I pray we find Priam still alive. Follow me!

NARRATOR: But, the Greeks had penetrated into the royal chambers high above. Pyrrhus, the bloodthirsty son of Achilles, led the pack. He found the royal family cowering and weeping in the upper stories.

PYRRHUS: A-ha! The crowned heads of Troy!

NARRATOR: A huge shrine filled the corner of the room. Hecuba and Andromache clung desperately to it. Priam sat—as if a stupor—upon its altar. Pyrrhus wiped the splattered blood from his face and advanced.

PYRRHUS: Old king! Face me! Face me, the son of the mighty Achilles.

PRIAM: *(weakly)* You have taken all that I love. What else can I give you?

PYRRHUS: Your head, old man. It will look grand hanging from my chariot.

NARRATOR: The Trojan king rose and began to slowly buckle on the faded armor that was at his feet.

HECUBA: *(frantically)* No, Priam! No! He will kill you.

PRIAM: He will kill me no matter what I do. There is no honor in him. There is no honor in any of these Greeks.

PYRRHUS: Silence!

PRIAM: You speak of Achilles, your father. You do him an insult. *He* was an honorable man.

PYRRHUS: Honor is for weaklings!

PRIAM: He honored the gods. He gave me back my son. Now, you will slaughter a family who claims the protection of the gods.

PYRRHUS: Cowards! You can't hide behind your shrines. This is war!

NARRATOR: Priam stared at the young man sadly.

PRIAM: I am ready. Come, and take me. I would not wish to live in a world where the likes of you are the masters.

PYRRHUS: Grrrrrrr.

NARRATOR: The son of Achilles ran forward and forced the old king to his knees.

HECUBA: *(crazy)* No! No!

NARRATOR: Grabbing a fistful of whitened hair, he brought his sword close to Priam's neck.

PYRRHUS: I never knew my father, you old fossil. But, when you see him, tell him what a shameful son he has. *(spits)*

NARRATOR: He spit into Priam's face, and with a grunt of satisfaction, drove his blade into the old king's side. A bit of air was all that escaped Priam's dying lips.

HECUBA: No! My husband! Noooooo!

NARRATOR: Shaking the body from his sword, Pyrrhus ran to the two weeping females. He pried them from their shrine and drug them away to his waiting troops. Merely minutes later, when Aeneas burst into the chamber, he knew that he was too late. A body lay face down in a pool of black blood. He lifted it and cried aloud.

AENEAS: My king! Those animals!

ACHATES: We must go, my lord. All is lost here.

AENEAS: Go without me. I must wait a moment—and mourn my king.

ACHATES: What are your orders for us?

AENEAS: Fight. Fight until all are dead.

NARRATOR: The men retreated to the fray once again, leaving Aeneas alone with the corpse in his arms. He had failed. After the soldiers had clattered back to the battle, Aeneas heard something stir in the darkness. A figure was crouching in the crevice behind the altar. It had gone unnoticed by all.

AENEAS: *(angrily)* You!

NARRATOR: Aeneas laid down the body of his king and, taking up his sword, moved toward the cowering form.

AENEAS: Come out of there, you coward! Come out and face what's coming to you!

NARRATOR: A royal veil moved from the shadows, a beautiful face covered with tears.

HELEN: *(sobbing)* Please, please. Spare me.

AENEAS: Spare you? Spare *you* when the royal family of Troy has been slaughtered at your feet! All for your lust! Why should you escape? Why should you ever see your home again, when the only home we Trojans have ever known is being destroyed all around us? You too shall know death.

NARRATOR: Helen wiped the damp hair from her face.

HELEN: *(sobbing)* You would kill a woman? You would be no better than they are!

AENEAS: I do not kill a woman. I kill a curse. No one would scorn me for that. They would praise me!

HELEN: No! Please!

NARRATOR: Aeneas raised his sword to strike, but a jarring light shone between the predator and his prey—a glow pooling into a silvery cloud.

AENEAS: *(angrily)* Mother! Don't interfere! This is has to be done!

NARRATOR: The heavenly figure of Venus appeared—her face in fear.

VENUS: *(forcefully)* Leave her, Aeneas! I came as soon as I heard.

AENEAS: Troy is lost. All because of her!

VENUS: Leave her, Aeneas. Helen did not bring down Troy. My Paris didn't either. It was the deathless gods. They have laid Ilium low. There is no hope for this city—but there still is hope for you, my son.

NARRATOR: As Aeneas lowered his sword, Helen scurried away into the darkness.

AENEAS: You have saved your darling princess, mother—but you're wrong. There is no hope for me. I will stay here until every last Trojan has died a valiant death, then I will lay my own body down next to theirs.

VENUS: Nonsense! If you die, Troy will die. Someone has to survive!

AENEAS: I have spoken, Mother. I will not run away like a coward.

NARRATOR: His mother floated forward and took his bloodstained face into her hands.

VENUS: You have stood your ground. You have done all that you know to do. Hecuba and Andromache have been dragged away to a life of unending torment. Will you doom your wife and your son to that as well?

NARRATOR: Iulus and Creusa flickered into his mind.

AENEAS: Look at all these who have died! Why should *I* survive?

VENUS: Because it is *your* fate to live on. Do not judge the will of the gods. Don't resist it. You struggle against the wind. Remember your dream. Remember your duty.

NARRATOR: Aeneas removed his mother's hands from his face.

AENEAS: Then, tell me what I should do.

NARRATOR: Below in the citadel courtyard, a bloodied group of surviving Trojans were throwing themselves against a Greek onslaught. One man fell back clutching the oozing stump of his arm, and another fell from a slash at the throat.

ACHATES: *(shouting)* We won't be able to stand much more of this!

NARRATOR: The citadel doors flew open, and Aeneas entered the fray—spearing left and right. Two Greeks fell instantly.

ACHATES: Prince Aeneas!

AENEAS: Flee! This battle is lost! Find the secret ways out of the city! Take your women and your children and flee! Meet me at Mount Ida in 3 day's time! We will reconvene there!

ACHATES: Yes, sir! As you say!

NARRATOR: The Trojans dispersed in chaos, and Aeneas thundered back toward his quarters. When he beheld the courtyard to his house, his heart stopped cold. The gate had been thrown down, and the entrance burned and badly scarred.

AENEAS: *(panicked)* Gods! Am I too late? *(yelling)* Creusa! Iulus! Father!

NARRATOR: His words echoed emptily back to him from the shadows.

IULUS: *(quietly)* Father?

NARRATOR: Timidly stepping forward came his young son. His wife was there holding his hand. When she beheld her husband, she ran to him and flung her trembling arms around him.

CREUSA: *(sobbing)* They—they tried to get in—but then it stopped—

AENEAS: Then you are safe?

NARRATOR: She nodded.

AENEAS: Gather what you can carry. We're getting out of here. The whole city will be in flames soon. Where is father?

CREUSA: He's in his chambers. Oh, Aeneas. What shall we do with him? We cannot leave him! But, he is too weak to survive any journey.

AENEAS: You tend to Iulus.

NARRATOR: Aeneas hurried to his father's chambers. The old man was propped up within his bed. Clutched in his sinewy arms was a nearly rusted sword.

ANCHISES: *(surprised)* Oh, son. It's only you. I was expecting Greeks. And, I was ready for them.

AENEAS: Father, come. We're getting out of the city.

ANCHISES: Yes, a wise plan—for you. I have decided to stay here. When the Greeks come to get me, perhaps I can drag a couple of them down into Hades with me.

AENEAS: *(angrily)* Father! There's no time to argue! Get up! I'm not leaving you here.

NARRATOR: The old man raised his eyebrows.

ANCHISES: The son orders about the father, now? Interesting. I think it is my place to decide when and where I will die. Not yours. I will die here with my city.

AENEAS: *(quietly)* Listen to me. We are meeting at Mt. Ida. I have no idea where we will go from there, but we will need ships. I know nothing of ships, but you do.

ANCHISES: *(small laugh)* Yes, I have built a ship or two in my day. But, that was very long ago. Aeneas, let's face it. I'm too old to make it to Ida. As much as I hate to admit it, my feeble body could not stand it.

AENEAS: I thought you'd say that.

NARRATOR: Aeneas moved forward—cradling the old man in his arms.

ANCHISES: What are you doing?

NARRATOR: He lifted his father from the bed and hoisted him upon his shoulder.

ANCHISES: Aeneas! Put me down! I won't have you risking your life for me!

AENEAS: Father. Keep that sword ready. Cover my back.

NARRATOR: He returned swiftly to the hallway where Iulus and Creusa waited expectantly.

AENEAS: Everything ready?

CREUSA: Yes.

AENEAS: All right. Stay close. Iulus, do not let go of your mother's hand. If we are separated, make for the shrine of Ceres just outside the city walls. May the gods protect us.

NARRATOR: And so, the family burst into the flaming night once again. The streets were even more chaotic than before. Aeneas hurried down trackless paths, pushing past fleeing servants and women wailing over the corpses of their husbands. Turn after turn through the winding streets of the city came and went, came and went. Soon the narrow doorway that led outside the city walls to the holy places came into view. Only Trojans and their allies knew of the exit.

ANCHISES: Aeneas! I don't see Creusa and Iulus behind us any longer!

AENEAS: What?

NARRATOR: Aeneas sat his withered father down upon the ground. He scanned the city street behind him frantically.

AENEAS: How long ago did we get separated?

ANCHISES: I do not know, my son! May the gods curse my old eyes! I did not see!

NARRATOR: Then—from around the corner—Iulus came into view, running as quickly as his little legs could carry him.

AENEAS: Thank the gods!

NARRATOR: But, no Creusa appeared. The boy ran into his father's outstretched arms. He was shaking from head to foot.

AENEAS: Iulus, where is your mother? Iulus! Listen to me. Where is your mother?

IULUS: *(frightened)* I don't know! I don't know!

ANCHISES: Aeneas, I will take the boy. The shrine is not far from here. We will hide there until you return. Search for her, Aeneas. Perhaps she is only lost.

AENEAS: *(in a daze)* Yes. Yes. Perhaps—

NARRATOR: Without another word, he dashed back into the crumbling city. Anchises rose, taking the hand of the trembling Iulus.

ANCHISES: Now, grandson. Let us walk—but not too quickly.

NARRATOR: The old man and the boy made their way into the open countryside, down a dusty path daily walked by the priestesses of Ceres. It was deserted now. As they drew away from the city, the clashing of blades and cries of those in pain died away, and only the night air greeted them.

ANCHISES: Did I ever tell you the story of how your father was born?

IULUS: No, Grandpa.

ANCHISES: Didn't I? Surely, I did. You see when I was a very young man, a beautiful woman appeared to me—right out of thin air! Do you believe that?

IULUS: I guess.

ANCHISES: A beautiful woman! You'll understand more when you're older, of course, but she was the most glorious thing I had ever seen. We loved each other very much. And, you know what?

IULUS: What?

ANCHISES: She was actually a goddess in disguise. I didn't even know it!

IULUS: Which one, Grandpa?

ANCHISES: Venus, of course. Venus is the best of the best, and she had picked me, out of all the mortals of the world to love. But, she had to go away, you see. Goddesses are busy people. And, 9 months later, she appeared to me again. Do you know what she had with her this time?

IULUS: What?

ANCHISES: Your father!

IULUS: Dad was a *baby!*

ANCHISES: Yes. Venus and I had made him together.

IULUS: How?

ANCHISES: Umm . . . perhaps we can save that part of the story for when you are older. But, when people tell you that you have a very special father, they're right. He's the son of a goddess.

NARRATOR: The two travelers—young and old—neared the sacred shrine. A gnarled tree grew up beside it, and they sat themselves down beneath it.

ANCHISES: *(groan)* Soon, your father and your mother will be here, and we will go to a new home.

IULUS: What about Troy?

ANCHISES: Ah, Iulie. This place will be better than Troy. It will be the best place that has ever been.

NARRATOR: A man soon appeared on the gloomy path.

ANCHISES: Aeneas?

NARRATOR: The old man rose and walked to his son. Aeneas' eyes brimmed with tears.

AENEAS: I looked everywhere. I filled the streets with my shouting. And, in the midst of it all I saw her. She was there, but not there—like a reflection upon the water.

ANCHISES: What are you trying to say, son?

AENEAS: Three times I tried to embrace her. Three times I only felt air. My wife is dead. She spoke to me. Told me to flee. Her destiny was to die, while mine was to survive. *(sob)* Oh, Father. Life has never been such a curse.

NARRATOR: Anchises draped his son's head over his shoulder, and the fierce warrior—the man who had killed time and time again—wept openly—his heart broken. Iulus watched this inquisitively. His young mind did not yet understand. He turned away, looking to the sky. A bilious cloud was moving through the night, twinkling as it went.

IULUS: *(laugh)* Grandma!

NARRATOR: Someone else was watching this cloud's course as well—someone higher up in the pitch black of night. In the dim halls of Olympus, Juno viewed the final moments of her victory.

JUNO: So, Venus. You think that you've achieved some kind of triumph by letting this ratty band of Trojans escape. After the Greeks have finished slaying all those in the city, they will hunt these others down like dogs.

NARRATOR: The cloud was too far away to answer—making its way toward the peak of Mt. Ida. In the darkness behind the queen of heaven, her husband, Jupiter, appeared.

JUPITER: So, I see you have gotten what you want. Troy is in flames.

JUNO: It was what needed to happen. Troy had grown too proud. It needed to be destroyed.

JUPITER: *You've* gotten too proud yourself, yet *you* are not destroyed.

JUNO: Dear, dear. Allow the rest of us some impulsiveness. *You* are always acting on *your* emotions—no matter how lustful they may be.

JUPITER: If I receive coldness in my own bed, I must search for warmth elsewhere.

JUNO: *(hatefully)* Go warm yourself on the fires of your beloved city! That is my warmth!

JUPITER: So quick to destroy, yet a city *you* love will one day perish . . .

JUNO: *(worried)* What do you mean?

JUPITER: The city-state of Carthage. It has always been your favorite. Am I right?

JUNO: *(worriedly)* What about it? Dido has turned it into a golden kingdom—one ruled by a woman—as it should be.

JUPITER: Women rulers are weak. Her city shall fall—just like my Troy has.

JUNO: How? *(angrily)* How do you know this? Who shall destroy it?

JUPITER: It will be many centuries from now, but it will. These Trojans survivors that you scoff at will prosper. They will sail across the sea and rebuild, and that new city will grow into an empire—one that will crush your precious Carthage.

JUNO: *(angrily)* No. I will stop it! I will bring all my anger against these Trojan whelps! Troy, have I not punished you enough? When will you lie down and die?

JUPITER: *(satisfied)* Great cities never truly die, dear. You will learn that in time.

NARRATOR: Beneath the silent slopes of Mt. Ida the survivors of Troy were gathering under the cover of midnight. The Trojan War had ended, but the journey for a new home was about to begin.

DISCUSS
- If you were Roman, would you want to be associated with the Trojan people? Explain.
- How is Pyrrhus, Achilles' bloodthirsty son, different than his father? Explain.
- How are the Greeks more villainous in the *Aeneid* than in the *Iliad*? Why is this so?

Building an Identity

Soon the United States of America will be 250 years old. Compared to the great civilizations of the world, it's still a newborn. We can't imagine our country without freedom ringing from sea to shining sea, yet not too long ago, freedom was still a dream. When the founding fathers officially declared their independence from the British Empire on July 4, 1776, they were taking a drastic step away from everything they had ever known. Up until then they were only British colonists. As soon as the ink dried on the Declaration of Independence, they were something else. They were Americans.

It's easy for us to sit here at the other end of our nation's history and act like we would be brave enough to take such a bold step. But, to most of their fellow colonists the idea of revolution was suicide. Everyone knew the British king would not take the colonies' separation lightly. He would do all in his military power to stop it. Death and defeat would come quickly.

In one of the biggest surprise victories of all time, the revolutionaries *weren't* defeated by the much larger British army. King George lost his mind, and American freedom was more than a possibility; it was a reality. One of the first tasks at hand was to form a national identity. *Who are we? What do we believe?* It was obvious that the founding fathers had plenty of strong ideas on the subject, but they had to be sorted out and streamlined. They took their final shape in the Constitution of the United States of America. Much blood, sweat, and tears went into that "We the people"!

History, a long record of names and deeds, is important to every nation. The founding fathers had divorced themselves from British history, so American history had to start from scratch. Along with American history a little American mythology grew up as well—some legendary tales that may have happened, but probably didn't. One example is a tale we've probably all heard about the young George Washington. He goes into a tree-chopping frenzy, only to realize that he cannot tell a lie. Another tale involves the revolutionary Paul Revere making his midnight ride shouting, "The British are coming! The British are coming!" He's tipped off by lantern code: One if by land, two if by sea. There are many more in this same vein. Betsy Ross sews the design for the American flag. Benjamin Franklin discovers lightning and suggests the national bird should be the turkey (not necessarily in that order). George Washington, sporting a set of wooden false teeth, skips a silver dollar across the Potomac River (even though the Potomac is half a mile wide and the silver dollar wasn't minted then).

These stories may seem unlikely, but they have been woven into the tapestry of our society. Although they may not be *factual*, they are *true* to the American spirit. They're ideals—conceptualizations of the first Americans—larger-than-life characters intended to make us more patriotic, to challenge *us* to be larger-than-life ourselves. Our country's founders started out as humans just like us, but have since become icons, legends, and myths.

Modern researchers have cast a skeptical light on the subject. Did these inspirational incidents really happen? Myth gives way to fact. But, should we stop telling these stories? Are we so tied down to facts that we can no longer learn from a myth?

Our stories and the people behind them are much like our nation. We strive for an incorruptible ideal, an unattainable goal. We want the George Washington who never told a lie. But, like George, we are not as great as our ideal. Our country, though we hate to admit it, is flawed. It will never be perfect, but should we stop trying to perfect it? Without an ideal before us, we have nowhere to go. George Washington and the others were ideal Americans because they stood for something bigger than themselves. We should do the same. Figure out what it means to be an American, and be the best one you can be. *America* should mean life, liberty, and the pursuit of perfection.

When he set out to write his epic the *Aeneid*, the poet Virgil was trying to create a founding father for Rome and solidify their national identity. The hero of his poem, Aeneas, is Rome's George Washington, a larger-than-life example of what it means to be Roman. Virgil roots his story in history *and* myth, and through this combination tells the story of a nation.

As you ponder this, think about America. Why is important that we have a strong national identity? What can happen when this identity suffers?

Enter the Romans

In the centuries following Classical Greece, a new world power was making its presence known. Rome began as an average city-state in the midst of Italy but through military conquest and political maneuvering came to govern the known world. At its peak the Roman Empire stretched from as far north as England, as far south as Africa, as far west as Spain,

DISCUSS

- What are some other pieces of Americana (symbols or stories that reflect the American spirit)?
- Do you agree that in some cases myth is better than fact? Why or why not?
- Do you believe the mythic stories of the founding fathers should be taught in school? Explain your reasoning.

READ

Read "Paul Revere's Ride" by Henry Wadsworth Longfellow. What are the patriotic elements? Is anything presented as larger-than-life?

RESEARCH

Create a presentation on an aspect of America's cultural identity (flag, national anthem, the national bird, national colors, national seal, national monuments, etc.). Present your information to the class, and discuss how these elements figure into our national identity.

and as far east as the Middle East. It was an impressive span even by modern standards. Assimilation into the empire usually improved a region's quality of life. The Romans were excellent engineers. They made aqueducts, which brought running water to cities. They built sturdy roads (many of which still survive today). Even small towns had public baths and amphitheatres. And, the greatest benefit the Romans brought with them was peace, the *Pax Romana* (Roman peace).

Even though the Romans were experts at broadening their borders, they weren't what we would call "creative types." They stuck to their strengths—subduing, organizing, civilizing, maintaining. But, politics and war left little time for philosophy and poetry. During its formative years, Rome borrowed much of its culture. Greek culture was in style, and the Greek ideas had spread throughout the known world. Almost every part of Roman life was a direct link back to Greece. The Romans even borrowed the Greek gods (with the names changed to protect the innocent). Zeus became Jupiter, Poseidon became Neptune, Ares became Mars, and so on. And, why think up your own stories about these gods when the Greeks already had some of the best myths ever told? Greek mythology became Roman mythology. When most historians refer to the common elements between Greek and Roman societies, they often use the adjective *Greco-Roman* because so many things were lifted, nearly unchanged, from Greece and placed in Rome.

It may seem unoriginal of the Romans to borrow a culture, but the modern world owes them a great debt for doing so. Without the Romans, the Greeks would have never had their far-reaching impact. Although the Romans had little to contribute to the Greek ideas, the Roman Empire was the conduit that spread those ideas throughout the world. If Rome had never pushed its borders into Gaul and Britannia (France and England), the Western world as we know it might not exist today. Once Rome officially became the unchallenged ruler of pretty much everything, some Romans were embarrassed to admit that their culture was a Greek knock-off. Romans were fiercely patriotic. Because Rome had proved to be the master of the world, Roman culture needed to be distinguished from Greek. *Roman* ideals had to be exemplified.

Often, a culture gets its identity from a central text, a work that one can give to a complete stranger and say, "Read this. It tells you what it's like to be one of us." The Greeks had the *Iliad*, a rousing story, one they could look to for inspiration, a chronicle of the good old days of Greece. The Romans had nothing of the same magnitude. They had plenty of political pieces, silly poems, and plays. What they needed was an epic. A Roman *Iliad* filled with an honorable legacy for the citizens to draw upon.

The poet Virgil was the man who rose to the challenge of creating a Roman epic. During his lifetime, Virgil had seen the Roman Republic transform into the Roman Empire. Julius Caesar, the most popular military leader Rome had ever seen, declared himself dictator for life, only to be murdered by a group of conspiring senators. A bloody civil war followed. At its conclusion, Octavian, Caesar's adopted son, arose out of the carnage to become the first Emperor of Rome and renamed himself Caesar Augustus. The times were changing, and the future looked bright. With its new emperor, Rome needed a new identity. It was time for Virgil to write.

The *Aeneid* of Virgil

There were several Greco-Roman legends concerning the Trojan warrior Aeneas, who only played a minor role in the *Iliad.* Homer mentions that it is Aeneas' destiny to escape the bloodbath of Ilium and lead the surviving Trojans to a new life. According to another legend, Aeneas and his refugees took to sea and sailed far to the west, landing in Italy. There he founded Lavinium, a new home for the weary souls of Troy. Yet another tale told how Aeneas' great-grandson Romulus founded the actual city-state of Rome.

With this fragmented source material, the Roman poet Virgil saw his opportunity. Just as the legendary Trojan War fascinated the Greeks, it also captured the imaginations of the Romans. Aeneas formed a link between a heroic past and a Roman future. The two major works of Homer, the *Iliad* and *Odyssey*, provided Virgil with his standard and his inspiration. He must create an epic as sweeping as Homer's—but his would be in Latin, the Roman language, instead of Greek. With this goal in mind, he made the voyage of Aeneas his storyline, an arduous oversea journey from Troy (modern-day Turkey) to the far shores of Italy.

Virgil, writing roughly 850 years after Homer, was operating under different conditions than the previous poet. The *Iliad* and *Odyssey* are oral in their make-up—even though they were written down, the poems are the result of a long history of oral storytelling. In other words, to be fully appreciated, they should be read out loud. Thanks to the advances of the Roman Empire, literacy was now flourishing across the world. Virgil's work could be *literary* from start to finish. It was designed *to be read.* Many readers have commented on the poetic styles caused by this difference. The introduction to a 2006 translation of Virgil's epic includes a statement by Alexander Pope, a 18th-century poet, concerning the artists, "Homer makes us hearers, and Virgil leaves us readers" (p. 389).

DISCUSS
- Are there any similarities between ancient Rome and modern America?
- Is American culture unique, or is it borrowed as Roman culture was?
- How was the problem faced by the Imperial Romans similar to the problem faced by America's founding fathers?
- How is American culture different than English culture? What caused these changes?

DISCUSS
- What is America's national epic? What piece of fiction clearly illustrates what it means to be an American? Support your choice with reasoning.
- What are some of the novels that have helped to shape America philosophically and politically? Explain.
- What writer has captured the spirit of America? What painter? What songwriter? Explain.

WRITE
Create a three-line poem that you will read aloud. Create a three-line poem that you will allow another student to read silently. How are the poems that are meant to be *heard* different than the ones that are meant to be *read?*

Unlike Homer, Virgil had a strong political purpose. Many Romans were leery of their new Emperor and feared they would be forced to give up many of the rights they had held under the old republic. Virgil chose to put his support behind the new leader. Rome had been at war for far too long. Caesar Augustus promised peace and a return to the original Roman family values. Virgil, therefore, had multiple purposes with his *Aeneid:* link a heroic past to the present, extol the glories of Rome, create a new national identity, and draw a correlation between the noble hero Aeneas and Caesar Augustus. It was a bold undertaking—taking him nearly 10 years to complete. He died with all but a few lines complete. Fortunately, his final order to burn the book was not carried out.

Although partially unfinished, the *Aeneid* was a success. Virgil was posthumously celebrated as the Roman Empire's greatest poet. His *Aeneid* became required classroom reading. A new sense of what it meant to be Roman was born. Patriotism thrived, and Caesar Augustus embarked on one of the most stellar reigns Rome would ever see. His rule brought the *Pax Romana,* and the Empire continued its unhampered growth. Upon his death, Augustus was declared a god, and the eighth month August was officially named for him. All emperors who followed him took his names *Caesar* and *Augustus* as part of their own. Virgil had helped to solidify the empire he so loved.

A Fate Worse Than Death

Who has words to capture that night's disaster,
tell that slaughter? What tears could match
our torments now? An ancient city is falling,
a power that ruled for ages, now in ruins.
Everywhere lie the motionless bodies of the dead,
strewn in her streets, her homes and gods' shrines
we held in awe . . .
Everywhere, wrenching grief, everywhere, terror
and a thousand shapes of death. (Virgil, 19 B.C./2006, p. 87)

These are the words Virgil uses to describe the Fall of Troy. Yet, the *Aeneid* does not show the reader what happens to a very important group of characters—the Trojan women. The following is a summary of their fates.

Once the fighting subsided, Troy lay lifeless, slow flames eating away its glory. The Greeks had won through Ulysses' (Odysseus) cunning. After every able-bodied or wounded Trojan man was put to death, the Greeks turned their eyes to the spoils. They gathered the Trojan women, wailing for their lost husbands and sons, into the city square. Queen Hecuba and Princess Andromache, desperately clutching her son Astyanax, were among the lot, their faces stained with blood and tears. Princess Cassandra was soon led there and thrown in with the others—her clothing torn and her face haggard. Between gasps, she told what had befallen her. As she sought sanctuary in the temple of Athena, a Greek soldier, ignoring the sanctity of that place, assaulted her, raped her, and then dragged her to the others.

As the women huddled together, the grim Greek officers came and pried the wailing boy Astyanax from his mother's arms. Out of all the children, his life would not be spared. As the last male heir to the throne of Troy, he was condemned to die. The men took Astyanax to the height of the city walls and, while the women shrieked, dropped him over the edge.

The female captives were divided between the Greek chieftains. Andromache was given to Pyrrhus, the son of Achilles. Hecuba was sent with Ulysses. Cassandra's fate was to journey back to Mycenae with Agamemnon. The remaining royal Trojans were separated forever.

Elsewhere, Menelaus hunted through the burning citadel for his wife. He planned to kill her—the rightful payment, he thought, for her unfaithfulness. When at last he found her, Menelaus raised his sword to strike, but Helen begged him to wait. Regaining her composure, she undid the clasp of her tunic and bore her breast. This unexpected sight softened Menelaus' anger, and he lowered his sword. Helen would live but only if she agreed to be his *faithful* wife once again. She agreed.

The Trojan Women

Euripides, one of the three greatest Classical Greek playwrights, never achieved the popularity of his contemporary, Sophocles. Euripides only won four first prizes for drama in his long career. Some attribute this to his choice of subject matter. More often than not, his plays were controversial, such as *Medea*, which cast the witch-wife of the hero Jason in a somewhat sympathetic light. The audience, predominately men, did not respond well to Euripides' depiction of the strong-willed Medea. In fact, the plays of Euripides frequently portrayed women as smarter than their husbands or slaves as smarter than their masters. Both of these concepts, to the male, slave-owning judges of the dramatic competition, were scan-

DISCUSS
- The Trojan horse saved the lives of many Greek soldiers, but did Ulysses fight fairly? Explain.
- Helen survives the Trojan War. Is this fair? Why or why not?
- Many of the people killed in the sack of Troy included innocent civilians. Astyanax, the infant son of Hector, was the most tragic victim of all. America faced a similar predicament near the end of World War II. Could they justify killing thousands of innocent Japanese citizens to stop a war? Do you believe this kind of action is worth the price? Explain.

WATCH
Now that you know the full story of the fall of Troy, watch the film *Troy* (2004) directed by Wolfgang Petersen. Analyze the director's choices in the way he presents the legend.

dalous. Because times and tastes have changed, Euripides' plays seem very modern.

When Euripides turned his sights on Troy, he chose not to focus on the brave kings and warriors who gave up their lives in the war, but on the surviving women. This was a set of victims the public may not have considered before. These women watched their loved ones die before being dragged off to a life of slavery—or worse. *The Trojan Women* also served a contemporary purpose: It was a scathing attack on Classical Greek war practices.

In *The Trojan Women*, Euripides gives voice to the female victims of Troy. Read the following monologues aloud.

> *Hecuba mourns the loss of her family and country.*
> Lift up your neck from the dust;
> Up with your head!
> This is not Troy; the kings of Troy are dead:
> Bear what you must.
> The tide has turned at length:
> Ebb with the tide, drift helpless down.
> Useless to struggle on,
> Breasting the storm when Fate prevails.
> I mourn for my dead world, my burning town,
> My sons, my husband, gone, all gone!
> What pride of race, what strength
> Once swelled our royal sails!
> Now shrunk to nothing, sunk in mean oblivion! . . .
> For those whom Fate has cursed
> Music itself sings but one note—
> Unending miseries, torment and wrong!
> (Euripides, 415 B.C./1973, p. 93)

> *Cassandra comforts her mother with a vision of the future. Agamemnon, which she refers to as her future husband, will be slain.*
> Mother, wreathe a triumphal garland round my head;
> I'm to be married to a king; rejoice at it!
> If you find me unwilling, take me, make me go.
> As sure as Apollo is a prophet, Agamemnon,
> This famous king, shall find me a more fatal bride
> Than Helen. I shall kill him and destroy his house
> In vengeance for my brothers' and my father's death.
> But let that go; my song shall not tell of the axe
> Which is to fall on my neck . . .

Therefore, dear mother, you must not bewail our land,
Nor weep for my lost maidenhood. My bridal-bed
Promises death to my worst enemy and to yours.
(Euripides, 415 B.C./1973, pp. 102–103)

Andromache, who bears the loss of husband and son, envies those allowed to die in war.
To be dead is the same as never to have been born,
And better far than living on in wretchedness.
The dead feel nothing; evil then can cause no pain.
But one who falls from happiness to unhappiness
Wanders bewildered in a strange and hostile world.
(Euripides, 415 B.C./1973, p. 111)

As the women of Troy ridicule Helen, she attempts to defend herself.
What happened in my heart, to make me leave my home
And my own land, to follow where a stranger led?
Rail at the goddess; be more resolute than Zeus,
Who holds power over all other divinities
But is himself the slave of love. Show Aphrodite
Your indignation; me, pardon and sympathy . . .
When Paris was in his grave,
And no god was concerned to find me a husband—then,
You will say, I ought to have left Troy and made my way
To the Argive [Greek] ships. I tried to do this. The gate-warders,
The sentries on the city walls, could testify
That more than once they found me slipping secretly
Down from the battlements by a rope.
(Euripides, 415 B.C./1973, p. 121)

DISCUSS
- Based on Cassandra's prophecy, what do you think will happen to Agamemnon?
- Is Helen's defense an effective one? Explain.
- Classical Greek city-states made slaves of their enemies' women and children. If you were a Classical Greek hearing these monologues, how would you feel about your city-state's war practices? Explain.

The Trojan War Find-It

By now, you should be familiar enough with the gods, goddesses, and other characters in the Trojan War to identify them. Using your knowledge of their attributes and roles, along with the profile pictures throughout this book, locate the characters listed on the handout on p. 152.

The Trojan War Find-It

Items to Find:

1. Athena
2. Apollo
3. Messenger Crow
4. Six Swords
5. Ares
6. A Copy of the *Iliad*
7. Thetis
8. Laocoön
9. Swan
10. Snake
11. Odysseus
12. Calchas
13. Golden Apple
14. Briseis
15. Ajax
16. Hermes
17. Achilles
18. Hera
19. Hector
20. Aphrodite
21. Hephaestus
22. The Name "Homer"
23. Paris
24. Old Nestor
25. Pitcher
26. Two Battering Rams
27. Apollo's Temple
28. A Sheep
29. Helen
30. Aphrodite's Cloud
31. Greek Ship
32. Peacock
33. Catapult
34. Two Horses
35. Ant
36. Poseidon
37. Egg
38. A Flock of Seagulls
39. Harpy
40. Zeus
41. Mythology Textbook
42. Pegasus Symbol
43. Artemis
44. Waldo
45. The Word "Styx"
46. Trojan Horse Structure
47. Six Hearts
48. Ladder
49. Chiron Flyer
50. Head of Medusa

Answers on p. 160.

The Saga Continues

Aeneas organizes the survivors of Troy, including the women and children, who have reconvened at Mt. Ida. The Trojans build a fleet and set out on a journey for their new home. Along the way the voyagers see many creatures previously encountered by other mythical seafarers such as harpies, the many-headed monster Scylla, the violent whirlpool Charybdis, and the Cyclops Polyphemus.

While Venus strives to protect Aeneas, the goddess Juno violently opposes the Trojans' progress. It has been prophesied that the Trojan descendants will bring about the destruction of her favorite city, Carthage. Juno bribes Aeolus, the Keeper of the Winds, to unleash a storm on the Trojan ships. It seems that the refugees will be destroyed by the ensuing hurricane, until Neptune, annoyed at his sister's interference, calms the storm. He then sends the ships sailing smoothly toward the one place Juno does not want them to end up: Carthage.

One of the reasons Juno loves Carthage so deeply is for its leader, Queen Dido. Building and ruling the city-state with her iron will, Dido is the epitome of female power in a male-dominated world. When Juno realizes that she cannot keep Aeneas and Dido from meeting, she strikes a deal with Venus, her enemy and Aeneas' mother. The two agree it would be in both of their best interests if Aeneas and Dido were to fall in love. For Venus, there is the danger that Dido will kill Aeneas if she feels that he is a threat. For Juno, if the two fall in love, Aeneas will stay in Carthage and never fulfill his destiny. The Romans will never exist, rendering them unable to destroy Carthage as prophesied. Both Aeneas and Carthage will be safe.

Using the talents of her son Cupid, Venus plants an arrow of love in Dido's heart. Even though the queen and her Trojan visitor now feel the same attraction, they both resist the temptation of beginning an affair. Using her own wiles, Juno waits until the two potential lovers are on a countryside stroll, then summons a storm that drives them into the shelter of a cave. There, their wills crumble, and they enter into a deadly tryst.

As Aeneas continues to be the lover of the queen, his fellow Trojans become restless. Jupiter too is agitated. Does Aeneas think he can escape his destiny over *love*? Jupiter sends Mercury to Aeneas with an ultimatum: Ship out immediately—or face the wrath of the gods. Aeneas is faced with a dilemma. Does he stay with the woman he loves and defy Jupiter? Or, does he abandon her and fulfill his destiny? In the end, he chooses to leave.

DISCUSS
- What similarities are there between the Trojan refugees and the pilgrims who sought religious freedom in North America?
- Was Aeneas right to abandon Dido? Explain.
- The Romans would admire Aeneas for his devotion to his duty. Do we see the situation differently? Explain.
- When Virgil was writing the *Aeneid*, Rome had just completed a violent war with Carthage's brilliant military commander, Hannibal. How is this event predicted in Dido's speech?

Dido, stunned by this news, numbly watches her lover leave. As her grief turns to anger, she sends her troops in pursuit—to destroy the unfaithful Trojan and his people. They soon report back that the Trojan ships have already sailed. In a mad rage, Dido orders a roaring fire be built and utters a curse against the future Romans:

"No love between our peoples, ever, no pacts of peace!
Come rising up from my bones, you avenger still unknown,
to stalk those Trojan settlers, hunt with fire and iron,
now or in time to come, whenever the power is yours.
Shore clash with shore, sea against sea and sword
against sword—this is my curse—war between all
our peoples, all their children, endless war!
(Virgil, 19 B.C./2006, p. 149)

Then, using Aeneas' blade, she takes her own life.

Far away, the Trojan ships see smoke rising from Carthage. The sight puzzles them, but Aeneas is resolved to his duty. As Aeneas and his men once again go ashore, the spirit of his father (who died early in the voyage) appears to him. Anchises tells his son to enlist the help of a strange oracular priestess who lives nearby, the Sibyl of Cumae, and seek for his soul in the Underworld. Once Aeneas speaks with the spirit of his father in Hades, the hero will truly understand his destiny.

Demeter (Roman Name: Ceres)
Goddess of Agriculture

The Greeks and Romans felt an extremely strong connection with Demeter. The goddess was responsible for providing them with their sustenance and livelihood. In addition to this, Demeter was one of the few gods who did not reside on Olympus. She lived on Earth, where she could be close to those who needed her most. Also unlike the other gods, Demeter's existence was bittersweet. In the fall and winter, she mourned her daughter, Persephone (Proserpine), who was taken into the Underworld to be the wife of Hades. Only during the spring and summer, when her daughter returned to visit, was Demeter truly happy. All of these qualities endeared her to her worshippers. Her sacred cult at Eleusis was one of the most popular, and the secrets kept so well that to this day researchers have no clue what their rites consisted of. From Ceres comes our word for grain-based food, cereal.

And, the Grand Finale . . .

After conversing with the spirit of his father, Aeneas returns from the Underworld with a renewed sense of duty. Sailing around the tip of Italy, the Trojans arrive at the land on the shores of Latium, the lands of the Latin people. *This* at last is the land promised to Aeneas and his descendants by the gods. Unfortunately, the goddess Juno does not take defeat lightly. Even though the Trojans have reached their destination, she hatches a plot to keep them from securing their new homeland. "If I cannot sway the heavens," she declares, "I'll wake the powers of Hell!" (Virgil, 19 B.C./2006, p. 223) The Olympian queen conjures up Alecto, the most fearsome of the three Furies, and gives her the task of stirring up war among the Latins. Alecto gleefully takes to her chore. From a very young age, Lavinia, the princess of Latium, has been betrothed to her cousin, Prince Turnus, the leader of the Rutulians. But, King Latinus keeps his daughter from honoring her engagement. A vision tells him that a stranger from a faraway land would arrive in Latium. This stranger is to be Lavinia's husband instead of Turnus.

Alecto arrives on the scene and sees her chance. She puts the torch of righteous anger into Turnus' heart. He has been wronged. Lavinia was supposed to be his bride. What does her father mean by saying that she will now be married to some foreigner? Fueled by the fury, Turnus begins to mobilize his troops and call on his allies. When the stranger arrives, Turnus says to himself, he will meet a swift death, and that will put an end to the old king's dream.

Once Aeneas and his men land on the Latin shores, they begin to entrench, putting up walls and defenses. With only the sea to their backs, they are not willing to take any chances. Their presence is soon discovered. Turnus and his newly amassed army arrive, eager to crush the Trojan newcomers. Two armies clash.

What then follows is a war of *Iliad*-like proportions. As the battle rages, Aeneas sails up the River Tiber to find friends among the peoples of Italy. When Aeneas returns with new allies for the besieged Trojans, the war reaches its bloodiest and most frenzied point. Venus arrives with new armor for her heroic son, forged by Vulcan himself. After he has put on this armor, Aeneas assumes supernatural strength and fights like a god. At last Aeneas and Turnus face off, man-to-man. Because of his new god-like prowess, Aeneas wins the duel and slays Turnus. With the prince dead, the hand of Lavinia will be his, and Aeneas will become the new ruler of Latium. The *Aeneid*, which was not entirely completed at the time of Virgil's death, ends here.

DISCUSS

- The final section of the *Aeneid* is Virgil's homage to the *Iliad*. What are some similarities and differences between the two?
- If the final section resembles the *Iliad*, the first part of the *Aeneid* most definitely resembles the *Odyssey*, Odysseus' 10-year sea voyage home. Based on what you know of the *Odyssey*, what are some similarities and differences between the two?
- Virgil basically created many of the events of the *Aeneid*. Even though the story wasn't particularly factual, the Romans warmly received it. Do you think Americans would like a fictional story about their past? Explain.
- Some have criticized Aeneas for being a little too perfect. He never seems to do anything wrong. Do you agree with this criticism? Explain.

READ

- Read the *Aeneid* (translated by Robert Fagles). Listen to Virgil's voice as he tells his story. Does he deserve the place he has received among the greatest poets of all time?
- Read *Lavinia* by Ursula K. Le Guin. How have the events of the *Aeneid* changed when seen from a different point of view?

DISCUSS

• Why do you think the Roman people put such a mystical importance on Virgil?
• Does the modern world have anything similar to the Virgilian Lottery? Explain.

Virgil, Tell Me My Future

During the centuries following its publication, the *Aeneid* was such a popular work that it eventually acquired a semireligious importance. Subsequent generations of Roman and European readers developed a technique called the "Virgilian Lottery." According to this practice, a person's future could be foretold by randomly selecting a passage from the *Aeneid* and taking it as prophecy. Several Roman emperors claimed to foretell their future successes through the Virgilian Lottery. Centuries later, certain Christian priests found references to a coming savior in Virgil's poems. They proclaimed Virgil to be a prophet because he had foretold the coming of Christ. Because of these associations, medieval Europeans revered Virgil as a kind of sorcerer.

DISCUSS

• Remember, the *Aeneid* was commonly read in schools after its publication. Would the inclusion of historical events on Aeneas' shield be a good way to teach history to young Romans? Explain.
• Homer included almost no true historical information in the *Iliad*, while Virgil frequently referenced history and current events. Why do you think this is so?

DRAW

Draw a circle on a sheet of paper, and illustrate it with famous events from your country's history.

The Shield of Aeneas

Aeneas receives his very own set of armor forged by Vulcan, the smith-god. This is Virgil's homage to the *Iliad*. If you will remember, Hephaestus made a similar set of armor for Achilles. The shield of Achilles depicted several interesting scenes, which were discussed earlier. To refresh your memory, gilded onto Achilles' shield was the images of two cities—one at peace, one at war.

Aeneas' shield is not so vague. The images upon it would be very familiar to Virgil's Roman readers. Instead of presenting a metaphor for the reader to unravel, Virgil places key scenes from Roman history upon Aeneas' shield. The history of Rome unfolds with great wars, mighty victories, famous leaders, and the seven glorious hills of Rome. Because these events all lie in the future, Aeneas himself has no idea of their meaning. They are Virgil's subtle wink to the audience, a way to remind them of their glorious heritage, of which Aeneas is a very large part. Remember, nothing was prized by the Romans so much as their ancestors, their emperor, and their beloved country.

Utopia

Utopia is a name used to describe a perfect society. This type of society is theoretical or imaginary because it has yet to occur. Will it ever be possible for humans to make a utopia? Does everyone have a different idea of what a utopia would be?

Thomas More, the writer who coined the term *utopia* and wrote a book by the same name, intended the title as a pun. The word is a combination of two Greek words and actually means *nowhere*. Even though there may never be an actual utopia on Earth, it's interesting to think what an absolutely perfect society would be like. Many authors have used their works in an attempt to describe a utopia. Plato wrote *Republic*, a description of the perfect governing body. St. Augustine wrote *City of God*, which describes the perfect Christian city.

In the *Aeneid*, a perfect society is actually Aeneas' goal. He sets out to create another Troy, but he also plans to solve its problems. The Trojans have learned from their mistakes. Never again will they be weak in will or mind. Their new race will cover the world and bring, at long last, peace to all.

Map of Utopia

Draw a map of your utopia. Make sure to include landscapes and buildings with the purpose of each building clearly labeled. For example, if you believe the perfect society should have a hot fudge fountain, first draw a picture of it on the map then label it so others can tell what it is.

Rule your utopia. Develop five laws that every citizen of your utopia must follow. List these at the bottom of your map. When you have finished your map, share it with your classmates.

Romulus and Remus

Livy was a contemporary of Virgil who attempted something very similar to the *Aeneid*. Instead of using epic poetry to extol the virtues of Rome, Livy utilized a historical approach. Although much of his information was legendary in nature, Livy's prose epic *History of Rome* was a great success and further united the Roman Empire behind their new leader. Below is a paraphrase from that work, which tells of Rome's legendary founding.

Aeneas' son Iulus had founded the city of Alba Longa, and a long line of his descendants ruled the city as kings and succeeded each other peacefully until the death of King Proca. Proca had two sons, Numitor and Amulius. Amulius drove out his brother and seized his male chil-

DISCUSS
- If you lived in the societies of the other students, would you consider it a utopia? Explain.
- Do you think developing a true utopia will ever be possible? Why or why not?
- Do you think the founding fathers of America thought they were creating a utopia?
- Can you find an example of a dystopia, the opposite of a utopia, from history?

READ
Read "Harrison Bergeron" by Kurt Vonnegut. Can too much equality be a bad thing?

WATCH
- Watch *Planet of the Apes* (1968) directed by Franklin J. Shaffner. How is this world a dystopia?
- Watch *The Island* (2005) directed by Michael Bay. How is this society both a utopia and a dystopia?

dren. Amulius also made his niece (Rhea Silvia) a Vestal Virgin, seemingly to do her honor, but actually condemning her to perpetual virginity to prevent the possibility of children.

But, it was already written in the book of fate that this great city of Rome should arise. The Vestal Virgin was raped and gave birth to twin boys. She declared that Mars was their father. Perhaps she believed it; perhaps she was merely hoping to cover up her guilt. Whatever the truth of the matter, neither gods nor men could save her or her babes from the savage hands of King Amulius. Their mother was bound and flung into prison; the boys, by the king's order, were condemned to be drowned in the river. Destiny, however, intervened; the Tiber had overflowed its banks and because of the flooded ground, it was impossible to get to the actual river. The men entrusted to do the deed thought that the floodwater, sluggish though it was, would serve their purpose. Accordingly they made swift to carry out the king's orders by leaving the infants on the edge of the first floodwater they came to.

A she-wolf, coming down from the neighboring hills to quench her thirst, heard the children crying and made her way to where they were. She offered them her milk and treated them with such gentleness that the king's herdsman found her licking them with her tongue. The herdsman, Faustulus, took them to his hut and gave them to his wife Larentia to nurse. (Some think that the origin of this fable was the fact that Larentia was called "Wolf" by the shepherds for her promiscuity.)

Romulus and Remus, after the control of Alba had passed to another king, were suddenly seized by an urge to found a new settlement on the spot where they had been left to drown as infants and had been then brought up. Unhappily, the brothers' plans for the future were marred by the same source that divided their grandfather and Amulius—jealousy and ambition. A disgraceful quarrel arose from an insignificant matter. As the brothers were twins and all question of seniority was barred, they determined to ask the gods of the countryside to declare by bird-sign which of them should govern and give his name to the new town once it was founded.

Remus, the story goes, was the first to receive a sign of six vultures, and no sooner was this made known to the people than double the number of birds appeared to Romulus. The followers of each promptly saluted their master as king—one side basing its claim upon being first, the other upon number of birds seen. Angry words came, followed all too soon by blows, and in the course of a fray, Remus was killed. This was how Romulus obtained sole power. The newly built city was called by its founder's name—Rome.

CONCLUSION

And so, this book comes to an end. These six chapters have only scratched the surface of Greco-Roman mythology. It's up to you to dig deeper. At the end of our journey, there are so many songs left unsung. What of Odysseus and his 10-year journey home? The revenge of crazed queen Clytemnestra? Phaethon's infamous ride across the sky? Or, even old King Midas' ears? The Muses reserve these for your own discovery.

Neither does mythology end with the Greeks and Romans. Many cultures have their own tales and their own way of telling them. Many voices wait to be heard.

I sincerely hope that along the way you have been entertained and enlightened. I hope you have seen beyond your own time into another—one riddled with the same problems we face today.

Who are we? It's an important question. The Romans thought the sun could never set on their great empire, yet it did. We read their history, and we hear their myth. Which speaks louder? How will our culture be heard by the cultures yet to come? Determine how *you* will contribute to the stories, the songs, and the sagas that will become the mythology for the ages yet to come.

The Trojan War Find-It Answer Key

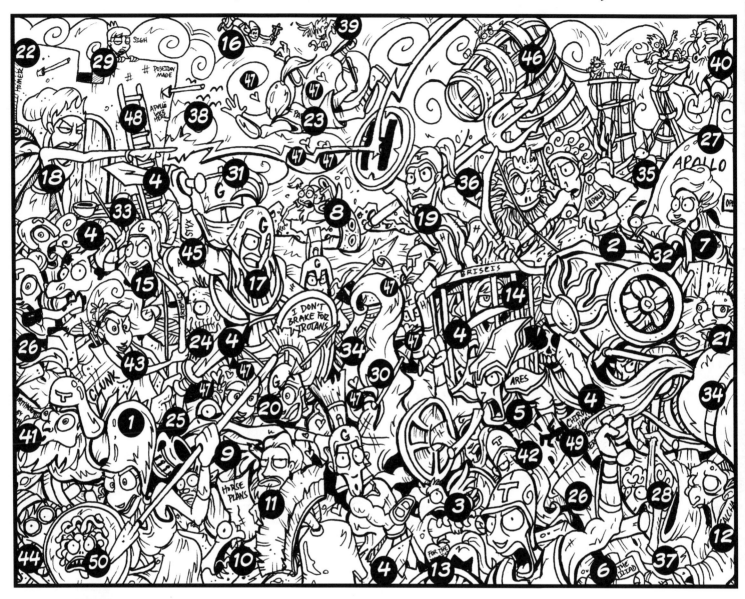

Items to Find:

1. Athena
2. Apollo
3. Messenger Crow
4. Six Swords
5. Ares
6. A Copy of the Iliad
7. Thetis
8. Laocoön
9. Swan
10. Snake
11. Odysseus
12. Calchas
13. Golden Apple
14. Briseis
15. Ajax
16. Hermes
17. Achilles
18. Hera
19. Hector
20. Aphrodite
21. Hephaestus
22. The Name "Homer"
23. Paris
24. Old Nestor
25. Pitcher
26. Two Battering Rams
27. Apollo's Temple
28. A Sheep
29. Helen
30. Aphrodite's Cloud
31. Greek Ship
32. Peacock
33. Catapult
34. Two Horses
35. Ant
36. Poseidon
37. Egg
38. A Flock of Seagulls
39. Harpy
40. Zeus
41. Mythology Textbook
42. Pegasus Symbol
43. Artemis
44. Waldo
45. The Word "Styx"
46. Trojan Horse Structure
47. Six Hearts
48. Ladder
49. Chiron Flyer
50. Head of Medusa

PRONUNCIATION INDEX

Achaean	(UH-KEE-UN)	**Aulis**	(O-LUS)
Achates	(UH-KAY-TEEZ)	**Briseis**	(BRIH-SEE-US)
Achilles	(UH-KIL-EEZ)	**Calchus**	(KAL-KUS)
Acrisius	(UH-KRI-SEE-US)	**Calydon**	(KAL-IH-DUN)
Aeneas	(EE-NEE-US)	**Carthage**	(KAR-THIJ)
Aeneid	(EE-NEE-ID)	**Centaur**	(SIN-TAR)
Agamemnon	(AG-UH-MEM-NON)	**Charybdis**	(KUH-RIB-DIS)
Alecto	(UH-LEK-TOE)	**Chimaera**	(KY-MEE-RUH)
Amata	(UH-MAY-TUH)	**Chiron**	(KY-RUN)
Amulius	(UH-MOO-LEE-US)	**Chryseis**	(KRY-SEE-ISS)
Anchises	(AN-KY-ZEEZ)	**Clytemnestra**	(KLY-TIM-NES-TRUH)
Andromache	(AN-DRAH-MUH-KEE)	**Colonus**	(KO-LO-NUS)
Andromeda	(AN-DRAH-MEE-DUH)	**Creon**	(KREE-UN)
Antigone	(AN-TIG-UH-NEE)	**Cronus**	(KRO-NUS)
Aphrodite	(AF-ROE-DY-TEE)	**Cumae**	(KOO-MEE)
Apollo	(UH-PAW-LO)	**Cupid**	(KEW-PID)
Ares	(AIR-REEZ)	**Cyclopes**	(SY-KLOPE-EEZ)
Argive	(AR-GYV)	**Danaë**	(DUH-NAY-EE)
Argos	(AR-GUS)	**Delphi**	(DEL-FY)
Ariadne	(AIR-EE-OD-NEE)	**Dictys**	(DIK-TUS)
Artemis	(AR-TUH-MIS)	**Dido**	(DY-DOH)
Astyanax	(AS-TY-UH-NAX)	**Diomedes**	(DY-O-MEE-DEEZ)
Atalanta	(AT-UH-LAN-TUH)	**Dionysia**	(DY-O-NY-SEE-UH)
Athena	(UH-THEE-NUH)	**Dionysus**	(DY-O-NY-SUS)

Dryad	(DRY-AD)	**Juno**	(JOO-NO)
Electra	(EE-LEK-TRA)	**Jupiter**	(JOO-PIH-TER)
Eleusis	(EE-LOO-SIS)	**Laius**	(LAY-US)
Eris	(EE-RUS)	**Laocoön**	(LAY-AH-KUH-WAN)
Erymas	(ER-IH-MAS)	**Larentia**	(LAR-IN-TEE-AH)
Euripides	(YOO-RIP-UH-DEEZ)	**Latinus**	(LA-TY-NUS)
Faustulus	(FAWS-TOO-LUS)	**Latium**	(LAY-SHEE-UM)
Glaucus	(GLAW-KUS)	**Lavinia**	(LA-VIN-EE-UH)
Gorgon	(GOR-GUN)	**Lavinium**	(LA-VIN-EE-UM)
Hades	(HAY-DEEZ)	**Leda**	(LEE-DUH)
Haemon	(HEE-MUN)	**Lemnos**	(LEM-NUS)
Harpies	(HAR-PEEZ)	**Lethe**	(LEE-THEE)
Hector	(HEK-TER)	**Leto**	(LEE-TO)
Hecuba	(HEK-YOO-BUH)	**Livy**	(LIV-EE)
Helenus	(HEL-UH-NUS)	**Lycomedes**	(LY-KO-MEE-DEEZ)
Helios	(HEE-LEE-OS)	**Maenad**	(MEE-NAD)
Hephaestus	(HEE-FESS-TUS)	**Medea**	(MUH-DEE-UH)
Hera	(HAIR-UH) or (HEE-RUH)	**Medusa**	(MUH-DOO-SUH)
Heracles	(HEER-UH-KLEEZ)	**Melanion**	(MUH-LAY-NEE-UN)
Hercules	(HERK-YOO-LEEZ)	**Meleager**	(MUH-LEE-UH-JER)
Hermes	(HER-MEEZ)	**Menelaus**	(MEN-UH-LAY-US)
Hestia	(HEST-EE-UH)	**Mercury**	(MERK-YOO-REE)
Hippolochus	(HIP-POL-OO-KUS)	**Meriones**	(MUH-RY-O-NEEZ)
Hyperborean	(HY-PER-BOR-EE-UN)	**Metamorphoses**	(MET-UH-MORF-O-SEEZ)
Idomeneus	(ID-AH-MAY-NOOS)	**Minerva**	(MIH-NER-VUH)
Iliad	(IL-EE-AD)	**Midas**	(MY-DAS)
Ilium	(IL-EE-UM)	**Minos**	(MY-NOS)
Iphigenia	(IF-IH-GEE-NEE-UH)	**Minotaur**	(MY-NO-TAR)
Iris	(EYE-RIS)	**Mycenae**	(MY-SEE-NEE)
Ismene	(IZ-MEE-NEE)	**Myrmidon**	(MER-MIH-DUN)
Ithaca	(ITH-UH-KUH)	**Naiad**	(NY-AD)
Iulus	(YOO-LUS)	**Nemea**	(NEE-MEE-UH)
Jocasta	(YO-KAS-TUH)	**Neptune**	(NEP-TOON)

Numitor	(NOO-MIH-TUR)	**Remus**	(REE-MUS)
Oceanid	(O-SEE-AW-NUD)	**Rhea**	(REE-UH)
Odysseus	(O-DIH-SEE-US)	**Romulus**	(ROM-YOO-LUS)
Oedipus	(ED-IH-PUS)	**Rutulia**	(ROO-TOO-LEE-UH)
Oeneus	(EE-NEE-US)	**Satyr**	(SAY-TER)
Ovid	(AH-VID)	**Scylla**	(SIL-UH)
Pallas	(PAL-US)	**Scyros**	(SKY-RUS)
Pandarus	(PAN-DARE-US)	**Sinon**	(SY-NUN)
Patroclus	(PAH-TRO-KLUS)	**Socrates**	(SAH-CRAH-TEEZ)
Peleus	(PEE-LEE-US)	**Sophocles**	(SAH-FAH-KLEEZ)
Perseus	(PER-SEE-US)	**Styx**	(STIKS)
Phaethon	(FAY-UH-THUN)	**Telemachus**	(TUH-LEM-UH-KUS)
Philoctetes	(FIL-OK-TEE-TEEZ)	**Thanatos**	(THAN-UH-TAS)
Phoebus	(FEE-BUS)	**Thebes**	(THEEBZ)
Plato	(PLAY-TOE)	**Thetis**	(THEE-TIS)
Polybus	(POL-EE-BUS)	**Tiber**	(TY-BUR)
Polydectes	(POL-EE-DEK-TEEZ)	**Tiresias**	(TY-REE-SEE-US)
Polyphemus	(POL-EE-FEE-MUS)	**Turnus**	(TUR-NUS)
Poseidon	(PO-SY-DUN)	**Tyndareus**	(TIN-DARE-EE-US)
Priam	(PRY-UM)	**Ulysses**	(YOO-LIS-EEZ)
Pyrrhus	(PEER-US)	**Zeus**	(ZOOS)
Pythia	(PITH-EE-UH)		

REFERENCES

Aristotle. (1891). *Nicomachean ethics* (F. H. Peters, Trans.). London: Paul, Trench, Trubner & Co. (Original work written 335)

Bulfinch. T. (1998). *Bulfinch's mythology.* New York: Modern Library. (Original work written 1855)

Campbell, J. (1970). *The hero with a thousand faces.* New York: Meridian Books.

Euripides. (1973). *The Bacchae and other plays* (P. Vellacott, Trans.). New York: Penguin. (Original work written 415 B.C.)

Franklin, B., & Sargent, E. (1855). *The selected works of Benjamin Franklin.* New York: Philip, Samson & Co.

Hamilton, E. (1942). *Mythology.* New York: Little, Brown.

Homer. (1990). *Iliad* (R. Fagles, Trans.). New York: Penguin. (Original work written 750 B.C.)

Marlowe, C. (2001). Doctor Faustus. In M. H. Abrams & S. Greenblatt (Eds.), *The Norton anthology of English literature: The major authors* (7th ed.). New York: W. W. Norton. (Original work written 1604)

Mill, J. S. (1874). *Dissertations and discussions.* New York: H. Holt.

Ovid. (2004). *Metamorphoses* (C. Martin, Trans.). New York: W. W. Norton. (Original work written 8)

Schuchhardt, C. (1891). *Schliemann's excavations* (E. Sellers, Trans.). London: Macmillan.

Spivey, N. (2005). *Songs on bronze.* New York: Farrar, Strauss and Giroux.

Strauss, B. (2006). *The Trojan war: A new history.* New York: Simon & Schuster.

Virgil. (2006). *Aeneid* (R. Fagles, Trans.). New York: Penguin. (Original work written 19 B.C.)

White, T. H. (1965). *The sword in the stone.* New York: Philomel. (Original work written 1938)

ABOUT THE AUTHOR

For the past several years, Zachary Hamby has been teaching mythology to high school students through the use of reader's theater plays. When he first began teaching his mythology course, he was discouraged by student reaction. Zachary felt the subject matter could be made much more interesting. After developing a series of plays covering the same material, Zachary has found that even secondary students enjoy reading aloud, role-playing, and learning together. He is also a consultant for the National Writing Project and has presented his reader's theater approach at multiple academic conferences. He currently lives and teaches in the Ozarks.

COMMON CORE STATE STANDARDS ALIGNMENT

Grade Level	Common Core State Standards in ELA-Literacy
Grade 7	RL.7.3 Analyze how particular elements of a story or drama interact (e.g., how setting shapes the characters or plot).
	RL.7.4 Determine the meaning of words and phrases as they are used in a text, including figurative and connotative meanings; analyze the impact of rhymes and other repetitions of sounds (e.g., alliteration) on a specific verse or stanza of a poem or section of a story or drama.
	RL.7.5 Analyze how a drama's or poem's form or structure (e.g., soliloquy, sonnet) contributes to its meaning
	RL.7.6 Analyze how an author develops and contrasts the points of view of different characters or narrators in a text.
	RL.7.7 Compare and contrast a written story, drama, or poem to its audio, filmed, staged, or multimedia version, analyzing the effects of techniques unique to each medium (e.g., lighting, sound, color, or camera focus and angles in a film).
	RL.7.9 Compare and contrast a fictional portrayal of a time, place, or character and a historical account of the same period as a means of understanding how authors of fiction use or alter history.
	W.7.3 Write narratives to develop real or imagined experiences or events using effective technique, relevant descriptive details, and well-structured event sequences.
	W.7.7 Conduct short research projects to answer a question, drawing on several sources and generating additional related, focused questions for further research and investigation.
	W.7.9 Draw evidence from literary or informational texts to support analysis, reflection, and research.

Grade Level	Common Core State Standards in ELA-Literacy
Grade 7, continued	SL.7.1 Engage effectively in a range of collaborative discussions (one-on-one, in groups, and teacher-led) with diverse partners on grade 7 topics, texts, and issues, building on others' ideas and expressing their own clearly.
	L.7.4 Determine or clarify the meaning of unknown and multiple-meaning words and phrases based on grade 7 reading and content, choosing flexibly from a range of strategies.
	L.7.6 Acquire and use accurately grade-appropriate general academic and domain-specific words and phrases; gather vocabulary knowledge when considering a word or phrase important to comprehension or expression.
Grade 8	RL.8.3 Analyze how particular lines of dialogue or incidents in a story or drama propel the action, reveal aspects of a character, or provoke a decision.
	RL.8.4 Determine the meaning of words and phrases as they are used in a text, including figurative and connotative meanings; analyze the impact of specific word choices on meaning and tone, including analogies or allusions to other texts.
	RL.8.5 Compare and contrast the structure of two or more texts and analyze how the differing structure of each text contributes to its meaning and style.
	RL.8.6 Analyze how differences in the points of view of the characters and the audience or reader (e.g., created through the use of dramatic irony) create such effects as suspense or humor.
	RL.8.7 Analyze the extent to which a filmed or live production of a story or drama stays faithful to or departs from the text or script, evaluating the choices made by the director or actors.
	RL.8.9 Analyze how a modern work of fiction draws on themes, patterns of events, or character types from myths, traditional stories, or religious works such as the Bible, including describing how the material is rendered new.
	W.8.3 Write narratives to develop real or imagined experiences or events using effective technique, relevant descriptive details, and well-structured event sequences.
	W.8.9 Draw evidence from literary or informational texts to support analysis, reflection, and research.
	SL.8.1 Engage effectively in a range of collaborative discussions (one-on-one, in groups, and teacher-led) with diverse partners on grade 8 topics, texts, and issues, building on others' ideas and expressing their own clearly.
	L.8.4 Determine or clarify the meaning of unknown and multiple-meaning words or phrases based on grade 8 reading and content, choosing flexibly from a range of strategies.
	L.8.6 Acquire and use accurately grade-appropriate general academic and domain-specific words and phrases; gather vocabulary knowledge when considering a word or phrase important to comprehension or expression.

Grade Level	Common Core State Standards in ELA-Literacy
Grades 9-10	RL.9-10.3 Analyze how complex characters (e.g., those with multiple or conflicting motivations) develop over the course of a text, interact with other characters, and advance the plot or develop the theme.
	RL.9-10.4 Determine the meaning of words and phrases as they are used in the text, including figurative and connotative meanings; analyze the cumulative impact of specific word choices on meaning and tone (e.g., how the language evokes a sense of time and place; how it sets a formal or informal tone).
	RL.9-10.6 Analyze a particular point of view or cultural experience reflected in a work of literature from outside the United States, drawing on a wide reading of world literature.
	RL.9-10.7 Analyze the representation of a subject or a key scene in two different artistic mediums, including what is emphasized or absent in each treatment (e.g., Auden's Musée des Beaux Arts and Breughel's Landscape with the Fall of Icarus).
	RL.9-10.9 Analyze how an author draws on and transforms source material in a specific work (e.g., how Shakespeare treats a theme or topic from Ovid or the Bible or how a later author draws on a play by Shakespeare).
	W.9-10.9 Draw evidence from literary or informational texts to support analysis, reflection, and research.
	SL.9-10.1 Initiate and participate effectively in a range of collaborative discussions (one-on-one, in groups, and teacher-led) with diverse partners on grades 9–10 topics, texts, and issues, building on others' ideas and expressing their own clearly and persuasively.
	L.9-10.6 Acquire and use accurately general academic and domain-specific words and phrases, sufficient for reading, writing, speaking, and listening at the college and career readiness level; demonstrate independence in gathering vocabulary knowledge when considering a word or phrase important to comprehension or expression.
Grades 11-12	RL.11-12.7 Analyze multiple interpretations of a story, drama, or poem (e.g., recorded or live production of a play or recorded novel or poetry), evaluating how each version interprets the source text.
	SL.11-12.1 Initiate and participate effectively in a range of collaborative discussions (one-on-one, in groups, and teacher-led) with diverse partners on grades 11–12 topics, texts, and issues, building on others' ideas and expressing their own clearly and persuasively.
	L.11-12.6 Acquire and use accurately general academic and domain-specific words and phrases, sufficient for reading, writing, speaking, and listening at the college and career readiness level; demonstrate independence in gathering vocabulary knowledge when considering a word or phrase important to comprehension or expression.